FROM KANT TO NIETZSCHE

From Kant to Nietzsche

by
JULES DE GAULTIER

Translated by
GERALD M. SPRING

THE WISDOM LIBRARY

A Division of
PHILOSOPHICAL LIBRARY
New York

Brief introductory essay on
JULES DE GAULTIER
by the translator.

In the English-speaking world two writers, one English and the other American, both bearing the surname of Ellis, have discussed Jules de Gaultier.[1] His works have never before been translated and the time seems ripe to present him to the American public.

Jules de Gaultier, whose dates are from 1858-1942, is essentially modern and might be considered a precursor. Even in this, his first work, written around 1900, he may be said to foreshadow in some ways the mood of the middle of the Twentieth Century. This French thinker's aesthetic philosophy is fundamentally a Monistic Idealism which can be traced to Berkeley as well as to Spinoza. Paramount influences in his development were Kant's CRITIQUE OF PURE REASON and Schopenhauer's THE WORLD AS WILL AND IDEA; he was very much in sympathy with certain aspects of the philosophy of Friedrich Nietzsche. Indeed, his somewhat Nietzschean attitude toward the Christian religion and his intrinsic aristocracy may partially explain why he remains to this day, relatively speaking, unknown.

DE KANT À NIETZSCHE, which W. E. Ellis

regards as a work "of monumental significance," appeared originally as a series of essays and was published by the Mercure de France. It was followed by LE BOVARYSME, which derives its name from the character of Emma Bovary in Gustave Flaubert's novel. Bovarysm is defined as "the power given man to see himself other than he is." De Gaultier's philosophy is that of an artist.[2] From his intellectual viewpoint life is illusory and fundamentally a good show. This spectacular philosophy he has elaborated in LE BOVARYSME.

One can agree with Wilmot Ellis that Jules de Gaultier's metaphysical interpretation of illusionism is original: "Schopenhauer contributed the concept of the will-to-live; Nietzsche that of the will-to-power; and De Gaultier that of the will-to-illusion."

In the work here presented the reader is brought face to face with two protagonists, the "Vital Instinct" and the "Instinct of Knowledge" and their respective counterparts, the "will to believe" and the "will to contemplate." Our author's relativism is allied to the fictionism of Hans Vaihinger, as found in The PHILOSOPHY OF THE AS IF, and to the PRAGMATISM of William James.

The English writer Havelock Ellis made an important point when, in THE DANCE OF LIFE, he called attention to the fact of Jules de Gaultier's philosophy agreeing with modern developments in Physics. In this connection, and considering the author's view of matter, one thinks of such names as Albert Einstein and Werner Heisenberg, of the theory of relativity and "the principle of indeterminacy." De Gaultier, too, believed that "the researcher, in observing the phenomenon, creates it."

Because of the degree of concurrence, for all the difference in their approach to philosophy, there is a temptation to compare Jules de Gaultier with Bertrand Russell. These thinkers could be characterized as, respectively, Introvert and Extrovert. In THE DANCE OF LIFE we find an interesting comparison between the two philosophers, between De Gaultier, the Idealist and Russell the Realist. ". . . , for the idealist thought means the creation of the world, for the realist its discovery."

Nothing in Jules de Gaultier's writings is more marked than his insistence upon Life meaning differentiation, diversity. This makes him cognizant of ethnic considerations. One cannot but be struck by the paradox of his stand, for he combines intellectualism, which he defines in his own way, with an especially keen appreciation of biology, its meaning and its rôle. In his system reason is seen as subservient to the ends of life. While appreciative of the need for an intelligent cosmopolitanism, this arch-sceptic is continually wary of becoming the dupe of "a general idea."

In my opinion an understanding of De Gaultier's philosophy can lead to a liberating tolerance helpful in resolving troublesome modern issues.

G. M. S.

CONTENTS

INTRODUCTION

What will be the object of these pages bearing the title FROM KANT TO NIETZSCHE? Is it to be a complete and erudite history of the metaphysical systems which have appeared in the time intervening between these philosophers, a summary or a sort of encyclopaedia of human thought during one century? By no means. Not that it would be without interest to treat philosophy like an historical science, to assemble impartially all its manifestations and to present them as documents on the diverse forms of mentality. But rather, aside from their value as physiological facts, as examples of the way in which a given temperament begs the question, to which most philosophical systems may be reduced and by means of which we are informed as to the ethnic peculiarities or cerebral categories of their authors, one will here with Kant concede to philosophy, when defined and restricted within precise limits, the value of an exact science, susceptible of a complete construction. With Kant philosophy is to be considered as a critique of Cognition, as a description of the modes and the limits of the faculty of knowing. Thus circumscribed it will benefit from the character of certainty belonging to all the sciences which, like mathematics, geometry and logic, treat of the form of the mind alone and do not venture, in the train of natural and historical sciences, to explore its content. Whereas the latter are reduced to a mere assembling of a more or less extensive system of causes and effects, without ever being able to attain a primal cause necessitating all the others and finally reabsorbing them into itself, whereas they are thus condemned to remain forever incomplete, the sciences which relate only to the form of Cognition permit an immediate and final construction, each of their propositions entailing a character of necessity.

It is this science of the form and the limits of our faculty of knowing of which we here propose to state precisely the conclusions, to define the rôle and the bearing, and for whose epic, so to speak, we set the stage. Now, we shall have to attain, through the detours of philosophical thought, to the CRITIQUE OF PURE REASON, simplified and fortified by Schopenhauer's analytical commentaries, in order to discover the axioms and theorems which constitute that legislation of the mind. Is there not cause for astonishment that so elementary a science and one which determines the legitimacy of all the others should have been formulated for the first time so recently and after so many centuries of metaphysical speculations? Have we not reason to be even more astonished considering that, scarcely established, this science was denied by the very one who had deduced it?

From the standpoint of this astonishment and the problem it raises the period between Kant and Nietzsche offers a spectacle of prodigious interest: for, whereas in the course of the preceding ages the laws of the intellect are hidden, they are then exposed to broad daylight. Now, leaving aside Schopenhauer and a few philosophical minds who were able thenceforth to confine themselves within the limits of science, one ascertains that there never was an epoch productive of a more abundant flowering of metaphysical systems conceived in defiance of all the laws of the intellect. Under a semblance of rationality all the concepts of ancient theology are, despite the condemnation banishing them, welcomed and restored to honor. Never did the philosophical mind display so much in the way of ingenuity, subtle ruse, obstinacy and ardor as at that time to assure the restoration of those dethroned principles. Never were such hollow ideas swelled with so pathetic a sentimentality. But that effort is symptomatic: it makes known to us that a great struggle is being waged between the hidden forces directing Life—and invites us to penetrate the mystery of those masked combatants. This study, then, will concern itself from the start with trying to find an explanation of a sort to anticipate astonishment and to make known the conditions of the contest which has been entered upon, as well as the nature of the stake which is in dispute. In the light of this initiation it will then become clear that, if it is not an equal match between scientific evidence and the ancient illusions, this is not the case in the way one might have believed.

Thus one will be apprised that no detail ought to be neglected, if the science of Cognition is to be disengaged from the snares laid against it and made to appear in its reality before a few minds more concerned with knowing than with believing—it is a category one is establishing there, and nothing more. Hence we shall profit by Schopenhauer's perspicacity and, having regained the high Himalaya to which he led the speculative mind, show the disloyal breach that Kant himself made in order to escape on the wing of old dogmas from the kingdom of the Intellect which he had circumscribed. We shall consider with some curiosity the same exodus made by a number of philosophers to the ancient lands of theology established as rationalistic provinces, then with a palisade close that breach by means of which the philosophy of state, exceeding the limits of scientific knowledge, continues, not without piety, to teach the bourgeois mythology of *practical reason.*

The fruit of this enterprise will be the collection into a luminous sheaf of the strict laws of the intellect. From the viewpoint of ancient metaphysics the projection of this assembled light, dissipating the phantoms of theodicy, will create a state of absolute nihilism. Now, this nihilism which leaves no room for any of the ideas of *thing in itself, first cause, final cause, substance, unity, good in itself, liberty,* this metaphysical nihilism was accepted in its entirety and without mental reservation by Nietzsche, foremost among idealist philosophers. Showing the progress of idealist Criticism from Kant to Nietzsche will, then, be the first stage of this journey through the realm of ideas. The one following it will be pursued across spaces in which are found to grow in obstinate profusion the interrogations and anxieties of human conscience with respect to its fate. For we must beware of forgetting that this anxiety alone is the mother of thought, that it alone has engendered all the resources of philosophical research. An infantile "why," having become urgent and dolorous in those attaining the puberty of the mind, is really the source and the justification of the most abstract speculations. Kant certainly understood it that way. To his definition of critical philosophy understood as the science of the limits of the faculty of knowing, he opposes another founded upon the concrete consideration of moral need. But, prejudging the conclusions of his first enquiry, he formulates them in this manner: "The inevitable problems of pure reason are God, liberty and immortality; the science whose final aim is the solution of these problems and all of whose dispositions are uniquely directed toward this end, is called *metaphysics."*

With the same concern in maintaining this research within the limits of its immediate and human objective we shall, nevertheless, show ourselves strictly respectful of the negative conclusions of the Critique. We shall ask ourselves whether those conclusions which, with Kant, remained a dead letter, mere algebraic formulas accessible to a small number of speculative minds and denied, moreover, by the *parti pris* of their author's ancient morality, are not with Nietzsche destined to accomplish a revolution in human perception. Kant was but a scientific mind ordered with perfection, evolving in the abstract, far from reality and destitute of anything like warmth or radiation. He possessed none of the qualities required to propagate his ideas in life, had he wished to do so. Nietzsche, on the contrary, is a sensibility of an extraordinary violence: the abstract idea, conceived by him with a marvellous clarity, has immediate reverberations in humankind in its entirety, letting loose the inner drama, transforming itself into feelings, passions, anger, disdain, in short into all things which live and expand. His scepticism of mind is dogmatism of will. His very indifference is frenzy. Nietzsche is a poet and the violence of his soul is transmuted entirely into the ardor of his speech. Through the words of foreign languages, as well as those of his native tongue, the vibration of his thought communicates its rhythm to the minds of his readers. It acts on temperaments themselves; it is a suggestion and a hypnosis; it stirs up wills and shifts them, the only effective way to change convictions. Therefore it is permissible to suppose that such a force of persuasion, put in the service of logical deductions, of evident and quasi-mathematical concepts, is called upon to invade a realm beyond the limits of a purely philosophical curiosity, to attain and to modify moral sensibility by making manifest the evidence, hitherto disavowed, of Kant's negative Critique. Assuming the realization of this prevision the philosophical problem will be put in these terms to which Nietzsche subscribed: granting that the thing in itself, that a simple and free substance are not objects of cognition, what is, on the one hand, the meaning of Life? Is an explanation of the Universe possible? Can metaphysical anxiety be satisfied and allayed? On the other hand, how should one live? Can a morality be established? If so, what will be its fundamental concepts?

CHAPTER I

THE VITAL INSTINCT, PLATO, JUDAISM

Recognizing the non-true as a condition of life.

(Nietzsche, *BEYOND GOOD AND EVIL.*)

    I. The non-true being posited as a condition of life, how is a science of knowledge possible?—

   II. The general law according to which the fiction necessary to Life is formed in a human group.—

 III. Monotheism, the vital fiction of the peoples of the West for eighteen hundred years. Its double source: Greece and Judea.—

 IV. Plato, transforming a theory of Cognition into an ontology, founds rationalistic theism.—

  V. The formation in the Bible of dogmatic monotheism; the God outside of the world logically becomes a God outside of reason.—

I.

Nietzsche initially hazarded the following hypothesis, which he subsequently elucidated with singular power: could it be that truth were not a condition of life? He propounded the problem of the value of truth and inferred the necessity of an enquiry. "Whatever," said he, "may be the value attributable to what is true, veracious and disinterested, perhaps one would have to concede to appearance, to the will of illusion, to egoism and to desire a higher and more fundamental value for all that concerns life." [1] "The falsity of a judgment," he further expresses, "is not for us an objection against a judgment . . . The question is the following one: in what measure does it maintain life?" [2] and he is inclined to think that the falsest judgments are the most indispensable to existence.

It is known that Nietzsche, reacting against Schopenhauer's pessimism, owing to an asceticism which was the determining principle of his acts and his preferences, made himself the champion of Life. Whether it be good or bad, it is given, it is that which exists; he wishes to be with it. He has resolved to rejoice in its exuberance, to love what favors it and renders it more intense, to hate what depresses and debases it. "If I have proof," said he, "that error and illusion can serve the development of life, I shall say "yes" to error and illusion; if it has been demonstrated to me that the instincts styled *evil* by the morality of

2

the present,—for example, hardness, cruelty, ruse, daring audacity, combative temperament are likely to increase man's vitality, I shall say "yes" to evil and sin." [3] It is not necessary, in the interest of what is to follow, either to declare oneself with Nietzsche in favor of Life or to condemn it with Schopenhauer. Both judgments are equally legitimate expressing, as they do, no more than the relationship to life of the one who makes them. Life is glorified or repudiated, affirmed or denied according to whether it is perceived as joy or as sorrow; that amounts to saying, according as it appears with intensity in this one and makes felt the proud joy of its vigor, or withdraws from that one and fails.—But that existence and knowledge imply antinomy, that the exuberance of life is directly proportional to the solidity of the fiction sustaining life, such are the postulates in favor of which one assumes credence until, after the analysis of the laws of Cognition, they appear as the necessary consequence or the substratum of those very laws.

To the hypothesis ventured and then accepted by Nietzsche, according to which life has an illusion, a fiction as a prop, we shall add this corollary: knowledge tends to destroy Life. Among all the instincts which, according to Nietzsche's true observation, tend by turns to philosophize, to set themselves up as first cause or first movement, the Instinct of Knowledge occupies a class by itself. It does not compete with the others, but rather on one side are all those instincts favoring Life, while the Instinct of Knowledge, which forever threatens to annihilate it, alone keeps in an opposite camp.

This verification explains the slowness of metaphysics to establish itself as the science of Cognition. Whereas it is of no utility whatever for maintaining and developing Life and even represents a danger for it, there are fertile illusions, namely those which have at all times been taught under the name of theology or philosophy, and it is only right for societies, states and governments to favor such teaching: indeed one could hardly be astonished to find them, as representatives of Life in humanity, endeavoring to propagate whatever strengthens Life. An old illusion is never destroyed and cannot be except by a new illusion taking command in its place. When a morality arises in opposition to a preceding one, its chances of triumph are tied up with the error it conceals, with the more or less fertile principle with which it endows humanity. Great men of action never fail to take their stand with this point of view. They are preoccupied with the efficacy of an idea, with its aptitude to produce acts. It is, on the other hand, understandable that artists should be engrossed with its representative beauty; but who could be interested in the truthfulness of an idea? Yet this concern is manifested by some: it is that which appropriately causes us astonishment and induces us to seek its justification. *How does Life leave room for the manifestation of its opposite, the state of Knowledge which, dissipating the illusion necessary to Life, imperils Life?*

This singular complacency can only be explained by an ulterior design, by a premeditated purpose, by a political aim, as it were. Granted that Truth, taken as the end of Knowledge, favors a state contrary to Life, it is comprehensible that the appetite for knowledge is going to manifest itself in those in whom Life is on the decline. Now, that this state of decline should manage to formulate itself, that it should be tolerated with the disclosures it permits, with the betrayal of Life's very interests, that can have but one meaning, that informs us that such a state may still be utilized—for Life. And, in fact, if truth never succeeds in establishing itself, one sees it at times to be marvellously efficacious in breaking the strength of ancient illusions. Thus it prepares and facilitates

4

the accession of a new fiction: "Give me then, I pray . . . , an additional mask, a second mask."[4] the enigmatic wayfarer of Nietzsche's work asks the curious sympathizer, who wishes to help him. Life is possessed by a more profound need of dissimulation than that passer-by, who from shame hides his wound. Whether it be hiding its nothingness or its mystery, it shows itself to be provided with an inexhaustible assortment of masks of all sorts. Hence, as soon as one of the latter begins to detach itself from its surface, it is no doubt better for it to be removed. The Instinct of Knowledge here fulfills its destructive office; it fulfills it completely: "I am the spirit who always denies" says Goethe's Mephistopheles in FAUST:

> "I am the spirit who evermore denies
> And justly; for whatever to light is brought
> Deserves again to be reduced to naught;
> Then better 'twere that naught should be."

The Instinct of Knowledge could hold the same discourse. It assumes responsibility for it without dismay. Its essence is nihilistic: it does not appear but what it ruins. But, in accomplishing this task in which it satisfies itself, it is in truth but a means utilized by a stronger instinct. For if the old idols are overthrown by it, Life, all-powerful and multiform, immediately erects new ones. So the effect of the intervention of Knowledge is, after all, to facilitate the advent of a new cult, which is more in keeping with the modified conditions of the spectacle, with the obscurity variable in degree, but always necessary to Life as long as it lends itself to the magical projections on the phenomenal screen of the shadows, in which it is represented and strives to apprehend itself.

The science of pure Knowledge, then, appears both as a means and a menace to Life: this double aspect explains at the same time how the CRITIQUE OF PURE REASON was possible, why it was conceived at such a late date and why, scarcely constituted, it was denied and then combated to the death. The fact that it may be a means will induce us to investigate whether it has on that score already accomplished its task. Is something, then, changed after its brief intervention, one will ask oneself, and is it not still the hour of a new stage-effect? The coming of a philosopher of the style of Nietzsche seems a reply to this enquiry and will actuate us to seek behind the actual illusion, supposing it to be really compromised and moribund, the possible modes of a new and more solid illusion, protecting Life better and maintaining more securely the obscurity in which it prospers.

Thus, beneath the abstract ideas which seem to occupy the philosophical scene through the ages, the most concrete realities lie hidden. Like mythological gods masked behind natural appearances, the Instinct of Knowledge and the Vital Instinct, dissimulated under metaphysical appearances, are at grips with each other. The pages to follow will be a sort of legendary narrative in which the personages have had to be presented and their vicissitudes foretold as in the mystery-plays of old. If the action calls for tragic episodes between the two antagonists, a transcendent comedy is not lacking in it either. On the other hand, the spectacle of Life continuing its course informs us in advance of the outcome of the duel which has been undertaken. We know that the Vital Instinct is always elected by fate to triumph. Doubtless that will not prevent there being some among the spectators of this contest, who will be disposed by some intimate analogies to side with the vanquished and to smile at the coarseness of the victor. They will, in the course of this account, find nutriment for their secret sympathy, for at no time was the Vital Instinct more dangerously threatened and never was its posture less noble than

6

during this period when, felled by the CRITIQUE OF PURE REASON, it employs in its defense the methods befitting the most discourteous form of strife, the most burlesque attitudes and the arguments of the most hollow kind of dialectics.

II.

In reality, when the Vital Instinct is formulated in a race, there is no question, in the beginning, either of the true or of the non-true, but solely of what is useful to that race.

A human group is at first like a natural body, endowed with chemical properties which it obeys blindly, like a plant requiring special conditions of atmosphere and light, which develops and multiplies under favorable circumstances and which a hostile milieu will atrophy. It is the true reality of this group to be an element *distinct* from other elements, provided with properties peculiar to itself, with precise and *special* actions and reactions. Thereby it is that mysterious thing, unamenable to investigation, Life. But the human group *itself* takes cognizance of *itself*, of what is harmful and what is useful to it. It is going to do for itself what every scientist does for the chemical bodies that he wishes to preserve, what every horticulturist does for the plant he is cultivating. The scientist places his crystals in the conditions of dryness which are propitious to them, and he protects them with glass casing hermetically sealed against any possible humidity of the air. He maintains around his mixtures the exact temperature suitable to them. The horticulturist evinces the same solicitude for his plants. If the soil around them is too poor or too rich, he modifies it. He also defends them against themselves, moderates the exuberance of their sap, trims their leaves and branches. The human group takes the same measure of defense against the surrounding milieu and against its own inner tendency. Everything useful to it it prescribes for itself and everything harmful it forbids itself.

Some great man appears at the beginning of every people which is establishing itself; he is the one in whom the instinct of the race shows the keenest inner perception of itself, of its needs, of its vital requirements. He is the legislator and the priest: he formulates a physical and moral hygiene in the name of the Vital Instinct, of the group's Instinct for happiness; he codifies all the measures apt to regulate attitudes, to determine acts with a view to assuring the strength, duration, happiness and power of the group. In order to ensure the observance of these precepts he gives them the character of external laws. He decrees a system of immediate penalties and rewards and then institutes fictions rich with promises and threats in order to act on the minds of men, beyond executory restraints, by means of images. Thus does the Vital Instinct in the plenitude of its strength, but foreseeing its decline, invest the preservative fiction with sovereign authority. Its only purpose is to live and to prolong its duration. So it grants real existence to everything that can serve it. It decrees with moral philosophies the aggregate of the ways of living favorable to it; in order to strengthen the ascendancy of the moral philosophies it invents paradises, founds theogonies, religions, an elementary philosophy comprising a more or less clear conception of the human person, of its destinies, of the world and the principle underlying it. This body of ideas is formulated outside of any intellectual control, any experimental datum; but by this very fact, and that is what one must firmly grasp, even when it calls for cruel constraints, painful observances and terrible and precise menaces as against vague and conditional promises, this system of ideas emanates from the best instinct of the social group, from its instinct which is the most preservative of itself. In the epoch of its formation and for a long time to come it represents the maximum of felicity and vitality realizable by this group. Everything that is undertaken against this whole will be combated by the best instinct of the group, by the element which has remained the most vital in it.

Thus the fictions, which will later be useful to the social group, present themselves from the very first as laws without troubling to justify their reality. They appear in the shape of dogmas. As long as the group remains animated with all its strength, it does not think of questioning them or demanding their qualifications. However, as soon as this strength wanes, as soon as an inferior vitality is manifested by a lesser aptitude for creating the illusion necessary to life, like a plant which is no longer maintained firm by its own sap, but has to be supported by a contrivance, the social group requires the prop of an argument for its faith. It no longer suffices for fictions to be useful to it; it must regard them as true. What was, for a particular group, an attitude of particular usefulness will, in order to keep its authority over this group, have to camouflage itself with the appearance of a universal utility. With this pretension the Instinct of Knowledge enters the scene: it is already armed to destroy, but it is entirely subordinate to the Vital Instinct, which deflects its growing strength for its own benefit. It is bound to form beside the dogmatic fiction a new fiction, beside the religious dogma a philosophical dogma. Its singular mission is to establish an identity between *usefulness* and *truth,* such as it has just been conceived. This task accomplished by the Instinct of Knowledge in the service of the Vital Instinct, is what is customarily termed a philosophy. The despotic will of the Vital Instinct, as it is sanctioned by the conclusions of such a philosophy, is what one is accustomed to call *truth.* Thus the Vital Instinct, foreseeing the future attacks of

9

the Instinct of Knowledge, endeavors to commit it in its pay, to pervert and deform it before it is full-grown. It compels it to construct, itself, one of the façades of the false edifice which it will later have to overturn, if it is ever to escape from the yoke oppressing it.

A religious fiction and a rationalistic fiction, a dogma and a philosophy, such are the double ramparts behind which every provident Vital Instinct shelters its petitions and its needs, assuring its duration beyond the period of its primal strength and spontaneity. Such are the phantoms which the glaring light of Knowledge will have to dissipate, when the time comes to organize the phenomenal scheme in conformity with a new fiction.

III.

The fiction established for approximately eighteen hundred years by the Vital Instinct to serve as the mainspring of its evolution among western peoples is, in one word, monotheism. A God outside of the world and creator of the world, a law revealed to the conscience of man either miraculously or naturally and intimating to him a good to practise and an evil to avoid, man provided with a free will which permits him to observe or infringe the laws imposed, hence responsible for his acts, capable of merit and demerit, liable to penalties and rewards conceived now in the spirit of the coarsest realism, now in more refined forms, such is the system of fictions which is embraced by the monotheistic conception in its Christian aspect after the simpler and more entirely dogmatic monotheism of the Moslems has been isolated from it. Just as it is, we must believe that this conception was the most apt to favor the development of the peoples which formulated it, that it was the attitude of utility most favorable to them. What, then,

10

was that utility? The following: *to elicit effort in races capable of effort.* Now this word "effort" is a deceptive term: at least it needs to be interpreted. It represents, in psychological language and applied to activity we call human, precisely the same phenomenon as does the word elasticity, when it is a question of an activity considered purely physical. The elasticity of a force is the property it has of evolving between a minimum and a maximum under the action of given circumstances. Now this evolution inevitably takes place as soon as opportune circumstances come in contact with this force. Any body capable of contracting under the action of refrigeration necessarily contracts as soon as refrigeration is given. It is the same with the more complex forces of the physiological world. Every living being endowed with an energy capable of growing under the action of a certain climate sees its energy grow as soon as the climate is given. Such is the case with the human being: but, since he becomes conscious of this increase of his energy at the precise moment when circumstances determine that effect, since he is himself the subject of the modification then producing itself, he believes himself to be its cause and meritorious author. It is in this sense that he designates as "effort" the reaction of his inmost elasticity under the action of external causes, a reaction whose initiative he attributes to himself and which he feels himself to be at liberty to produce at will. Now, for this being, who thinks himself free and responsible, and in the special case of our races of the Occident, the monotheistic fiction with the retinue of the other fictions it commands—free will, merit and demerit, responsibility—is going to represent the external phenomenon which will make the external phenomenon "man" produce its full yield. The faith with which he attaches himself to this fiction and the authority he accords it, will represent the exact degree of his elasticity and the measure of the growth, of which his energy will prove capable under favorable circumstances. Thus one may conceive how the resistance, which the Vital Instinct opposes to the Instinct of Knowledge threatening to destroy the useful fiction, will be the stronger, the more intact and the more favored by the milieu the energy of the social group in which this fiction was formed. Hence the superior utility represented by this fiction will account for its influence on all the healthy parts of the social group and explain how it can make the most obviously fallacious reasoning acceptable to minds concerned in believing it. It will, moreover, render clear how, in its service, the rustiest and most ancient weapons turn into the most formidable tools, as soon as it employs them to combat the assaults of Knowledge.

*

Every vital instinct which becomes objective derives, we have said, the fiction manifesting its strength from a double source. The monotheistic fiction does not escape this law and shows itself with two distinct roots, one of which, vigorous, straight and profound, plunges into the most ancient bedrock of Jewish soil, while the other, dispersed in a thousand radicels, shrivels on the surface of Greek terrain. One, with the Bible, will nourish the spurious tree with the sap swelling the fruits of dogmatism, while with Platonic dialectics the other will form with its essences the sweetish fruits of rationalism, whose insipidness the half-breeds of Knowledge and Dogma will know how to relish.

It is at this second source that we shall at first have to study the origin of the monotheistic fiction. Formed by the solicitude of philosophers it grapples, in due order, with Cognition. Therefore we shall see how the latter, temporarily domesticated and forcibly coupled with the Vital Instinct, engenders the prescribed fiction, a deformed and lame fiction, however, seeing that it is wounded by the incisions of the steel and mutilated by the forceps of the sophisms which had to be employed in order to wrest it from the matrix of pure reason.

IV.

One is no equitable judge of minds, if he does not take into consideration the epoch in which these manifest themselves and the degree of inner constraint they undergo. The conclusions of Platonic philosophy invite a smile, but the improbability noted therein today and which, in point of fact, shocks only a few discerning minds, has for its cause the despotic influence exerted in that epoch by the Instinct of the races, who were aspiring to live. Monotheism is formed in the bosom of polytheism, from which it actually differs little. It maintains its essential means, namely anthropomorphism taken as a principle explanatory of the Universe. It finds in it the ideas of creation and first cause which, between the milieu where it is being prepared and the one in which it is going to develop, betoken both as to aspirations and form an identical mentality. Plato, in his capacity of philosopher in the service of the Vital Instinct, is bound to give a body to these fictions. Now, despite this necessity which compels him, he has nevertheless, in the train of the Eleatic philosophers, put in its true light and partially resolved the problem of Cognition.

To propound the problem of Cognition means to wonder and be concerned for the first time about the relation between objects such as we perceive them and objects as they may be; it means suspecting for the first time that the *object* may differ from its *representation*. What degree of resemblance is there between the molecular movement produced in the brain and the appearance of an object in space? In the formation of this appearance, what part must be accorded the elements themselves which constitute the object? What is the share of the cerebral apparatus? Endeavoring to analyze the processes of the phenomenon, science observes between objects and different parts of the human body, the retina and the tympanum, undulations being transmitted with varying rates of speed. How do these invisible and silent undulations become transformed in the brain into perceptions of color and of sounds? Whose is the share of sound and whose of color? Is it that of the object or that of the brain? What part do magic and illusion play in the deformation? Does the object even have an existence outside of the way in which it is perceived? With growing disquiet one comes to perceive that the molecular movement in the brain, or at least a part of this movement is still no more than a means of perception, thus a new screen between the object and knowledge thereof. At what instant and how does the subject of knowledge itself arise? How is the subject opposed to the object, *percipere* to *percipi?*

If the birth of philosophy as science is marked by such an anxiety, it is precisely because of the necessity it entails of a preliminary Critique of Cognition. Called upon by Socratic doubt to solve this essential problem Plato applies himself to it straightway. But other tasks engage him, tasks which force him to abandon this enterprise, though not without having distorted it. The time is not ripe; having doubted is already too much, even if it was in the manner of dialectical procedure: the people of Athens have just signified as much to Socrates, and not without reason did the Vital Instinct of the race put itself on the defensive, since this dialectical procedure introduced into

14

the arsenal of the mind by Socrates will prove the very instrument by means of which Knowledge will later bring the sacred fictions to ruin.

Presently and with Plato it is the Vital Instinct itself, that is going to wield that subtle instrument and assign its object to psychological curiosity. It will be the same until about the time of Kant and during that entire period one witnesses this singular spectacle: with every philosopher worthy of that name the marvellous instrument, animated by a magical clairvoyance and divination in somnambulent hands, searches with dexterity among the tissues of the living phenomenon, interrogates it with its point, removes fiber by fiber everything which hides the organs; it is going to lay bare the most secret system and unveil the mystery. But, all of a sudden, the philosopher has awakened from his lethargy and his hand, once more submissive to an imperious will, makes the indocile instrument deviate and he concludes in conformity with the ancient formulas, having retained nothing of the investigation which it seemed to direct.

The enigma of Knowledge presents itself under a threefold aspect. Scientifically the problem is posed with the objects of the external world. But, beside these objects, the Vital Instinct has already created in rudimentary fashion other categories of objects, those of the moral, those of the metaphysical world. It requires of the philosopher that he complete this rude outline. Now these objects, by the very fact of their being purely intellectual creations, lend themselves to being easily wielded. They are concepts, which appear neither in time nor in space. One readily believes them to be of the same nature as the intelligence which conceives them: supposing that one has the boldnes to grant them life, the audacity to declare once and for all and with eyes closed, never to retract at any future time, that these objects, fabricated by the intellect itself, have a real existence outside of the mind which formed them, then the problem of Cognition will, under these altered terms, be close to solution. At the same time the essence of Reality will be defined according to the desire of the Vital Instinct. The ruse, then, consists in that artifice of the mind, which, finding itself unable to explain the fact of Knowledge by the fact of Existence, inverts the terms of the problem to grant Knowledge the power of creating Reality. This procedure, as practised by a superior intelligence, is the very one used by primitive man who, constructing idols with his hands, persuades himself that he owes them his existence. It is a procedure which, in view of its ancient appearance, must be regarded as essentially human and as representing the very mechanism of the Vital Instinct. It will be found again and again wherever life has a chance and a future. Is this, moreover, not the evident sign of life, namely the power a being has to dispose of it, to endow with it objects and all the things he touches superabundantly? Plato does not hesitate before this affirmation, but in the service of this dogmatic *coup d'état*, whose authority he will maintain on every occasion, he employs the perfect dialectic method familiar to us; he makes ingenious use of the instrument of precision which the Instinct of Knowledge has astutely let fall into the hands of philosophers.

Knowledge of an object, he remarks with Socrates, supposes that a definition can be given of that object, —and to define is to class and circumscribe under the category of a general idea. But that general idea, that idea which alone renders possible the knowledge of the object, which really grants it knowable existence, that idea could not pertain to the object. Neither does it derive from the senses, which provide us in the form of sensation with but incomplete information about objects, showing them to be in a state of perpetual change, and which, in a manner of speaking, allow us to see only their ephemeral and unstable shadows. Where, then, is Plato going to situate those Ideas through whose interposition we know? In human reason? No, since he teaches us that they are its objects. Now, just as external objects are independent of the senses, so are ideas independent of human reason. It is in divine reason, whose attributes they are, that Ideas, eternal archetypes of the particular entities perceived by the senses, live with a real and substantial existence. Here then, introduced under the pretext of an explanation of the mechanism of Cognition, is the procedure upon which in the future all theology is going to be founded. It consists, as one can see, in considering real what is abstract. The forms of Knowledge are given an objective existence the supreme reality of which is in God. Conversely existence is denied the particular objects that we perceive. They are vain appearances. They are merely, through the idea of genus, the latter being already endowed with a reality greater than the individual entity which it explains, the manifestation, or more properly, the deformation of the typical Idea of the object situated in divine reason, which alone possesses and bestows real existence.

This theory is of interest to us because, in the part which is susceptible of a legitimate application, that is to say as far as it concerns external objects, it sanctions the notion of *phenomenon,* the notion of a possible and probable discrepancy between our perceptions and the object we perceive. The platonic *Idea,* taken as a means of knowing external objects, agrees accurately enough with the concepts of the understanding which Kant will deduce. It furnishes us with the precise meaning of the word *idealism* which comprises nothing else than the notion of a deformation whose importance remains to be evaluated, but of a necessary deformation undergone by the object as the subject apprehends it through the apparatus of cognition, the ideological instrument. The dialectical method, although it is applied by a hireling of the

17

Vital Instinct, is already bearing fruit and progressing toward the disclosure of the Illusion implicit in every knowable state of existence.

In order to disengage and differentiate Ideas from the phenomena of the external world and from the conceptions of our understanding in which they are reflected, Plato already uses the procedure which will be Kant's, namely abstraction. From the representations to which our perceptions give rise, he eliminates what is particular and maintains only what is general, what embraces an ever more considerable number of particular objects. This procedure is perfect for determining the forms of Knowledge and for taking apart all the pieces of the apparatus of mental optics through which the content of Knowledge is apprehended by the mind. For Plato, however, it is no more than a means of attaining the metaphysical objects which he feels it to be his mission to define and whose reign he must as a herald prepare. With the collected materials of a *science of cognition* he constitutes an *ontology*. His work of propaganda, then, is going to consist in applying on every occasion the aforementioned substitution, in perpetually taking the form of knowledge for its content, in endowing the concepts formed by his mind with all the more substantial an existence for having, by a series of abstractions, the more completely emptied them of their substance. Indefatigably he is going to take Piraeus for a man,[5] as if the frequency of that illusion were to have the effect of rendering it legitimate and efficacious.

*

The maneuver is flagrant; the procedure would be impudent, were it not naïve. Nevertheless, this attack against the laws of logic has been universally ratified. The error it imposes is the fertile source from which has sprung all theology without distinction of churches, all rationalistic philosophy, the encyclopedic doctrine in its entirety, all free thought if one takes this phrase in the sense toward which its adepts have slanted it, all state philosophy, all legislation. This success apprises us that a great spectacle is here presented: it is precisely the one to which we called attention at the beginning of this study, endeavoring, as we were, to anticipate the astonishment to which it might have given rise. In order to justify the constant triumph of the non-true over logic we have invoked the all-powerfulness of the Vital Instinct which, being what it is, is fated to triumph in every living entity over the Instinct of Knowledge. It is lord and master and well aware that its most frivolous insinuations will for its courtiers always be reasons without rejoinder.

The coarseness of the means employed by great tragedians or comedians to institute their dramas and their comedies and to show us life, only imitates this informality of Life. Are very complicated circumstances required for Othello to kill Desdemona? No, all that is necessary is for Othello to be jealous and passionate. All the spectators *know* Desdemona to be innocent. They *know* Iago's treachery. But Othello does not *know* it. That he should condemn and kill the one he adores on a mere rumor seems absurd. But he is obliged to obey the vindictive jealousy, the passionate violence animating him and these essential elements of his character must find a pretext to break through. Molière shows his characters to be subject to the same blindness as soon as a passion or an interest or a clearly pronounced trait dominate them. His Sganarelle of THE SCHOOL OF HUSBANDS thinks he has secured Isabelle's heart by keeping gallants away from her and having her confined to her home and busy with household duties,

"Or else knitting some stocking for pleasure."

19

His presumption makes him the easiest of dupes and is enough in itself to render the success of his victim's ruses acceptable. Without being astonished he believes in the tokens of her feigned tenderness, transmits to the amorous Valère the letter that is going to ruin him and marries the two lovers by mistake. Orgon, dominated by Tartufe, who has been able to exploit his simplicity and his terror of celestial punishment, is as easy a dupe as Sgnaraelle. His credulity is so strong as to lead him to doubt the testimony of his senses. Under the table where he is hidden, he witnesses the well-known scene of seduction; but, however importunate Tartufe may become he is not proven guilty, inasmuch as Sganarelle believes neither his eyes nor his ears and, despite the impatience of Elmire, who urges him to show himself, he wants to see and hear ever more until Tartufe rightly says to Elmire:

"C'est un homme entre nous à mener par le nez;
De tous nos entretiens il est pour faire gloire.
Et je l'ai mis au point de tout voir sans rien croire." [6]

Alceste [7] has just had the proof of Célimène's frivolity and perfidy and thereupon, believing only his own passion, he clearly and definitely offers to take her with him to the desert, where he wishes to live. His blindness is complete enough to make the coquette's refusal a stunning blow.

These scenes provoke the mirth of the spectator. Is it by their improbability? No, but merely because the spectator has purposely been placed in the playhouse and has through the author's exposition come to know the circumstances and the motives of the characters. Conversely the characters represented by the actors, Sganarelle, Orgon, Alceste are enclosed in the absolute of their passional presumption, which puts a screen between their view and reality, a screen on which is inscribed the imaginary vision which deceives them. The contradiction existing between the Vital Instinct and the Instinct of Knowledge is thus revealed to the spectator. It is the sudden view of that deviation that provokes his laughter. But in leaving the play-house he himself is going to become an actor again, and if some violent passion drives him, he will surpass in power of illusion the personages whose blindness struck him as so ludicrous; for every vehement passion, of whatever kind it may be, sees and believes what is in its interest to see and believe. Hypnosis governs everything living. Every instinct forms at the same time its atmosphere, in which it breathes, and its clouds which hide from it, what it wishes and ought to ignore. The myth of Titania pressing to her bosom the asses' head of her lover only specifies by means of the exaggeration of a spell the power of deformation peculiar to every desire. Moreover love which, in propagating life, shows itself as a direct manifestation or even paroxysm of the Vital Instinct, indicates better than any other passion this essential power of deformation. For a lover there is no such thing as knowledge of his sweetheart. He invents her through his own optimistic presumption or his inborn hypochondria, either the one or the other multiplied by the degree of his desire, and when two real passions meet, it is across the barrier of that double deformation that the lovers embrace, while continuing in ignorance of each other.

Sganarelle derided, every lover betrayed and wishing to ignore it and, with his instinct for happiness, outdoing in cleverness at inventing his own reasons for being duped all the ruse of the faithless one, here are the examples one must conceive and keep in mind in order to admit the extraordinarily naïve and gross procedure by which the Vital Instinct of humanity defying the Instinct of Knowledge, obtains the metaphysical illusion, which seems until now to have been indispensable to it.

*

May it then be for us the occasion of a comedy to have seen formed in Plato's philosophy the fiction, whose consequences still dominate us. Let us penetrate behind the coulisses of that philosophical theatre and consider more closely the devices by means of which the plot's strong yet fragile knot is fashioned. The fiction, we have said, consists in realizing abstractions, in confusing the form of Knowledge with its content, in granting existence to the properties of the mirror through which existence appears. The procedure of this fiction is an arbitrary use of abstraction. Now abstraction is a faithful instrument of Cognition and, as soon as its employment is pushed to extremes, it gives its creations for what they are and thus threatens to end the quid pro quo.

After having established with Plato that such a particular phenomenon is apprehended only through the general idea of the genus with which it is connected, that Alcibiades' dog is to be grasped only through the genus dog, dog in general through the idea of animal and that the latter is founded on the still more general idea of existence, one is compelled, if the logical use of abstraction is to be exhausted, to abstract the fact of existence itself from the *idea* of existence, and all that remains is the pure concept of the *idea* giving itself candidly for what it is, for an empty form, for the means rather than the content of knowledge. Then one perceives that he has done an excellent piece of work in so far as it is considered to be an attempt to order hierarchically the degrees and the forms of the understanding. But it is not so understood by the instinct for happiness, which

22

animates the philosopher. It must elude this last consequence of abstraction giving the Idea for an empty form, inasmuch as it breaks the will of Life. By what stage-trick or what cue will it achieve its purpose? "One does not think what is not real," the school declares, and here is the magical assertion which is going to permit the Vital Instinct to believe in the reality of its creations. One does not think what is not real, hence everything the mind thinks has actual being, hence genera exist and the concept of existence engenders real existence, existence in itself, absolute existence. Thus thought creates Being. The concept of God creates God. The pretension is so strong that one senses in it the preconceived opinion of a will, with the result that a secret tact restrains the too easy reply. A scene is played in the arcana of metaphysics between two instincts and, seeing the passion animating one of the actors, one guesses that no mere argument could sway him. "Everything the mind thinks, exists," cries the vital instinct. A voice replies: "You conceive nothingness, therefore nothingness exists." But the instinct for happiness speaks so loudly that it does not hear and will never hear the ironical and truthful reply of Knowledge. It is upon this deafness that platonic philosophy in its entirety is going to be founded and eventually all of theology, then all rationalism which, outside of dogma and without its excuse, will maintain the fallacies of theology. Plato is indeed the true creator of the theological illusion on which we live and this illusion may be perfectly summed up in a single idea, the Idea of God, of God provided with his attributes, absolute good, absolute beauty and absolute truth, that trinity of spiritualistic philosophies.

With Plato all the ideas of moral and intellectual perfections, abstracted from the phenomena of the visible world and the moral world and completed by the Idea of power borrowed from the phenomena of nature, all these Ideas become the apanage of God, of the Νοῦς, in whom they receive existence with the same logic one would show in endowing with existence the concept of nothingness, the legitimate product of the same process of abstraction. "To be and to be known amounts to the same thing" is Aristotle's formula when he establishes as doctrine the very principle of illusion from which will result the *Ens realissimum* of scholasticism, the Supreme Being acknowledged by the Encyclopédie, revered by Robespierre, bequeathed by the Savoyard Vicar to the cult of M. Homais.[8] Plato's establishment of the Idea of God is, then, the triumph of the Vital Instinct over the Instinct of Knowledge. The constant application of the quid pro quo by virtue of which the forms of knowledge, listed and described in the course of the dialectic, are taken for the attributes of existence, issues in the Idea of God. This triumph does not prevent the Instinct of Knowledge at times from threatening suddenly to destroy this strong rampart behind which Life prospers. This rebellion of the intellect against philosophical and religious dogma gives rise to the dramatic episodes we know: the inquisition performs its office and the pyres are stirred. But those tragedies have been invoked and described too often and there is no need to linger in recollecting them. Nevertheless, it should be pointed out as curious that those, who are called upon to represent the old faith in its renovated form and the one best adapted to the present, namely the ideologists of philosophical deism and free thought, have obtained from them the best and most oratorical effects and in the most indignant tone.

It seems more original, while disregarding that heroic and tragic legend, to indicate to those, who are inclined to take sides for Knowledge, that the violent passion of the Vital Instinct and the blindness resulting therefrom have also produced a superior comedy. It was the genius of Flaubert who, in such works as

24

LA TENTATION DE SAINT ANTOINE and BOU-
VARD ET PÉCHUCHET, inaugurated this transcendent comic art. But there are few philosophies in which
it is not discernible and without the preparative of a
literary stage-setting, as soon as, becoming indifferent
to the concerns of life, one views the intrigues it
institutes as a spectator.

Canon Roscelin was, in the sixth Century, the hero
of one of these episodes of philosophical comedy.
However, it is not at his expense that he has set us
laughing. One likes to think that Roscelin was one of
those sincere, naïve and clairvoyant souls that were
found in the cloisters of the Middle Ages. Doubtless
scholasticism seemed to him an honest and positive
science, which it is permissible to deduce without
circumspection, like mathematics, without mental reservation and with no need for being on guard against
the consequences of its theorems. That is wherein he
showed himself to be naïve. Undertaken in such a
spirit the study of scholastic philosophy led him to
discover that genuses are categories formed by the
mind, abstractions without real existence, words,
flatus vocis. He eagerly made his discovery known:
that was, as we know, *nominalism,* which well nigh
entailed tragic consequences for its author. Now under
this dispute between nominalism and realism, which
may appear to represent idle discussion, one can imagine, according to what preceded, that a struggle of an
exceptional gravity was at that time waged between
the Vital Instinct and the Instinct for Knowledge.
Roscelin's discovery amounted to nothing less than
placing in broad daylight the essential vice upon
which the entire theological edifice was established.
He was showing that there is an insuperable abyss
between *existence* and *knowledge* and that it is not
legitimate to give life to abstractions. Inasmuch as
he was divesting genuses of all real existence, he was
imperilling the existence of Ideas, which were them-

selves conceived by abstractions obtained from genuses, and ultimately the supreme Idea of God himself. Orthodox theologians immediately perceived the danger, but without becoming fully aware of its extent, and it seems as if nothing could give a clearer idea of the possible deformations of reason subservient to the Vital Instinct than the conclusions at which they arrived. If genuses are nothing but words, they judged, then existence must no longer be granted except to individual entities: divine Unity, which absorbs in its essence the three persons of the Trinity, is destroyed. The three persons alone survive. Thus it was that pagan anthropomorphism remaining in dogma preserved a whole part of the theological edifice and the gleam of good sense, which should have annihilated all metaphysics, appeared as no more than a partial heresy tending to distort the idea of the divine without destroying it. These conclusions did not cause astonishment in their day. To confound Roscelin Saint Anselm wrote a treatise on Unity in the Trinity and the canon, ordered to appear before the Council of Soissons, had to retract *metu mortis*. One must be grateful to him for that retraction: it did not prevent his clear and pellucid thought from coming down to us, and that dénouement without any tarnish of spilled blood permits us a good laugh.

This hearty laugh, this abstract laugh which is characteristic of the Instinct of Knowledge when it has become conscious of itself and cognizant of its rôle, when, having renounced any pretension of organizing life, it is enjoying as a spectator the vicissitudes of phenomenal representation, this silent laugh amidst the admirable deafness of the living runs through the entire metaphysical parade. The Vital Instinct cramped in philosophical breeches and seeking to adorn itself with the nobility and the haughty coldness of Knowledge is for him, who is able to trace his evolution, no less comical a "Bourgeois gentilhomme" than the other. But the humor is idealized, if one sees him accompanied by some old retainer, himself a dupe of his fine manners, signalizing by a redoubling of respect the slips in which he fails. M. Cousin plays the part of this old servant to perfection and it is marvelous to see him in the course of his HISTORY OF PHILOSOPHY, as a guardian of the monotheistic formulary, reject with a grave gesture the metaphysical systems which are injurious to etiquette and, as if he were in an unctuous tone announcing a great name, introduce authoritatively the *petitio principii*. He gives orders to keep apart sensualism and idealism, those vagrants of all the schools, who are already roaming in India around the Vedas, whom one finds again in Greece frothing the Ionian seas, or enlisted as partisans in the train of Pythagoras in the provinces of Elea,—who penetrate even into the medieval monasteries, always undisciplined, exaggerated in their gestures and incapable of either tact or moderation. But he takes especial care that the Instinct of Knowledge be rigorously excluded from the place where one imitates its postures, since the comparison imposed upon minds by that vicinage would make our false gentleman run the greatest risk.

This danger we have just seen appear in the Middle Ages with nominalism. But it was already present and no less great among the philosophers of the Alexandrian school. Plotinus, carrying to extremes the logical use of abstraction, uses it to the point of depriving the Divine Idea constituted by Plato of such adventitious ideas as Intelligence, Good and Power with the result that only the supreme concept of Unity is allowed to remain, the logical end of a description of the limits of the faculty of knowing, a concept as negative as the very idea of nothingness and in which abstraction sincerely shows the nature of its creations. Although Plotinus preserves a nominal trinity in his system, he really situates the idea of God in absolute

Unity, a Unity which is determined by no accident and which leaves no place for the useful God of Plato. That is a great danger, but M. Cousin points it out and with one word puts things back into place and reassures all his followers. He knows exactly what use is to be made of dialectics; he knows where abstraction may be applied and where it must be withheld. It is good for disengaging from the particular phenomenon the ideas which will constitute divine perfection, but beyond that it becomes pernicious. Only an uninitiated mind can overstep that boundary and, in doing so, he is culpable. Such is the case with Plotinus. "Plotinus went astray by carrying Platonic dialectics too far and extending it beyond the limit where it *should* stop." [9] Here, properly stigmatized, we have a want of good breeding. That is not the way to employ dialectics. "In Plato," M. Cousin continues, "it terminates with the idea of God and produces a God, who is intelligent and good; Plotinus applies it without restriction and it leads him into the abyss of mysticism."

＊

This attitude on the part of M. Cousin is symptomatic and tends to confirm the importance of the monotheistic idea from the standpoint of Life. The idea of God, such as it was conceived by Plato, imposed by the Bible and altered and completed by Christian theology, is the most contradictory idea and the one best suited to retard the solution of the problem of Cognition. Philosophically speaking, it is the very abode of the absurd. One gains access to it through a sort of courtyard of miracles in which, mutilated and deformed, all the metaphysical notions stolen during the youth of societies from the Instinct of Knowledge by the Vital Instinct, meet to contradict one another.

The first of the antinomies implicit in the divine idea stands at the apex of the system of abstractions devised by platonic philosophy. The celestial heights have just received their host and away down below, humiliated in the depths and having fallen on his knees from lassitude, appears man who has just created God, *the finite coexists with the infinite*. The theological mind will long sharpen its wits on this problem, but can never overcome it except by hypocritically substituting, yet without changing the labels, a pantheistic theory for the monotheistic fable. Plato already wondered why God representing, as he did, infinite perfection, infinite power and infinite happiness, had created the world and answered his own query without embarrassment: by reason of his goodness, thus introducing a moral anthropomorphism, which is going to complicate the rational antinomies with new and irreducible contradictions. The theologians, who were imprudent enough to follow him on that path, were presently obliged to justify the infinitely good and infinitely powerful God for having created suffering. Dogma came in very handy there to furnish the notion of sin. Suffering, according to theologians, was the punishment for error. God, being just, chastises and they pretended not to see that they would have to justify the good and omnipotent God for having made man fallible, fatally destined to transgression and chastisement, since one sees man punished and the world in the grasp of woe. Nevertheless an attempt of that sort had to be made and, since chimerical ideas engender monstrous conceptions, the free will attributed to man came to have the mission of justifying God for permitting human suffering. Man, free to choose between good and evil, between suffering and joy, chose evil and suffering. The absurd itself is here idealized and attains its own perfection. Reason searches in vain for what cause or by virtue of what singular motive man, who was free in his volition, made so strange a choice and attached himself by preference to evil, which was to cause him suffering. If it was done knowingly, the mind is confounded, for this is the psychology one would expect to find in a madman's cell. If it was through ignorance and, as Pascal and the Jansenists thought, for having drawn some unlucky number, there again one would have to blame the just God and ask him why he instituted that game of chance and made himself its manager.

It is difficult to avoid the appearance of some indelicacy in accepting the too easy task of showing the incoherence of such a system of chimeras, and good sense here seems like tactlessness. With God's infinite perfection, his infinite justice, his omnipotence, his prescience, with man's liberty and the existence of evil and suffering, rationalism has embroidered on an unreal fabric conceptions more fantastic than the fauna painted by Chinese image-makers on the embroidered silk of fire-screens. Thus covered with fabulous concepts that metaphysical fabric also forms a precious screen, since it is destined to intercept the light of Knowledge.

Yet it should not be forgotten that, unless they are forced to confess their antinomies, those conceptions give themselves out as the legitimate daughters of reason and pretend to convince. As soon as they are unmasked there is a change in tactics and theologians, entrenching themselves behind mystery, vaunt the powerlessness and incoherence of reason in order to make the necessity of revealed dogma felt and to impose it. Then it behooves us to remember that the chimerical conceptions of deistic philosophy come, as has been shown, from a reason that was purposely mutilated, so that they could not compromise pure reason.

When one considers with what advantage the
Vital Instinct is able to turn to account the share of
philosophy in the formation of the deistic Idea, one
could not admire too much the skill and the superior
strength it manifests in utilizing so compromising an
ally. It must, however, be noted to the honor of human
good sense that the monotheistic conception in its
philosophical form did not at first have any social
influence. From Plato to the formation of Christian
dogma it had no hold on the Greeks, nor later on the
people of Rome.

Both remained faithful to their gods, to all their
plastic gods, unscathed by dialectical pretensions, sufficiently explanatory for the imaginations that had
begot them, national and therefore suiting exactly
the needs of the race, not exclusive, but rather en-
larging their circle and, with a benevolent curiosity,
making room for new-comers, as soon as it was a question of augmenting the fatherland with the contingent
of a new people. The idea of Plato's God could then
enter only into the paradoxical brains of a few scholars
and professional philosophers interested in confounding knowledge and conception with the free play of
thought, formed, or rather, deformed in the abstract
atmosphere of the schools and taking pride in a still
esoteric prejudice, through which they thought they
were rising above vulgar prejudice.

For the idea of the one and only God to impose
itself and to become the glue of a whole new civilization, as polytheism had been the sufficient support of
ancient culture, the contribution of Jewish dogma was
needed and, upon leaving the examination of the
monotheistic idea as conceived by philosophy, it is a
release for the mind to see this same idea giving itself
in dogma for what it is, to find that it imposes itself
in a pure and simple commandment of the Vital In-

stinct, as an attitude of utility. With the Bible, indeed, the monotheistic idea is promulgated and ordained; it takes great care not to belittle itself by referring to reason. The Vital Instinct, here endowed with all its intuitive sagacity, regards reason as a danger.

In contrast to Greek anthropomorphism, the dogma, which is formulated in the Bible, tends to deprive God of any human characteristics: it does not suffice for him to forbid reproducing his image and giving him an appearance were it the most noble; he sets out to destroy in the human mind anything like a presumption of an analogy between the conceptions of human intelligence and the decrees of divinity. It is true that in the epoch in which it creates God, the Jewish people, as Nietzsche saw very well, makes of him first of all the representative of its will to power. God approves and counsels Jacob in the ruses he invents in order to deceive Laban and appropriate his flocks. When Jacob fled with Rachel carrying off the riches he was able to seize, God himself appeared to Laban in a dream in order to frighten him as to Jacob's power, thus persuading him not to attack him. In every circumstance the Jewish people has Jehovah himself approve or suggest the measures useful to it. Later, when taken into captivity, it imagines that it is expiating the faults committed against its God. A noble idea on the whole and, after all, an ingenious one to spare its pride: for in that way, by attributing all-powerfulness to a being who is outside of any comparison with men, it denies its enemies the benefit and the honor of their victory. They were but the instruments of God's vengeance on his people. This people, then, because it is enslaved and oppressed, judges itself to be guilty and recognizes the need of an atonement: if it accepts punishment, it will be forgiven and reestablished in its ancient glory, for it has confidence in divine justice which, moreover, it appreciates according to its own sense of justice.

32

This last trait of resemblance upon which man might rely in order to attain God is also going to be effaced. The book of Job makes us witness the perfect constitution of the divine person, such as it will be bequeathed to Christian dogmatics by the Old Testament and such as it must be conceived to save it from intellectual analysis. Job, overwhelmed with misfortunes, pours out his lamentations in the midst of his three friends, who have come to appease him and here now, in the several conversations, appears beside previous conceptions of divine justice, the idea of a power out of all proportion with human intelligence, a justice incomprehensible to the reason of man. Nevertheless, it is at first the ancient theme: Job's friends infer his guilt from his misfortune: "Behold, happy *is* the man whom God correcteth: therefore despise thou not the chastening of the Lord."

Job protests his innocence in vain; his friends do not believe him. Can God destroy justice? Does the Almighty overthrow equity? God does not reject the righteous man. He does not strengthen the arm of the wicked one. Job has sinned and his friends are indignant, because he is not willing to repent. But he invokes the Lord's judgment. "I shall multiply the proofs of my innocence," he says, and the three old men no longer answer Job "because he continues to believe himself innocent." Here then is a first attitude which implies the ancient belief in an identity between divine and human justice; but, from the flood of violent words and the chaos of ideas clashing in this poem, the new theme disengages itself. "God strikes equally the just and the unjust," says Job, and that does not astonish him; he takes care not to accuse God. "God is not a man so that one could answer him or enter into judgment with him." And Elihu, expressing the same feeling, cried: "Will God take you as a pattern of his justice? Is he bound to hate what

33

you hate and to choose what you choose?" Thus there is no common measure between man and God. Job may not know his fault, yet it exists none the less in the eyes of God, and when God himself intervenes in the middle of this dispute and manifests himself to Job, his words show that this very evaluation is still not pleasing to him. If he reproves Job, his anger is stronger against Job's friends, who dared to "speak in God's favor." "Who is the one," he asks, "who obscures wisdom by senseless talk?" Making no mention of his justice and showing but his power, he is finally appeased only by the following statement of Job: "Yes, I wanted to explain wonders that I did not understand, marvels surpassing my intelligence: yes, I accuse myself and shall do penance in the dust and in the ashes."

Here, then, is the divine idea from the point of view of moral conceptions and absolutely detached from any anthropomorphism: between man and God the disproportion is absolute. Man cannot equal God even with his loftiest ideas, not even with those on which he thinks he can most legitimately pride himself, not even with the idea of justice. Hence, from the viewpoint of revealed dogma neither moral wrong nor physical ill will any longer prove anything against God. God is safe from the attacks of Knowledge and the conception of the God, who is outside of the world, here becomes logically *that of a God outside of reason.*

When one considers this outcome of the biblical doctrine, there is a temptation to allow the Jewish people some prerogative analogous to the divine mission which it attributes to itself in its prophecies and which, on the testimony of the scriptures, Christian dogma assigns to it. Parallel to the orthodox legend of the people of God destined to spread over the universe the principles of the true faith, an analogous construction may be made from the standpoint of abstract mythology which is employed here. From this point of view the Jewish people does indeed appear as the champion of the Vital Instinct. The Vital Instinct seems in it to become conscious of itself, of its needs and especially of the danger that threatens it. ". . . Of every tree of the garden thou mayest freely eat: But of the tree of knowledge of good and evil, thou shalt not eat of it: for in the day that thou eatest thereof thou shalt surely die." Here then, at the threshold of the book of Life, is posed the fundamental antinomy between *being* and *knowledge,* an antinomy which the science of Cognition will confess to us with the same sincerity as the Vital Instinct does here. Then, in order to avert this danger, we find the Vital Instinct in the course of prophecies and legends fashioning, with the idea of God, the most opaque screen as a shelter in order to protect itself against Knowledge. This idea, which in Greek philosophy proved the most contradictory, the most false and the most destructive of all the forms of the faculty of knowing imaginable, the Bible imposes in the name of revelation and contrary to all rationalism, with the result that a necessary state of hostility between dogma and reason is created. At the same time this most false idea emerges as the strongest for organizing society. For two thousand years it has been easy to recognize the connivance of the Vital Instinct with monotheism by this fact of *power* being exclusively vested in the nations possessed of this illusion. Christians and Moslems prosper to the detriment of the peoples whose philosophy, like that of the Hindus, rejects the idea of a creative God outside of the world and shows itself to be dominated by the Instinct of Knowledge. The symptom is flagrant: not one great conquering people, that is to say one capable, secure in its strength, of embroidering the texture of civilization, has come out of the races of Buddhist religion since they have entered into competition with the monotheistic peoples. The principle

35

of knowledge, which is at the basis of their mentality, is the cause of their weakness.

VI.

The triumph of monotheism, with Christianity and the strong concentration realized by Roman power may, then, be said to date from the encounter of Greek rationalism with Jewish dogma. Never would Plato's deistic philosophy, with the flagrant contradictions it implies, have succeeded by its own virtue in becoming an efficacious religion and a principle of authority. But by means of the state of faith created by dogma and with the help of consenting wills and the aspiration of consciences it is henceforth going to be possible to introduce fraudulently the singular counterfeit of the science of Cognition fabricated by the Greek genius. As palates undergo a gradual perversion by that adulterated draught, they will take it for the real wine from the intellectual vine, and minds intoxicated by the vaporous abstractions burdening it like a superadded alcohol, will in the turbid light of their disordered reason come to see the phantoms appear to which the obscurity of dogma alone gives an appearance of reality. Some of these alcoholics of the mind will even reach the point later, where they refuse the help of any dogmatic hashish mixed with their beverage. A long-standing intoxication, inducing a natural lesion of the cerebral centers, will have conditioned their minds to deform objects without the help of the poison. They will be seen to take pride in that privilege: spiritualists, rationalists, free-thinkers, deists make up this singular category, whose pathology we shall have the leisure to describe at greater length in connection with the doctrines which will arise between Kant's CRITIQUE OF PURE REASON and the integral critique of Nietzsche.

But before venturing to appear alone outside of the limits of dogma, platonic philosophy practices and fortifies itself within that orbit. The authoritarian Jewish God has espoused the varnished metaphysics of Greece: by its tinsel, by its rouge and by its contortions and ogling this promising courtesan attracts into the tabernacles of Jehovah transformed into cathedrals, temples and Sorbonnes, a clientèle of weak, erudite and unsound minds. Their vital instinct is no longer strong enough to engender their faith; this faith acts only with the help of the thongs and the allspice of a simulacrum: philosophy imitates for them the chaste attitudes of pure Knowledge.

Thus, within the Church definitely constituted by the union of dogma and philosophy, a double attitude is manifested. On the one hand Jewish dogma, whose mission it is to protect the Vital Instinct against the danger of Knowledge, is reabsorbed in the *Credo quia absurdum* of Roman Catholic dogma and intrenches itself as in a fortress in the conception of mystery, which, according to the definition of the catechism, is "a truth we cannot understand and must believe." Rational theology, on the other hand, proposes to unite two forces mutually excluding each other; it wishes to compel Knowledge to lend assistance to Life. To be sure, this rational theology could not stand up without the bulwark of dogma, behind which it takes shelter every time that too direct an argument is going to strike it. But it is found, after all, to render in its way a considerable service to the theistic idea. It rather than dogma degrades minds, for it deforms reason, the instrument of Knowledge, whose efficacy dogma is content to deny and, when the dogmatic rampart weakens and menaces ruin, the entire race of minds which, we know, was prepared by its attentions, a race of minds as deaf and blind as one could wish, in such a way as to enable them, without danger to their ideological belief, to affront the broad daylight of Knowledge and heed neither arguments nor quibbles.

So it is thanks to this falsification performed by the philosophical spirit on the mind itself, that the theistic fiction with the consequences favorable to life it permits,—ideas of justice, good and evil, free will, effort and responsibility,—was prolonged and will still be able to continue beyond the duration of the dogma which imposed it. Hence with Saint Augustine and the Fathers of the Church, with Saint Anselm, Saint Thomas, Saint Bernard, Saint Albert and the Doctors of the Middle Ages and then with the help of theologians like Bossuet and Fénelon, philosophers like Descartes and Leibnitz and with the powerful aid, despite a superficial antagonism, of vulgarizers like Voltaire and the Encyclopedists, the platonic and deistic philosophy succeeded in living and growing. By means of this confluence of all the streams united by the defense of the Vital Instinct it erected its monumental façade variegated, by way of ornamentation, with the diverse motives of its metaphysical pretentions, all decorated with specious appearances, false windows and false doors designed to cloak the entrance to the dangerous, lethargic and silent necropolis of Knowledge which it is its mission to conceal.

§

In opposition to these sophisticated minds incapable of believing without motives who, trusting only reason to confirm their desires, wretchedly mutilate reason, another species of minds, a rare and precious one, is formed under cover of a more profound faith in revealed dogma. They are those, who sincerely refer to the Bible and the absurd set up as a creed, those whose awareness of an antinomy between what is vital and what is knowable leads them to

38

resolutely embrace Life. Having nothing to fear from the conclusions of reason, since they do not credit them, they sometimes consider them with amusement and some curiosity. Their intellectual integrity delights in it so much the more, as they do not think of deriving their faith from that source. When this attitude is idealized, they can become impassioned as for a beautiful chess-move on the occasion of a good piece of reasoning inferring the contradiction and absolute negation of revealed dogmas.

Their instinct for happiness is so strong that it does not need to produce extraneous titles. For them reason is disqualified and by the very fact of its contradiction with dogma, which is synonymous with the interests of Life itself. But, if they undoubtedly reject it as a basis upon which to ground Life, they do not pervert it. It is by the disinterested speculations of those pure dogmatists and with the most intransigent element of dogmatism that the instrument of Cognition, warped by the rationalists of theology, will nevertheless become perfected during the theological period. It is this *parti pris* of robust faith which permits the blossoming of some authentic fragments of the doctrine of Cognition such as they are exhibited in the nominalism of Roscelin, destructive of all theism, in Luther taken only as a dialectician and independently of the practical consequences of his reform, in the Jansenism of Port-Royal, denying free will in the name of Grace and focus of an asceticism that will bear still better fruit, and in Pascal, a superior type of those minds in which the duel engaged between living and knowing became apparent and who, without dishonoring reason, were able to sacrifice it to revealed faith.

Surely one must not forget the services rendered the Vital Instinct by those, who wished to be heroes of will-power and bear witness by martyrdom in the manner of men like Bruno, Ramus, Vanini and

Galileo. But these, like saints, perfected the ascetic attitude more than they sharpened the instrument of knowledge. Nietzsche gives philosophers precious advice on this subject: "Beware of martyrdom! Of suffering "for the truth's sake"! even in your own defense! It spoils all the innocence and fine neutrality of your conscience; it makes you headstrong against objections and red rags; it stupefies, animalizes, and brutalizes, when in the struggle with danger, slander, suspicion, expulsion, and even worse consequences of enmity, ye have at last to play your last card as protectors of truth upon earth." [10] Emanating from an excessively brave spirit, as was Nietzsche's, this advice signifies that, in order to be a perfect workman of Knowledge, one must have gone beyond asceticism and renounced the great joys of pride and the warlike joys it gives. Now, in an artificial way and by an occasional method religious dogmatism pushed to the absolute did engender that fine spiritual neutrality demanded by Nietzsche: the security which faith provided, the *parti pris* to consider reason incompetent, the absence of all fear which was characteristic of the way it was wielded by some great believers, created a disinterestedness which is the very essence of the scientific spirit and it is thus that the instrument of Cognition, dulled, rusted, impaired by the liberals of theology, was maintained with a meticulous care and sharpened and polished by some dogmatists, as though there were a possibility of co-existence between the most contrary things when each of these is perfect of its kind. In considering the event, is there not a temptation to imagine a secret alliance between pure dogma and pure reason against rational philosophy and theology and could one not regard as a sort of revenge on the part of dogma the care with which it maintains the instrument of knowledge destined to extirpate like a cancer the purulent compromise of the syllogism grafted on the imperative?

VII.

Nevertheless it was from a dogmatist, a believer and not from an independent philosopher that pure reason received its canon. Kant, however, it must be acknowledged, was not a dogmatist after the manner of those we have described. Kant is a Protestant and Protestantism already permits a falsification of the dogmatic coin. It virtually contains rationalism, for it is based on that *petitio principii* which assumes a necessary accord between revealed religion and reason. Therefore it is permissible to suppose that a Catholic Kant would not have dishonored the CRITIQUE OF PURE REASON by the CRITIQUE OF PRACTICAL REASON, nor by the reticences which, in his first work, already prepare the possibility of a return. He would have established that there is a divorce between reason and revelation and would have sacrificed one to the other.* On the contrary, he is so imbued with protestant dogma that he will unhesitatingly maintain its formula against an evidence which he himself has displayed. Thus, by that absolute faith that he has since proven, he joins himself from the outset to the dogmatists of the preceding kind, and it is to that absolute faith that Knowledge

---

* The sentence, as it occurs in the original essay version of DE KANT À NIETZSCHE, is as follows: "Il eût constaté qu'un divorce existe entre la raison et la révélation et eût sacrifié l'une à l'autre." (Mercure de France, Revue Mensuelle, janvier, février, mars 1900, Section VIII.) Owing to a typographical error the second "et," required from the sense of the passage, does not occur in later editions.

is indebted for having been so well served by the analyses of the first Critique. When Kant undertakes to determine the laws and the precise compass of the faculty of knowing, he does not suppose for an instant that his faith can be brought into question by the results of his inquiry. Dogma guarantees for him the concurrence of reason and faith. That is the source of his strength and, when he engages in his enterprise, he sees reason in the light of an ally; he has, so to speak, the treaty in his hand.

So he thinks that it is beneficial to restore it, to give back to it its true and venerable image, to disencumber it of the varnish and the cosmetics with which a false theology has overlaid and painted it. It is in this frame of mind that he presents himself before the platonic façade embellished with false windows and false doors, before that façade whose threshold no one can cross, but behind which there dwell, in palaces described by philosophers, all the theological idols. With his critique it did not take Kant long to discover all the artifices of the façade and, despite the splendor of the great doors surrounded by colonnades, despite the real appearance of the porticoes and the marble stairways covered with precious fabrics and which are strewn with flowers exhaling their sweet scent towards some temporary altars, he discerns that these are but deceptive perspectives, paintings in a solid wall, and he is led by his deductions to a low door carefully hidden near a corner without any sign to distinguish it from the partition-wall in which it is set. But at the first thrust the door opens and behold the philosopher in the true palace of Knowledge. How different it is from the descriptions that have been made of it! Instead of the showy rooms, carefully arranged and communicating by spacious galleries which, becoming ever more sumptuous, reach the throne-room, it is a labyrinth which, once one has entered it, seems to have neither entrance nor exit. One does not encounter in it the heralded idols, no divinity either in the form of first or final cause or in the form of the absolute; emptiness takes the place of the infinite and of perfection; in it free will, good and evil are indiscernible and justice invisible. By way of compensation causality, time and space stretch out therein in illusory perspectives and become endlessly entangled, propagating mirages in which one perceives the continuous flight of the phenomenon. Kant faithfully describes the arrangements he observes, all the absolutely empty forms he encounters. He is well aware that that is the apparatus of Cognition and he carefully indicates its scope; he willingly confesses from the start that the study of that mechanism could not give us information about the Being in itself. But, having ventured so far, trusting in the final accord between dogma and reason, he nevertheless begins to be frightened. Already under the control of fear his view grows dim and he begins to lie: while he is compelled to concede that the forms of Knowledge do not inform us as to the Being in itself, he even now conceals that by their very nature they denote the impossibility of knowing the Being in itself. That, however, is what is implied in the description he gives us, for, thanks to the complete blindness of his faith, which prevents his suspecting any danger, he has freed the Instinct of Knowledge from its servitude. He would have compromised Life, if it were not ludicrous to think that Life can be compromised by an argument. Besides, after having accomplished that decisive task, Kant, availing himself of the voluntary reticence that he has just pointed out, came back and placed himself in front of the platonic façade, where, with a disconcerting bonhomie, he reestablished on one point, from which he deduced all the others, the philosophical illusion he had just overthrown, and restored the idols. Yet, since it is based on recourse to reason rather than on a command imposed on our wills, his categorical imperative, his new dogma betrays its fragility on all sides. The question of what may be the chances of duration of an illusion presented in this form will be investigated in its proper place. But now is the time to recall the glorious part of Kant's work and, by developing according to their logic, the conclusions of his analysis, to expose without ambiguity what the laws of Cognition teach us about themselves and about Existence.

The entire beginning of this study had to be devoted to a description of the illusion created by the Vital Instinct and we showed its double origin in dogma and in philosophy, compelled to serve Life with the very weapon of Knowledge. It could not be otherwise, for Knowledge, far from being creative, makes everything that appears return to nothingness. Life, then, had to be and the Vital Instinct had to begin by triumphing, by furnishing the motive for a charade, and it was under these conditions that the platonic décor was delineated. Here with Kant we have Knowledge manifesting itself with all its destructive force. Does this apparition mean that the colors of the old décor are faded, that the canvas is perforated to admit light and can no longer deceive? However that may be, with Kant a spectral manager has come to the front of the cosmic stage and has uttered the words of Mephistopheles understood by some: "I am the spirit who always denies and surely with reason, for everything that exists is good only to disappear in ruins, and it were better if nothing existed."

CHAPTER II

THE INSTINCT OF KNOWLEDGE
KANT AND HINDUISM

Apollonius—Leave him, Damis; he believes like a brute in the reality of things.

(Flaubert. TENTATION DE SAINT-ANTOINE.)

   I. The defect of Kant's work: by the way he destroys the theological ideas Kant, from the *Critique of Pure Reason* on, betrays the interests of Reason.

  II. In opposition to this betrayal, the deliberate work of the moralist, the unconscious and genial work of the logician. How he deranged the philosophical point of view: mental laws, considered until then an apparatus qualified to apprehend existence, prove themselves to be one adapted to instituting the illusion of the Universe.

  III. This conception of illusionism founded, with Kant and Schopenhauer, on psychological analysis, contains the essential principles of the science of Cognition.

The events which for eighteen hundred years, and with the rule of God, marked the triumph of the Vital Instinct over the Instinct of Knowledge have just been exhibited as on a stage. We showed the monotheistic fable rousing human effort, furnishing a principle of movement, instituting a plot and thereby fulfilling usefully its function of temporary impresario of the cosmic spectacle. This efficacy of the fiction justifies it and obliges us in compensation to accept, as an integral part of representation, all the bloody conflicts to which the divine idea, in its religious form, gave rise and which history shows us. For one

46

could not without vanity criticize Life for what it shows of a popular taste for circuses, battles and melodramas.

But ought this absolution in behalf of the monotheistic idea, pronounced by reason of its utility, to induce any partiality in its favor? Are we to hesitate to pierce and expose the old fiction or attenuate the blows which are going to be dealt it by the Instinct of Knowledge with Kant's weapons? For such a compromise the presumption would be lacking. The servants of Knowledge are not like the ordinary servants of Life: the latter are disturbed if one dares derange anything in its ancient order. As Elihu took the defense of God, they intercede in favor of Life; they counsel and protect it. But the philosophers in the service of Knowledge know that Life is multiform, that it is infinitely supple, pregnant with numberless potentialities, as rich in moral as in physiological accommodations; they couldn't have the presumption to spare it, nor are they able to believe it at the mercy of a reasoning-process. In ruining the ancient fictions they are conscious of still being enthralled to some useful task and of clearing the ground for architectures of a new style. Their perspicacity informs them of the rôle destined for them, since the rigorous price of their supremacy in the order of Knowledge is the fact of not being able to be dupes. Even when their individual passion tends to destroy Life, their lucidity condemns them to know that they are fortifying it and that the violence of their hate is but a zeal suited to renewing it. Here, then, the destructive Instinct of Knowledge will be shown in its best light. Without either presumptuous consideration or nihilistic illusion we shall join in its passion for destroying, enjoy the immediate satisfactions granted it and yet not be unaware that, on the accumulation of the decomposed ancient fictions, there will have to rise in effervescence some new

47

fabrication for the pain and the joy of a future humanity.

I.

What is, with regard to the Instinct of Knowledge, the great merit of Kant? Is it the fact of having overthrown the conclusions of theism? Is it because he showed that pure speculative reason can not attain the entities of metaphysics: *God, the soul, liberty?* Is it his warning that the false paths traced by theology toward these postulates do not issue in them, that the guide-posts *God, soul, liberty* lure the meditative voyager into an impracticable route without egress?

This task Kant accomplished in the course of the transcendental dialectic. In presenting the Ideal of pure reason he explains, as is well known, that for speculative reason there are but three possible proofs of the existence of God. He refutes the ontological proof and shows how the concept of the *ens realissimum* could not imply existence except at the price of a tautology, by means of a deliberate and pre-established confusion between the terms *reality* and *existence*. Having demonstrated the inefficiency of the ontological proof, which was the argument of Saint Anselm, Descartes and Leibnitz, Kant establishes that the two other proofs, the cosmological and physico-theological, are confounded with the preceding ones and attain their object only through the latter, whose inanity he has just exposed. On the other hand, the antithesis of the second and third antinomy show, one, that no simple substance exists, hence no soul in the theological sense, and the other, that there is no liberty and that everything happens according to natural laws.

So it seems that Kant first of all infers the non-existence of those three metaphysical hypotheses,

God, the soul, liberty, by reason of which he instituted his enterprise of critical exploration. Yet did he in his refutations furnish a force, an evidence and arguments unknown until then? That is what one could not grant. If we have indeed seen the theological fiction formed in platonic philosophy, scholasticism and rationalism, it is already known that the ontological argument consists in the bold realization of an abstraction. The proofs, on the other hand, which are invoked by Kant in the antitheses of the second and third antinomy against the existence of the soul and of liberty, derive from the most elementary principles of reason. Consequently we cannot credit him with the honor of a task which any impartial mind would have accomplished as successfully and which had many times already been achieved. But there is more and it is important to note right now that this part of Kant's work conceals intentional snares, that it plots a betrayal of the interests of pure reason and contrives a possible restoration of the ancient fictions.

With respect to the existence of a Supreme Being, first cause of all other beings, uniting in itself all the perfections and assimilating all reality, Kant limits himself to establishing that it is impossible for speculative reason to attain such a Being and prove its existence. But he carefully avoids adding that the hypothesis of such a Being, provided with all the theological attributes, contradicts all the laws of reason. That, however, is what should of necessity have been said from the standpoint of a disinterested science of pure reason.

In fact, when we cease considering the relations of phenomena among themselves and make a transcendental hypothesis of such a nature as to explain the existence of the aggregate of phenomena, it is very certain that no experience will ever come either to affirm or to deny the reality of our hypothesis, and precisely because we have taken our position outside of the realm of experience. So we shall never have the assurance that a being exists where we think it does. In compensation and by a different means of experience, it will not only be possible for us, but we shall be imperiously commanded to deny all reality to certain concepts and to affirm that, under certain hypotheses, no being exists. For in that rarefied atmosphere of transcendental speculation in which concepts are no longer rendered fruitful by experience, they do remain subject to the principle of contradiction and continue to depend strictly on the legislation of reason, so that any concept formed in contravention of its laws is disqualified by this fact alone and confesses its unreality.

Now what Kant carefully avoids saying, however strongly the evidence may coerce him, is that the idea of a *first cause*, taken as a transcendental concept, charged with explaining phenomenal existence, is in the highest degree one of those concepts formed in contradiction of rational laws and which need only to be formulated to be disavowed. Reason gives us, for managing the phenomenon, the principle of causality: *everything that exists* exists by virtue of a cause. Now a cause being *a thing that exists,* one must, in order to show the law here in its blinding light, deduce *that every cause has a cause.* That is the principle of reason which it is not permissible to transgress and which the idea of a first cause, a cause without a cause, directly violates.

When reason seeks an explanation of the Universe, it goes without saying that this explanation must be intelligible to reason. In the presence of mystery the intellect is in a state of ignorance; its query demands a response which dissipates ignorance. Now trying to dissipate ignorance by applying the principle of causality, according to its legitimate form, to the *ensemble* of phenomena taken as the *effect* of a cause situated outside of that ensemble, that is, on the one hand, a kind of anthropomorphism, but above all that explains nothing, since the form of the principle of causality is going to oblige one immediately to inquire into *the cause of that cause outside of the world* and to go back indefinitely into the void from cause to cause. If, moreover, in order to obviate this disadvantage, theology forms the concept of a *first cause,* it does not explain any more, for an added word hasn't the power of changing the nature of reason and of rendering intelligible to it what wasn't before: one does not explain mystery by the incomprehensible. So the state of ignorance remains the same, but reason has in addition been profaned by this attempt at an explanation which distorted its laws. The concept of a first cause, as Schopenhauer observed, is tantamount to the notion of iron in wood. To explain the existence of the Universe by that concept amounts to proposing to reason that two and two are five, by insinuating that at the price of this concession problems until then insoluble will be solved; it means that reason should comprehend beyond its limits and in contradiction with its laws. In the ideological realm the idea of a *first cause* is a concept befitting a masquerade, one of those artless disguises, such as those crude masks, which shock without deceiving and which the hue and cry of a carnival pursues in the streets.

"The principle of causality which has value only in the field of experience and which, outside of this field, is unavailing, even meaningless, would here (that is to say, as a principle of transcendental explanation of the phenomenal Universe) be entirely distorted from its destination." Thus does Kant express himself on the subject of the use in theology of the causal idea and he deduces *the impossibility* of attaining by that course a being which would be a first cause. Now, as we have just seen, that is well, but it is not enough and logically he should have added that the notion of a first cause offends the laws of pure reason by its very enunciation, *so that, if such an idea could be attained by a route other than that of speculative reason, it would from the standpoint of pure reason have to be considered an illusion and refused all credit.*

Now what Kant has formulated, is precisely the opposite of these conclusions of simple scientific honesty. Far from acknowledging that the existence of a Supreme Being, first cause of the Universe, is an irrational concept, he grants against all evidence that this concept, if it cannot be considered real in the light of *speculative* reason, cannot be regarded as empty either, so that, in case its objective reality should happen to be discovered by another method, this reality would be validly established with regard to human consciousness. Here then, as a precautionary measure, Kant made the breach through which he will be able to escape from the scientific rampart in which he had enclosed his mind. He declared all the proofs of speculative reason inadequate to attain the idea of God, but failed to show that this speculative reason does not tolerate the hypothesis of such a Being. In that way he continues free to hearken to the argumentations of the moral proof based on the existence of a *categorical imperative* indicating to human conscience a good and an evil. It is known that, in order to increase the authority of these claims and in lieu of seeking the roots of the notions of good and evil in experience, he assigns to them as their origin a new form of reason, *practical reason* designed for the purpose of consummating the incomplete work of pure speculative reason.

The value of that hypothesis will be examined in its proper place, but what concerned us here was to show that, without a preliminary falsification of the conclusions of speculative reason, such a fable could not have been hazarded, inasmuch as its consequences would have been condemned in advance. There would then have been no pretext for composing the CRITIQUE OF PRACTICAL REASON, for which it will be seen that there is no excuse.

*

This silence, imposed upon the rational conclusions to the extent they reveal the impossibility of constructing the idea of a Supreme Being, is not the only artifice employed by Kant in the CRITIQUE OF PURE REASON for the purpose of favoring the claims of the second critique. The imaginary conflict he sets up in reason, on the occasion of the cosmological ideas, has no other design than to bring discredit on reason by assigning inappropriate pretensions to it, and to put it in contradiction with itself, in order to be able to introduce a hypothetical principle of conciliation, which becomes entirely superfluous as soon as the apparent contradiction created by him is rejected. All the theses representative of the theological spirit admit of a presumption, an extension of rational laws beyond their limits; they are irremediably false. But it is only by ascribing to the antitheses positive affirmations, of which they are not susceptible, and exaggerated negations unattributable to them that Kant manages to compromise them and weaken their evidence.

It is well to note in the first place that Kant, intent on giving a semblance of reality to the theses of the antinomies, introduces into the conflict, as a regulatory concept, the idea of the absolute totality of the conditions of the world. Now, the antitheses are employed in all their force and constructed entirely without recourse to this concept, whose negation they, on the contrary, imply. For they aim precisely at establishing that in no direction of the mind is it possible to attain a reality encompassing the absolute totality of the conditions of the world. So this concept is an artifice by means of which the theses are going to be able to present themselves. Kant also makes use of it to compromise the antitheses by attributing propositions to them that they cannot express.

Thus, after having demonstrated the falsity of the thesis of the first antinomy, *the world has a beginning in time and in space,* Kant misconstrues the antithesis in order to be able to prevail over it. Actually the antithesis expresses only a negation: *the world has no beginning in time, nor limits in space.* Kant translates: *the world is infinite in duration and extension.* Now, by the concept of the infinite, he means a fixed quantity implying the totality of the conditions of the world. Therefore, having defamed the antithesis in that way, it is easy for him to incriminate it and he does, in fact, rightly condemn its pretension to attain by pure thought the absolute magnitude of the world by means of a regression whose legitimate rôle consists only in ascending *indefinitely* from one condition to another higher one. But, and it could not be repeated with too much insistence, such a pretension imagined by Kant is in flagrant contradiction with the pure and simple negation to which reason obstinately confines itself.

Likewise the antithesis of the second antinomy, expressing a strict principle of reason, is contained in its entirety in the following proposition, which admits of no reply: *every body is indefinitely divisible and there exist no simple ones.* But Kant misinterprets this proposition, as he did the foregoing one; he wishes to add: *a given whole is composed of an infinite number of parts.* Now reason has no need of the fact that a given whole is indefinitely divisible, so that it is impossible to attain quantitatively anything simple, and it carefully avoids deducing that this given whole is composed of an infinite number of parts. Not only does reason not use this term *infinite*, in so far as it expresses a fixed quantity, but it explicitly contests the legitimacy of its use.

So it is by distorting the antitheses of the first two antinomies to the point of compelling them to a contradiction of themselves that Kant succeeds in showing them to be vain.

It is known, concerning the third and fourth antinomies, that Kant prides himself on establishing that the theses and antitheses are equally true. But, whereas the antitheses [1] are justified by themselves without recourse to any hypothesis and move in the free air of reason, the theses [2] became animated with only an apparent reality and breathe in an artificial milieu. Kant has to create for their use an imaginary world which, in opposition to the sensible world, the only one attainable for us by Cognition, Kant terms *the intelligible world*. The hypothesis of the intelligible world rests, as we know, on that of the noumena, which are things in themselves as opposed to things such as they appear to us. In possession of these hypotheses Kant grants that the laws of our mind apply rigorously to things such as they appear to us, to phenomena, and that the phenomenal world admits of no law other than that of natural causality. He also recognizes that in the sensible world and by virtue of the causal law, it is impossible to attain a necessary being. But, he adds, things such as they are in themselves, noumena, are not subject to phenomenal laws; noumena have their own laws, those of the intelligible world, in which the hypothesis of a free causality and of an absolutely necessary being no longer encounters the plea in bar, with which such concepts are opposed by the laws of the sensible world. Kant pretends in that way to bring about a conciliation and so, according to him, a human act considered as an effect in the sensible world and subject as such to the law of natural causality, could, as a thing in itself, be freed from this servitude.

We shall demonstrate in due order that in the mental world there does not exist any notion which, unexplained by natural laws, receives any clarity from the hypothesis of an intelligible world. It will be shown that Kant, after having devised that useless hypothesis, saw himself constrained, in order to give it an object, to alter the notions of duty and of the imperative which, easily decomposable by analysis into their positive elements, have become in his system and as intelligible things in the sense in which he uses this word, things totally unintelligible in the sense in which this word admits of any acceptance. First there will be occasion to demonstrate that the hypothesis of the noumena is irreconcilable with the Kantian theory itself. Finally it must already be discerned that the idea of law is valid only in the phenomenal world, in time, space and cause, and that, if it is entirely allowable to say that the laws governing phenomena have no currency outside of the sensible world, it is not to assume laws outside of this sensible world and to imagine that a free causality and an absolutely necessary being, by the mere fact of their being notions unintelligible for the mind, are susceptible of a meaning in a hypothetical world to which, by Kant's admission, Cognition has no access.

Our immediate object here was to show that the supposed antinomies of reason, set up by Kant as a pretext for a mediation, do not exist and could have been conceived only by exaggerating and misrepresenting the antitheses. Reduced to their legitimate import all the antitheses are sound: they are the real theses against which there is no argument. Constructed, moreover, in conformity with the laws of reason, they prove to be respectful of the mystery which they allow to subsist in its entirety. They recognize the boundary where reason's power of explanation ends, a limit beyond which the faculty of comprehension is without an object. That is what rationalistic dogmatism, for which Life must have no secret, will not accept. And so, where the intellect refrains and where religious dogma explains mystery by mystery and by appealing to faith, which amounts to putting the patient to sleep for the duration of the metaphysical anguish, rationalism subjects reason to torture and puts the question to it until it confesses the irrational.

All that remains for it is to produce a race of minds, for whom the irrational is a principle of explanation. Kant has contributed singularly to the fostering of minds of that type. The theses of the antinomies, which he ventured to set forth in opposition to the antitheses and which are so many sophisms, have no other aim than to distort reason, to discredit a form of cognition that refused to speak in the sense of the fiction founded of old by the Vital Instinct.

Our purpose in recalling here those chapters of the "Transcendental Dialectic" relative to the antinomies and to the Ideal of pure reason was only to show, in the constraint there imposed on the laws of logic, the maneuver which will render possible the return to theological conceptions. It was important to designate those pages of the Critique as the place of the shipwreck. They mark the point at which Kant, seized with fear, perceives that he has broken all the moorings between theological dogma and pure reason and where he sees himself borne away adrift on the mysterious sea of the mind far from the artificial cities built by the hand of man on familiar coasts. It is then that he hastens to cast towards the land, from which he is already detached, and as a substitute for the rigid chains of dogma, new cables fabricated by means of the assemblage of the grossest sophisms hurriedly discovered in the store-rooms of dialectics.

If Kant had left all their force to the antitheses of the antinomies, it would have compelled him to give up for ever reconciling dogma and reason, and the vital fiction, unmasked by Cognition, would have lost its power of illusion. One could not be too insistent on this point: it is there, at the very heart of the CRITIQUE OF PURE REASON, at the moment when he is delivering the most decisive attack on the old fiction, that Kant blunts the weapons he is using and himself deflects the blows he is dealing from the regions where they would cause death. As in popular novels the traitor, who was thought to have been slain, is able to arise once more and, by his intrigues, amplify the feuilleton which seemed concluded, with a final vicissitude. It is under the cloak of the *Categorical Imperative* that he will be seen, equipped with levers and false keys, stealing into the CRITIQUE OF PRACTICAL REASON.

II.

Thus, from the standpoint of the Instinct of Knowledge, we have no reason to thank Kant for the manner in which he directly combatted the postulates of platonic philosophy. His will to remain the servant of the Vital Instinct intervened in his undertaking to pervert it. By falsely showing reason in conflict with itself he tried to conceal the evidence. But, whereas his volition caused him suddenly to give unexpected conclusions to his analyses, the fatality of his philosophical genius compelled him to institute these analyses with such a force that their legitimate conclusions necessarily imposed themselves afterwards on all minds that were no longer dominated by a *parti pris* of ancient morality. He did far more than refute the claims of theology by new arguments; he displaced the philosophical point of view and created a new perspective. He removed minds from the penumbra in which they were dupes of metaphysical appearances, and situated them in a clear spot from which they saw the phenomenal mirage being formed according to the laws of illusion governing it.

Henceforth this mirage is going to present itself for what it is, and the laws which determine it will, in future, confess that they exhaust their entire efficacy in instituting illusion. If their extremities outreach the phenomena they have evoked, they will acknowledge that these extensions lead nowhere and have no other aim than to create perspectives in which the eye is drowned. The phantoms of first cause, creative and anthropomorphic divinity, liberty and absolute truth are going to be dissipated in this luminous atmosphere. The questions which arose at their appearance will no longer have any occasion to be posed, and metaphysical anxiety will be concentrated in this unique interrogation, before which the mind of Nietzsche remained haggard: Does phenomenal existence, which alone is given us, absorb the totality of existence? Does it leave room for the possibility of the thing in itself? Are we to conceive an eternal return of things? Or is an unknowable, a nirvana opposed to the phantasmagoria of the knowable universe?

Such a displacement of the anxiety is the substitution of the Hindu perspective for the Jewish perspective, of a viewpoint of knowledge for a vital viewpoint.

The significance of this metaphysical vicissitude can preoccupy us later. Here we can only establish and describe it. Now it is certain that the Aryan races, which for two thousand years established their fulcrum for living on a fiction borrowed from the dogma of another race, have for a century seen the thought peculiarly their own revive in German philosophy with Kant, with Schopenhauer and with Nietzsche, who enriched it with a singular energy and a new anguish.

Did Kant foresee all the consequences of his work and the new orientation it was to give to philosophy? There is reason to doubt it: like all great discoveries this strong conception came from the Unconscious, and the man of genius, in whom it became manifest, was not too conscious of the fact. Schopenhauer, freed from the dogmatic prejudice which enthralled the mind of Kant, rectified the Kantian philosophy on many points. The circumstances of his day were also helpful to him: the discovery and translation of the Hindu books, whose substance was unknown to his predecessor, permitted him to connect critical philosophy with its true origins and to discern the direction in which it was destined to develop. Thus, if we are to get a complete idea of the philosophy of pure Knowledge, such as it is in contradistinction to platonic philosophy, we must set aside the last propositions toward which Kant directed his analyses and consider only those analyses themselves, the consequences which logically follow from them, the interpretation thereof furnished by Schopenhauer, the extended currency that philosopher gave to the new point of view and the clarifications he contributed. Finally, a comparison of the system thus formed with Hindu metaphysics, such as it appears to us in its great lines, will show us the existence, in a remote past, of a mentality similar to the one we are reconstituting and will illumine our conception of the world with the radiance of an analogous conception.[3]

*

One can say of the greater number of philosophical systems comprised between Hinduism and Kantism, that they all present themselves as ontologies. If, like platonic philosophy, they concede in some measure the unreal character of external objects, it is to accord all reality to metaphysical objects and to create a supersensible ontology. If, like atomistic philosophy, they neglect the objects imagined by the preceding philosophy, God and the soul, it is to endow the objects of the external world with real existence, it is to create a new metaphysical being, matter, and thus found a sensible ontology. Such, then, is the characteristic trait of both of them: they think that the cerebral laws in consideration of which we see objects appearing in space and ideas in reason, attain genuine realities, the Being in itself of things. Conversely, the distinguishing mark of the philosophy of Knowledge is the following: it takes these cerebral laws for an apparatus of deformation designed to make us see the Being in itself other than it is, to make an imaginary spectacle arise. The hypothesis of the first philosophers contributed to strengthening life by creating the illusions, which make it progress, but it results in a system of contradictions in which the concepts of finite and infinite, liberty and necessity clash in irreconcilable conflicts.

The philosophers of the first manner always arrive at inferring a relationship between cause and effect, creator and creation, between the laws of thought and those of being. The philosophy of Knowledge infers a relationship between the thing represented and representation. Now it eventuates in this ascertainment that every phenomenon of representation is of necessity a phenomenon of deformation, a phenomenon of illusion, so that the representation of the Being in its own view is in its essence a systematic falsification of the Being in itself, supposing that such a being, conceived by the preceding philosophy, is endued with reality and that something exists outside of the phenomenon. Therefore it is going to study the laws of the mind, considering them as the means of that deformation: to the ontological system of the preceding philosophers it is going to oppose a system of illusionism.

The philosophers of the theological group are like naïve spectators, who are being shown for the first time the figurative spectacle in a panorama. They are on a circular platform in an attenuated light and, before their eyes, in interminable spaces illumined by an intense light, there unfold scenes, representations of battles, of festivals and sinister events, entire cities, flat open country with rivers, fields and verdure: behind those landscapes the horizon widens. And, once the first astonishment of these naïve spectators is dissipated, after admiring the beauty of the prospect, they are seized by the whim of contemplating at closer range all the details of the region and plan to go as far as that steeple on the hill. They estimate the length of the way as perhaps half a league and start out, for they trust in the indications provided by their eyes and are convinced that their perceptions evaluate exactly the distance to be covered.—Contrariwise experienced spectators enjoy the panoramic illusion without being its dupes. They know that they are in a place, which has been arranged to produce illusion, and that they are witnessing a spatial representation. They know that their perceptions do not correspond to any equivalent realities and that, were they to leave the circular perimeter where they are placed and run toward the distant steeple, the vision would be immediately destroyed; they know that the miraculous leagues, along roads surrounded by landscapes and light, would vanish and that, after a bound of a few meters, their *élan* would strike the painted cotton material, where vision is condensed in a system of lines and colored surfaces. They are aware that the plans formed to proceed to the end, notwithstanding its being visible to them through the deforming and creative mirage, are vain and disproportion-ate for attaining an object without reality, whose deceptive appearance one can touch with one's hand, as soon as one withdraws from the circuit, where the illusion is born, to come a few steps closer. Instead of forming such unreasonable designs these experienced spectators are going to examine the procedures, which determine illusion. They will discover the artifices of light and tricks of perspective constituting the spectacle and realize that the information conveyed to their minds by their senses, as well as the whole apparatus serving to transmit this information, do not have as their purpose to put them into relationship with real objects, but rather to create, with the aid of some material signs, a purely ideal representation essentially different from the model serving as its pretext.

The philosophers in the service of Knowledge resemble these disabused spectators. They view the spectacle of the Universe with the same clear look. But how much more perfect and better arranged is the gigantic illusion whose enigma is proposed to them. The one just described, which is instituted by man, deforms only a fragment of space. It lures but a single one of our senses, deceiving only our sight and, when we leave the circuit in which the illusion is formed, to enter the place itself, where the spectacle appears to be situated, then, if the spectacle itself disappears, the painted fabric inducing it remains to explain our error to us: the illusion allows its material remnant to be grasped; it appears as an aggrandizement, a deformation, but as a deformation of *something*.

The spectacle of the universe is created by means which are far more powerful and complex: these means are the artifices of space, time and cause. There is, further, the mirage of abstract representation and of mental laws. At least it is as such, as artifices and means of illusion, that philosophers in the service of Knowledge are going to consider these laws governing our mind. To be sure, this new point of view will not dissipate the mystery of phenomenal appearance. But in these new philosophers the cult of and the jealous respect for mystery are the supreme form of the religious sentiment interpreted as a constraint exerted upon oneself and converted into intellectual probity. A counterpart of their passion for knowing and their will not to be dupes, this respect, originally resigned, soon turns into a new will to maintain the mystery at the origin of this cosmic spectacle, whose intrigue, they know, wishes to remain secret. By this *parti pris* the philosophers of Knowledge identify their desire with the indefinite forms of the laws of Cognition; it is in that way that they accept and realize their destiny.

III.

The philosophy of Knowledge is, therefore, really the study of the Universe taken in its entirety as a system of illusions. Describing our faculty of knowing means, for such a philosophy, disassembling the different lenses of an apparatus. This is the apparatus through which Being, becoming conscious of itself, appears in its own view.

The suspicion of an illusion steals into the philosophical mind on the occasion of the objects of the external world, and it is expedient to note here that the science of Knowledge, which is destined later to destroy all theism, owes its establishment to idealistic schools alone, to the exclusion of materialistic schools, whose credulity concerning the immediate results of perception would have been an obstacle to the critical progress of the mind. This is why one could not give even the most summary history of that science without naming Plato among its founders. Although he was also the principal inventor of a completely contrary philosophy and must be considered as the father of theology, he none the less cast a doubt on the truthfulness of our perceptions and Schopenhauer did him appropriate homage by recapitulating his thought, such as it is expressed in many a place in his works, in the following maxim: "The world which strikes our senses does not really exist; it is but an incessant becoming, indifferent to being and not being: perceiving is not knowledge so much as it is illusion."

The principle of deformation glimpsed by Plato is known to reside in the rational apparatus with its power of producing what Kant later calls the concept: it inheres in our faculty of abstraction and our ability to form general ideas. Our senses, Plato observes, furnish us nothing but contingent data; it is through the *idea* that we grasp and establish particular things and convert them into objects of knowledge, for there is no true knowledge except of the general. Here we have, then, with reason in which the idea is reflected, a first lens signalized by philosophy, a first prism through which the reality we ascribe to things is deformed before becoming manifest to our minds.

With Locke another anxiety arises. What is the value of perception itself? In what state are these particular objects, objects whose contingency was already established by Plato, transmitted to us? A perception is formed only through the mediation of a sensation, and a sensation is a state of the cognizant subject. Thus sensation is a new prism through which the object is modified before appearing before the mind. Locke, who made a distinction in bodies between first and second qualities, considered the latter as the contribution of sensation, that is to say, as a property of the subject. These secondary qualities are, as we know, color, sound, scent, taste and low or high temperature. Now experience itself permits us to touch here the deforming power of sensation and to verify philosophical induction. The anomalies presented by sensory functions in certain individuals, inform us through pathological exaggeration as to the normal behavior of the function. Do we not see certain particular cases of vision augmenting or diminishing the clarity or the dimension of objects? Does not Daltonism go so far as to modify their color?

Here, then, we already see the real existence of the object singularly reduced, inasmuch as all the concrete qualities just enumerated must be withdrawn from it and attributed to a disposition of the subject. There remains scarcely anything equivalent to that painted fabric of our panorama, which created the complete illusion of a landscape. But with Kant even this remnant will disappear. Everything still recognized by Locke as an intrinsic property of the object, as primary qualities, such as extension, contour, form and motion vanishes before Kant's discovery, for such properties can only be manifested in space and in time. Now the great work of Kant, accomplished in the fifty pages of the TRANSCENDENTAL AESTHETIC, consists in his having demonstrated that space and time do not, on the one hand, have substantial reality and that, on the other hand, they are not properties of the object either; that, on the contrary, they belong to the knowing subject and that they are the forms of this subject's sensibility. According to Kant's observation, indeed, it is possible by thought to withdraw from time and space a specific object or all imaginable objects without altering the texture of time and space. In his view time and space remain unimpaired after that subtraction and ready to envelop new objects and render them apprehensible. But it is impossible to abstract time and space themselves, and that means precisely that they are a part of the apparatus through which the object is apprehended.

Here then, with space and time, still another lens of the apparatus of Cognition has been disjoined and set aside. According to Kantian terminology this new lens is sensible intuition; space and time are the two pieces of glass superimposed one over the other, which give it its power. But at this point Kant must be rectified by Schopenhauer, because the lens of sensible intuition could not perform its office without being completed by a third piece of glass. Time and space cannot produce an objective representation unless they are put in relation with each other, as well as with the subject of cognition, by the cause. That is what Schopenhauer demonstrated clearly in his FOURFOLD ROOT OF THE PRINCIPLE OF SUFFICIENT REASON and in his supplements to the first book of his great work. Sensation, the raw material of all perception, can indeed become an object situated in time and space on but one condition, namely that it be considered the effect of a *cause* different from itself. Hence it is on this condition, by means of the mechanism of causality, that the subject is going to externalize the modification he feels and create the material object. Kant wished to make of space and time the only forms of sensible intuition, whereas causality included among the twelve categories was to be considered one of the *a priori* forms of another faculty, reason properly speaking. Schopenhauer considers causality to be one of the forms of intuitive representation by the same right as time and space, and views all these forms as being of an intellectual nature. He reserves for reason the rôle of forming concepts and abstract representations.

The essential thing, after all, is that Kant should have kept for causality its character of an *a priori* element, rendering experience possible and not deriving from it. In that he did not fail. Schopenhauer's analysis only permits us to discern more clearly the composition and the disposition of the different media through which the object is deformed before it is apprehended by the subject. The state of perfection, to which this philosopher elevated the science of Cognition, reveals three screens interposed between the object and its representation in consciousness: these screens are a sensation, the primal source of the whole process here described, an intuition objectifying the sensation in the mirage of time, of space by the mediation of cause, transforming it into internal or external perception, and finally reason with its systematic apparatus of concepts, which converts the experimental datum into thought, into an object of knowledge.

What, in view of this threefold apparatus of deformation, remains of the objects in themselves? Nothing appreciable really, since these objects, which seem to us to be situated in space and in time, linked among themselves by relations of cause to effect, appear as such only by virtue of the structure of our mentality and do not fulfill those conditions any more than colorless substances seen through green or blue spectacles would fulfill those of being in reality green or blue. Therefore Kant's discovery, which resulted in showing time, space and cause as forms of the subject's faculty of knowing, suffices to place before the imagination in its concrete value the conception of the universe taken as a system of illusion, to compel us to assume a difference between things such as they appear to us and things as they are in themselves. By that discovery Kant transformed the aspect of metaphysics; he created a more baleful and destructive suspicion of all ontology than the most direct attacks could have done.

*

And yet, would one be justified, after this description of the several pieces of the apparatus of Cognition and despite the information apparently conveyed in addition by certain sensuous anomalies, in dogmatically inferring a positive discrepancy between the object and its representation? Would there not be some warrant for minds, offended by such a conclusion, imagining up to this point that an identity, though not subject to any check, may nevertheless exist between the representation of objects in the mind and real objects? That was the hypothesis of Malebranche and, however hazardous and improbable it may appear, one still could not call it impermissible, for it implies no contradiction and the Kantian analyses do not up to this point authorize dogmatic negations. Besides, persuaded by analogy and considering that all representation in the phenomenal world implies some model, the mind still affirms and with some appearance of justification, that the existence of phenomena necessarily presupposes the existence of some reality, hidden behind those phenomena, and serving as a pretext for their manifestation. It was in yielding to this instinct of analogy that Kant laid down, over against phenomena, the hypothesis of noumena, objects such as they are in themselves.

If such hypotheses are still permitted, that comes from the distorted manner in which the philosophical problem was approached, that is to say from the ontological presumption created by platonic philosophy, which had previously disguised the aspect of this problem and falsified its terms. Plato, Locke and Kant begin by regarding this presumption as sound: it is only after psychological experiments and analyses that they come to feel its fragility and discover the flaws revealing its improbability. Presently the science of the faculty of cognition was completed by a final proposition which, by a series of logical deductions, manifests the unreal character of all representation with an evidence, against which no quibble could prevail. Schopenhauer may claim the honor of having made this proposition known. However, it is certain that Kant knew it and it seems as if, in the first version of the *Critique,* he were close to formulating it. If, in the following amended editions, he seems chiefly concerned with evading and obscuring it, one must see therein his preconceived opinion of ancient morality and the determination to conceal a truth which, clearly formulated, would have made a return to theology impossible. From a point of view of equitable criticism one must accord to Kant the glory of that discovery because the best part of his philosophy renders it indispensable and draws its clarity from it.

Schopenhauer's merit lies in an intellectual probity, which subordinates the interests of Life to those of Knowledge and which no prepossessions of social interest can any longer suppress.

There is no representation except of an object for a subject, that is the supreme principle of the science of Cognition formulated by Schopenhauer. By means of analysis we have already been able to distinguish three kinds of apparatuses, through which reality seemed to become deformed in order to constitute an object of knowledge: sensation, intuition in time, in space and in causality, and reason with its faculty of generalization and abstraction. The necessity of a preliminary distinction between object and subject, in order to render a representation possible, is going to account for the true nature of these apparatuses through which we have seen knowledge filtered. Besides, it will confirm their deforming rôle and place the knowable Universe definitively before the mind as a system of illusionism and no longer in a hypothetical manner, but with all the certainty implied by an *a priori* science.

We owe to the genius of Schopenhauer the introduction into philosophy of the conception of the

Universe *as representation*. It is his best claim to glory. To be explicit, it is again his peculiar and rare originality that he should have devoted his initiative in metaphysics to a notion of simple good sense and given it a scientific value. Now Schopenhauer's teaching did not consist exclusively in the notion that the world is representation; he added that the world is *my* representation, thus affirming the identity of the knowing subject and the object. But it is well to establish that he based this second assertion, in the manner of Kant, on an observation derived from psychological experience. His point of departure is the *self*, the immediate subject. It is in the *self*, in each individual *self*, that he discovered the confusion of object and subject. I say *myself*, he observes, of my sensations, as I say *myself* of the knowledge I receive from them. They are *my* sensations, which become *my* perceptions, and he establishes that man with his capacity for reflecting and abstracting possesses "the absolute certainty of knowing neither a sun nor an earth, but only an eye which sees this sun, a hand which touches this earth." Again, in order to rightly grasp the philosopher's exact meaning, one must substitute for that eye which sees and that hand which touches, the sensation that is ascribed to the one or to the other. It is on the occasion of this sensation that the mechanism of time, space and causality is unlatched and that the *self* as subject places its own sensation, that is to say its own *self*, outside of itself under the form of earth and sun in space, thus giving itself the representation of the external world.

But it is also at the same moment that the self as subject comes into being in relation to that self as object, that external world which, having suddenly appeared, determines it. If it tries to apprehend itself without having recourse to this determination by means of space, here it is constrained to a new division of itself, projecting into distinct moments of time this *self*, which it destines to become an *object* of knowledge and this *self as subject*, which wishes to know. Instead of placing itself as an object for a subject in space, the self as subject, in order to take cognizance of itself, places itself as an object for a subject in time. But the new subject thus formed tries in vain to add the knowledge of itself to that of the self newly objectified, so as to possess in that way the knowledge of the total self, for it can no more escape the disjoining process than did the preceding subject. The very desire of every subject avid to apprehend itself involves an alteration of its reality and the necessity of fixing a part of itself on the pedestal of the past, of separating and withdrawing from it in order to see and to know it. Thus, from the point of view of the microcosm, does the principle of the distinction into object and subject reveal, by pure psychology, the necessarily imperfect, incomplete and unachievable character of any state of knowledge, the impossibility for the self of apprehending itself integrally in cognition.

IV.

This psychological deduction is perfect for rousing the concrete perception of the spell of any phenomenal representation and the hallucination it implies. It shows in a definitive manner all the laws of Cognition converging to render impossible the integral knowledge of Reality, constructed expressly in such a way as to fortify the mystery of its origin, instead of conducing to dissipate it. Now it is well to observe that such results, which sanction the propositions of the antitheses, have been attained by purely psychological means and without the intervention of any hypothesis. Possessed of this ensemble of laws directing the mechanism of Cognition we are now going to show that, by complying with the dialectics of Kant and accepting the employment of his metaphysical hypotheses, one comes, with respect to the macrocosm and in an even more palpably obvious manner, to the same conclusions which have just been reached through psychology. Thus it will be seen that the premises of Kantian philosophy making known the idealism of time, space and cause necessitate a purely phenomenalist interpretation of the Universe excluding all possibility of Reality apprehending itself as such and being resolved into a state of Knowledge. There is more: in imitation of Kant we shall resort to the concept of the absolute totality of the conditions of the world invoked by the philosopher as a serviceable hypothesis qualified to render possible a metaphysical construction of Reality; now this concept, confronted with the laws of Cognition such as they have just been briefly set forth, will require rigorous deductions in absolute opposition to those which Kant intended to make.

*

Once in possession of this hypothesis it becomes possible to form the concept of the Universal Being, *that outside of which nothing exists*. Within this concept, and in contrast with the Phenomenal Being, Schopenhauer's *world as representation*, which experience gives us, it is further permissible to introduce the concept of the *Being in itself*. However, if there be need to enunciate it, the formation of this latter concept by no means presumes that it corresponds to any reality. We are here in the domain of pure metaphysics, where no experience ever enters in, either by inflating the hypothesis with life or nullifying it, to confirm or dispute its reality. But the principle of contradiction, whose impact has ruined theological conjectures, is of such a nature as to make known within what limits the concept of the Being in itself remains apprehensible, what it is permissible to express regarding it and especially, and with entire logical certainty, what one must deny its including. If of these three concepts of unequal value that of the Universal Being is considered first, one ascertains that it also forms Unity in itself, since *that outside of which nothing exists* implies a totality to which, under the hypothesis, nothing can be added and from which nothing can be abstracted. If we then go back to the principle of Cognition, which was stated above, it will be seen that this unity can only represent itself to itself by becoming distinguished into object and subject. What that amounts to saying is that unity only represents itself to itself in multiplicity, in diversity and it can be formulated that the Universal Being necessarily and in the most radical fashion conceives itself other than it is. And here we have, necessitated by the *a priori* laws of reason and with respect to the Universe, the deformation whose mechanism had been revealed by psychological experience in the intimacy of consciousness.

*

The Universal Being necessarily conceives itself other than it is. It is important to draw from this first conclusion the integral consequences it permits. Now the following one, which will determine the concept of the *Being in itself* by means of a negative description, imposes itself as a corollary: the *Being in itself is unknowable to itself.* Indeed one cannot conceive a state of knowledge without a state of representation, without a subject confronted with an object. Outside of these conditions the term *knowledge* is for the mind devoid of all meaning, all intelligibility. It is then no more than a word failing not only to represent any reality, but any concept whatever. On the other hand, it is impossible to attribute to the *Being*

74

in itself the distinction into object and subject: that would be identifying it with the world as representation and would, therefore, amount to abolishing it. Thus one is compelled to affirm of the *Being in itself* that it is unknowable for itself. Now what has just been affirmed of the *Being in itself* may also apply to the Universal Being. For, unknowable for itself as it is, in so far as it is considered as being in itself, the cognizance it takes of itself is false in so far as one considers it in the world as representation, since, distinguishing itself into object and subject, the Single conceives itself as multiple. So we must conclude, after all, that knowledge is not an apanage of Being and that *there is an essential antinomy between existence and knowledge.* It goes without saying that the knowledge, with which we are concerned here, is absolute knowledge proposing absolute truth to itself as an object, knowledge such as it was conceived by the old metaphysics. Henceforth it will have to be regarded as an hysterical aspiration of humanity, as probably one of the means of serving the manifestation of phenomenal life and assuring its movement in duration. In compensation the true science of cognition will have to be defined as the enunciation of the laws of illusion, the description of the illusory perspectives, according to which the Universal Being deforms itself in so far as it represents itself to itself. It is the science of the *non-true,* the law and condition of phenomenal life, according to Nietzsche's formula.

The concept of a *Being in itself,* of which one could not say if it admits of any reality, may then be accepted as a regulatory concept devised for the useful purpose of serving to make comprehensible the nature of phenomenal representation. Whether the phenomenal universe really has Being in itself as a counterpart prior to the distinction into object and subject, or whether this concept is only a logical form of reason, it may still be maintained that such an hypothesis is legitimate as a purely logical concept and that, by its intervention, the phenomenal universe is impelled to show more clearly the necessary principle of deformation, which presides at its genesis, the illusion calling it forth. Every thing that knows itself knows itself other than it is; the universe we know takes cognizance of itself in us other than it is. Illusion is the law of Life such as we know it experimentally. Such are the avowals of the phenomenal world, when it is interrogated, trusted and compelled to speak through the hypothesis of the Being in itself. Therefore this hypothesis of the Being in itself and that of the absolute totality of the conditions of the world, in so far as they are circumscribed within the limits in which they imply no contradiction, show themselves very apt to make known by a magnifying process the illusory character of phenomenal representation.

V.

These first ascertainments are going to give rise to new deductions; they will authorize, or rather prescribe some negations. The Kantian hypotheses will in effect have to be denied. The object and the subject and the different objects and the different subjects have no existence in themselves, no noumenal types corresponding to them. There is no object except for a subject, no subject except in the presence of an object. Objects and subjects are purely appearances. The material object no more has its noumenal equivalent than does the simple substance called soul, of which one makes the subject. For the Being in itself, the only possible home of the noumena, is conceived as anterior to the distinction of the Being into object and subject, so that diversity could find no place in it. The diverse objects and subjects of the phenomenal world could not, then, have a noumenal correlative, even if it were to be conceived in the manner of the Platonic Idea as a very general type and in the status of a genus: the existence of noumena would improperly introduce diversity into the Being in itself. So we are compelled to deny the existence of noumena with the result that only two kinds of conceptions are possible: that of phenomena whose reality is certified for us by experience (the reality of an appearance),—and that of the Being in itself. All transcendental metaphysics is reduced to deciding whether or not this conception of the Being per se, of which we know only that it is unknowable for itself, conceals a real existence.

*

After the hypothesis of the noumena has been rejected, there still remains for us to contest another assertion of Kant's, which until now was accepted as true by reason of its opportuneness and because it tended to destroy in people's minds the belief in the reality of things. One could not really concede to Kant that time, space and causality are necessarily properties of the subject. If we see rightly that these properties do not belong to the object, how could they be attributed to a subject, to which existence in itself cannot be ascribed, which exists only in its relation with the object and which manifests itself and allows itself to be apprehended only through these very properties, with which we wish to endow it. Therefore, from the standpoint of illusionism to which in the wake of Kant and of Schopenhauer we have been led by the science of cognition, that claim could not be upheld: rather may it, on the contrary, be said with verisimilitude that time, space and causality must by the same right as the distinction between object and subject, of which these properties are the consequence, be regarded as the very procedures of phenomenal illusion, as the panoramic laws engendered by the attitude of the Universal Being in so far as it represents itself to itself.

This conception may be determined by the following considerations. We have said that the Universal Being can take cognizance of itself only by means of an alteration of its own essence, that it necessarily conceives itself other than it is. At least we must think that this representation, however inadequate it may necessarily be to its object, is perfect as representation and as complete as it can be, that it exhausts all the possible combinations in order, through an indefinite series of clichés, to consummate the description of its model and that it imitates the aspect of the total unity by a multiplicity that discourages any effort of experimental numeration. One does indeed see the modes of this representation being realized at all the stages of the Universe. It ranges in form between an inanimate and immobile world, whose unique rôle it apparently is to be forever an object—and all the eyes, all the senses, from those of the lowest animals to those of man, organs serving an infinity of distinct subjects which perceive that inanimate world. But all these perceiving subjects are objects themselves, for themselves and for all the others, and the figurants of a vaster spectacle, which, with the new artifice of reason, attains in the human self the greatest complexity and generality. Now, as soon as the Universal Being plays the part of an object for a subject in some particular being, is it not clear that this distinction necessarily entails, as complementary means of representation, the entrance upon the scene of time, space and cause? Whatever may be the number and the position of the elements forming on one side the spectacle and, on the other, the spectators, is it not evident that time, space and cause arise with the very fact of the division, according to which this distinction was established? For that reason, while sensation may be regarded as the reciprocal action of the object on the subject, as bringing the content of experience and signifying the relationship in quantity and position pursuant to which the Universal Being was divided into subject and object, time, space and cause appear as direct consequences of the determinate attitude in accordance with which this division was effected; in no wise connected with either subject or object they specifically constitute the perspective, by which the Being in itself deforms itself in order to apprehend itself. They are, as we have said, the very laws of phenomenal illusion.

If Kant's assertion, which made of the three faces of this prismatic mirror a property of the subject, has not been sooner contested, it is because it tended, as well as the actual description, to show these forms of intuition as the laws of phenomenal appearance and no longer as the laws of things. Now this essential viewpoint—time, space and causality considered as an apparatus of deformation, as purely representative means,—sufficed to destroy the ancient philosophy and to substitute for the conception of the world according to Plato and Judaism, the scientific conception which was that of the genius of Hinduism.

VI.

When one already knows, by the consideration of the concept of the Universal Being, that such a Being can only conceive itself in a manner radically different from what it is, the intervention of this apparatus of deformation takes on a clear meaning. One then discerns that it represents itself sincerely for what it is and confesses its illusory mission by its very form: time and space admit no limits, and cause, which supposes indefinitely a cause engendering it, does not support any first principle. Do not these forms give us in that way an intimation that they lead nowhere and correspond with no object, that they are something *through which*, an optical apparatus by whose means a mirage is formed—and not vehicles toward a given point? The ancient philosophers, who had resolved to make of time, space and cause rigging, upright masts and stretched ropes in order to ascend toward metaphysical ideas, were astonished to be forever mounting and never arriving: they came to persuade themselves that they had hit the mark, when they were seized with giddiness. Contrariwise the new philosophers, who know that these ideas of time, space and causality are the prisms through which phenomenal representation is diversified, find them marvellously adapted to this use. They are not astonished by the magnifying quality of a lens, nor surprised that colored glasses should tinge. They are like informed spectators of the panorama, who interpret the play of light and perspectives deceiving them as laws of illusion for an illusive representation.

VII.

Evidently the importance of the Kantian conception regarding the forms of intuition did, in despite of Kant's intent, give a new direction to the metaphysical point of view. The law of causality, which served to connect the universe with a creative cause, shows its true nature, inasmuch as it professes to be a means of representation in space and in time. The conception of a world created by a force outside of itself gives way to that of a Being, which represents itself to itself. The idea of representation is substituted for that of creation. All the mental monstrosities brought forth by the preceding hypothesis, such as dualism, conciliation of finite and infinite, of liberty and fatality vanish and the metaphysical problem presents itself henceforth under the following aspect: existence is given us as representation and we *know* it only as such. Has the concept of an existence per se any reality? Do the thing in itself of Kant, Schopenhauer's world as will, the Brahma or Nirvana of the Hindus exist?

That this Being in itself, by whatever name one may designate it, is unknowable for itself the Kantian deductions have compelled us to confess and that is the only certainty we have so far been able to acquire pertaining to it. That was also the conclusion of Hinduism, which preceded us by such an interval on that metaphysical path and formulated the science of cognition from the first, such as the German genius recovered it. Long before the speculations toward which we tended only after a long effort to throw off the theological yoke, the same position of the mind to which we are but now acceding, had become established in the Brahminical philosophy. And it is not a question here of a fortuitous coincidence of conclusions: they are indeed the same deductions, which compel like minds to the same ascertainments. The same intelligence freed from the yoke of the Vital Instinct shows itself to be more preoccupied with knowing than with living and ends with a like detachment and a like perspicacity.

The philosophers of India were no dupes of the artful rôle of causality, inasmuch as they saw in it continuously the means of an illusion: there was no trace in them of the imagination of a first cause. They believe that Life, however, has a fomenter: ignorance, here a synonym of illusion, of that state of rapture under the ascendancy of which, in attributing duration, extension, permanence and reality to things, we create the world of appearance. But this ignorance, which engenders desire, is itself born of desire, for in this state of ecstasy from which phenomenal life arises, the twelve causes discerned by metaphysics are embroiled in a mutual interlacement, now causes, now effects. From this confluence of desire, motivated by sensation, born of contact, which is the seat of sensible qualities, with perception—we find arising the name and the form by which things are distinguished and become objects of knowledge. Now this knowledge, the daughter of ignorance, is accompanied by suffering, which determines the aspiration to Nirvana in which the vital frenzy is to be dissipated and the hallucination of Maya to vanish.

Whether it be a question of the return to Brahma of the first masters of Hindu metaphysics or of the method of annihilation preached under the name of Nirvana by the heirs of the doctrine of Buddha, one must see in either term an identity—just as in Kant's *thing in itself* or Schopenhauer's *will*. All these terms have metaphysical value and accord with the ensemble of the system they express only on the condition of being entirely stripped of their customary meaning, so that they render no more than the idea of what is unknowable for us and for itself. By neither one of the terms they used did the Hindus ever intend to signify anything but a negative state, namely what is opposed to the relative or the composite, what is abstracted from the conditions of phenomenal life and of knowledge. This is what some expressed abstractly by the idea of the void and others represented by concrete descriptions, numerations and prodigious exaggerations of a kind to confound the imagination. But neither side contested that a different state, one in opposition to the phenomenal world, was possible. The existence of such a state even impressed them as indispensable: it seemed to them that a world in itself should of necessity be opposed to the world of representation, to the world engendered by the Maya. They regarded phenomenal life as an accident, a malady of true life, one which was to be cured by the return to Brahma or by annihilation in Nirvana. The transmigration of souls through duration could, then, end some day, the nightmare was to cease; the concatenation of causes showed its fragile vanity and the awakening was to take place secure from the mirages of cognition.

VIII.

It has been said that with Nietzsche a new metaphysical anguish was born: under the idea of the eternal return, which strikes Zarathustra in his cave with such despondency, there is indeed hidden the aforesaid metaphysical interrogation, an anxious interrogation this time and one presuming no response: if it be accepted as a datum that the world exists as representation, is another mode of existence possible? Does not the world as representation absorb the entire substance of Being? Does not the phenomenon with its laws exclude the hypothesis of an existence in itself? Does man return forever? "Does little man return forever?" Such is the anguish oppressing Zarathustra and on which, in lending him these thoughts, his prating animals comment, these creatures who are already accepting and becoming resigned before exerting themselves to the stage of a joyous will:

"But the plexus of causes returneth in which I am intertwined,—it will again create me! I myself pertain to the causes of the eternal return.

I come again with this sun, with this eagle, with this serpent—*not* to a new life, or a better life, or a similar life:

—I come again eternally to this identical and self-same life, in its greatest and its smallest, to teach again the eternal return of all things." [4] These words of Zarathustra imply the belief that it is impossible to withdraw from the circle of the phenomenal world; they set up a sudden doubt before the hypotheses of Hinduism and renew religious disquietude in the most poignant way.

The question as to whether or not it is possible

to decide between Nietzsche's hypothesis and the Hindu solutions is one into which we shall inquire in its proper place: these conceptions, however diverse in their consequences, derive from a like origin and lend themselves to comparison with each other. But our first concern should be to draw from the science of cognition, such as we have seen it reconstructed with German philosophy, the nihilistic conclusions it commands. The antinomy that we have seen manifested between Existence in itself and the state of Knowledge apprises us of the fiction necessarily implied in all phenomenal manifestation. We shall discover that the science of Cognition, by disclosing the futility of the springs communicating its movement to the phenomenal apparatus, paralyzes the illusion which made it move, and threatens the Vital Instinct with death.

CHAPTER III.

IDOLS OF THE LOGICAL HEAVEN
TRUTH

What is Truth? Pilate said unto him.

Gospel according to St. John.

I. The idea of Truth is formed by means of a confusion of the form with the content of Knowledge: the infallibility of the Intellect, in so far as it comprehends itself, is attributed to the Intellect as it is applied to experience.—

II. Philosophy of empirical Knowledge: Claude Bernard.—

III. The relativity of Knowledge, founded on the non-existence of a first cause, has been manifest from the simplest sciences of observation: for example, astronomy.

IV. The uncertainty of the sciences grows in ratio to the degree of empiricism that is implicit in their object: morality, the most uncertain of the sciences.

V. To that science, the richest in empiricism, there has been applied the conception of Truth formed on the occasion of the *a priori* sciences of reason.

VI. Truth, a principle of fanaticism and combat, is the substitute for the principle of differentiation, which engenders Life.

In our first chapter we showed the monotheistic fiction in its vital rôle. It was regarded as the support of the illusion necessary to moral life during the eighteen hundred years of our occidental civilization. We took it at the stage of its formation in dogma, saw it grow stronger and followed its evolution therein until it was formulated under rationalistic guise outside of the theological egg, in which it had originally germinated. This amounts to saying that we have seen it little by little substitute for a unique fiction which appealed to imaginations and commanded without explanation the whole series of useful acts, an ensemble of abstract fictions pretending to derive their authority from the laws of reason. These abstract fictions, divesting themselves more and more of their primitive appearance, have come to the point of ridding themselves of the idea of God, which had created them. But those among the rationalistic philosophers, who made the definitive attack on divinity, did not fail to despoil their victim: they seized its attributes with which they covered, as with an emblem of command, the ideas they were enthroning. Imitating the attitudes and the procedures of the ancient God the rationalistic fictions set themselves up as real entities, as the laws of Life which, in reality, utilizes them as means and artifices.

We intend to show that these abstract ideas proceed from theology and that one must see in them slips from the dogmatic plant; apparently thrust into rational soil they traverse this thin layer of artificial soil to strike root in the deep compost of faith, in the hot manure of credulity in which they are really immersed and on which they thrive. Taking their semblance into account we here call them,—in order to distinguish them from the theological idols,—logical idols. These idols are the ideas of *Truth* and *Liberty*. The Science of Knowledge, which does not have for its aim the organizing of Life, but inquires into the way Life is made and organized, considers them like the idea of God, and by the same right, as fictions. It is going to show us their inanity, while at the same time recognizing their vital utility. Did we not take the non-true to be a condition of Life? There will, then, be no occasion whatever for astonishment at this condition here producing its consequence.

The ideas of Truth and Liberty are fictions, but natural fictions begotten by Life, which begins to lie as soon as it stirs. The bunch of fresh grass attached, for purposes of training, in front of the nostrils of the horse which, in a riding-school at the fair, makes the circle of wooden horses turn, does not by itself have any power to make the apparatus move, but the horse, put there and harnessed, darts after the fresh grass fleeing before him with a speed equal to that which he is attaining in order to reach it. Thus with his effort he drags the entire circle of wooden horses with its childish riders, its girlish equestriennes on a holiday, amid the noise of words and songs, the fracas of organs and cymbals and under the light of multi-colored oil lamps. Truth and Liberty are for man equivalent to those bunches of fresh herbage: man believes that a fixed truth is assigned as a goal for intellectual effort; he believes he is possessed of a free will, that is to say the power to modify himself, to determine himself in the direction of the Truth he will have found. And man too starts after those flowery promises, which regulate the speed of their flight by the energy of his zeal. In that way the infinitely complex diorama of the moral world is put in motion, amid the procession of civilizations, the clamor of prayers, the frenzy of acts and the meditation of philosophers.

I.

Rationalistic mythology, in which the idol Truth finds its place, is constituted in the same manner as theological mythology was formed with Plato. It results from a confusion of the form with the content of Knowledge.

In the number of relations among things grasped by the mind there are some, that have fascinated men beyond all the others: they are those which impose themselves upon every one's attention with equal rigor. Now, what has been overlooked, is that the universal similarity of that vision comes from the fact of its pertaining to the very form of the intellectual act. In so far as the mind formulates those relationships, it is apprehending itself and describing its own mechanism. This mechanism, as we have seen from Kant, is a system of illusions, inasmuch as it is precisely the apparatus by whose means Being, distinguishing itself into object and subject, deforms itself in its own view. The mathematical, geometrical and logical propositions are the detailed description of the diverse lenses composing this apparatus; they set forth the properties of time, space and causality, the rational modalities, in a word, the laws of perspective, according to which Being presents itself as an object for a subject. All minds agree on these laws, because all minds are subject to them, being, as they are, the very rules of the game of the intellect and anterior to all empiricism. They are *that through which* the phenomenal illusion is going to arise, they are *that* prior to any appearance, and

88

that is common to all and placed before the eyes of every subject, *that* being equivalent to the circular balustrade, which keeps all the spectators of the panorama at the same central point where the creative illusion of the spectacle is formed.

Now, in lieu of perceiving like initiated spectators, that it is the mission of this fixed system of perspectives to falsify Being in its essence and to engender the phantasmagoria of the non-true, men have been struck by these facts alone, namely the unanimity and the agreement of their vision regarding the laws of representation themselves and the absolute, immutable and quite definite character of these laws. To this concurrence of all intellects regarding the laws governing the mind they have given the name Truth. In this sense it is a legitimate appellation. It cannot be denied to the mathematical, geometrical and logical laws, which have brought it into operation. For these laws do, with respect to reason, constitute that outside of which the mind ceases to move.

Up to this point and in so far as it sanctions this infallibility with a special term, human intelligence is merely exercising its right. But it is precisely here that the mistake is made, and it behooves us to note its phases now. For the most part men derive little mental satisfaction from the contemplation of these logical and mathematical laws, since they in no wise concern their active emotion; the universal consent they engender is, in effect, compensated by the little joy they procure to men plunged in life. Consequently the latter scarcely linger to envisage them; they consider them just long enough to counterdraw them, to take them as models of the idol they are going to set up and to deprive them of the appearance of their properties. Having become infatuated with this power inherent in the intellect to grasp rigorously the formal laws of its own working, to be, from that point of view, in harmony with itself, they attribute this power to it in regard to its content, which the intellect has precisely for is object to render indiscernible by indefinitely diversifying it, by altering it, by making it appear through the deceptive still-life painting of becoming and amid the perspectives of space.

Of a view pure and simple, which science prolongs as by means of a telescope or renders sharper with a microscope, but whose sole function, as far as it applies to phenomenal reality, is to perceive relations knit together indefinitely, men have made a machine for the production of truth, that is to say that kind of certainty and perfect repose enjoyed by the intellect in so far as it takes cognizance of itself and of itself alone. Therefore, when men invoke Truth and ascribe a despotic power to it, they are not referring to logical or mathematical truth; it is not truth in the only sense of which this word admits, but the idol they have put in its place and conceived in its image. What they have in view in their inquiry is a first cause of the physical phenomena from which to deduce the world, a universal moral law, a cause primal in its class deciding sovereignly as to good and evil. Now the hypothesis of a first principle or a first cause is shattered by the inflexible form of the law of causality, whose essential interrogation only ceases making itself heard when the life of the mind ceases equally, when the power to know, exhausted by the effort, renounces being gratified.

II.

The domain of truth, then, is circumscribed within clearly determined limits. These limits are those of the formal laws of the intellect themselves. Truth is the exclusive attribute of the science of the forms of Cognition and the final lesson of this science consists in teaching us that its mechanism, as soon as it goes into action and makes the Being become manifest

90

to itself, distorts the Being into a system of infinite perspectives with the inevitable effect of rendering it indiscernible and refractory to any construction.

As soon as the mind ceases describing the different mechanical means, which direct its operation, to consider what appears through the play of this machinery, its work ceases to be the science of Cognition and becomes the science of the phenomenon,—Science, in the ordinary sense of the word. And this science ceases immediately having truth for its object. Its aim is to describe the succession and concatenation of the phenomena, which compose the cosmic mirage in conformity with the laws of illusion produced by the distinction of Being into object and subject. It is evident that never, among this ensemble of phenomena, will it discover the one which would be explanatory of all the others, since that phenomenon cannot exist, seeing that the explanation of the Universe, not being involved in the mirage of causality, consists in the very fact of the distinction of Being into object and subject and is thus out of the reach of Cognition.

In contrast with the science of Knowledge, whose object is truth, one may assign as an object to science proper the notion of mystery. To understand scientifically is to become more capable of astonishment. A profession of agnosticism is at the threshold of all scientific thinking worthy of the name. A scientist reveals the measure of his mind when he conceives the indefinite progress of science as advancing, not toward the discovery of Truth, but toward a more direct view and a greater sense of mystery.

Human intelligence with its laws, whose importance for deformation has been recognized, epitomizes the attitude of the Universal Being taking cognizance of itself, giving itself as a spectacle to itself. The means of this phantasmagoric enterprise have confessed their aim and their essence, inasmuch as we

91

have seen them disposed in such a manner as to perpetuate the spectacle indefinitely and know them to be so arranged as to guarantee eternal sustenance to curiosity. Would it not be strange to expect truth from an apparatus instituted for the purpose of begetting illusion? Would it not be wronging the laws of the mind and amount to considering them ill-made, defective and poorly conceived, to imagine that they are going to fail to live up to their mandate and suddenly cease engendering phantoms, that they are going to reveal the enigma which it is their mission to perpetuate?

The spectacle of science and that of its procedures completes the dispersal of such a reverie. For science, by discerning the immediate causes of phenomena, has no other effect, after every link has been added to the causal chain and every explanation has been furnished, than to show that ignorance has remained the same: thus the consciousness of mystery is amplified by the fact of every effort to dissipate it succeeding only in making it more obscure and more impenetrable. On the part of scientists the pursuit of Truth would amount to the violation of the laws of the intellect. It would, in fact, be irreverence, if it were not in its essence stupidity. So it gives way in them to an attitude of a very different sort, a curiosity that is sated with its own tension and acquiesces to never being gratified. The habit of dealing continually with the mysterious laws of the universe and the constant effort to rise above intelligences in order to see, beyond the common enigma, the formation of new enigmas develop in them, after a resignation perhaps stoic in principle, a resolute partiality in favor of *what is*, of that *"amor fati"* of which Nietzsche made the appropriate measure for appreciating the greatness of a spirit. From this point of view and this posture there comes into being an intellectual mode in absolute antagonism with belief, with aspiration toward Truth, with respect for Truth. That word, having become suspect, is no longer found except on the lips of those, who expect from Science what it cannot give, on the lips of those latter-day believers, those dogmatists of the most recent and blindest species, who, in the intellectual world, are situated at the antipodes of scientific minds.

I am tempted to think that in the course of this century scientists, and principally in this country, have furnished minds of the most noble and the most philosophical kind. This will become evident and by contrast, when we consider during the same period,—from Kant to Nietzsche,—the effect of philosophers bent solely on adulterating the laws of reason and on restoring the theological spirit. True philosophy, indeed, does not consist in the creation of a terminology and an algebra by means of which official diviners, men who do not laugh, exchange untranslatable formulas, ready to explode, like ill-made chemical compositions, as soon as, despoiled of their esoteric character, they are exposed to the free air of good sense. True philosophy consists in knowing the power and the limits of the mind, in not confounding its categories and in not asking it what it cannot give.

Now, of this power and of its limits, scientists seem to have been more aware than philosophers. In them the very practice of science does, at least in a potential fashion, imply this precise notion. As proof of their possessing it most of them have given us no more than the direction of their research itself and have been content with the testimony of their work. However, one of the most illustrious among them was able to bring out this substratum of universal thought in striking fashion and in pages of a perfect clarity. In the second chapter of his INTRODUCTION TO THE STUDY OF EXPERIMENTAL MEDICINE

Claude Bernard gave a veritable canon of the scientific mind in its relations with the universe which it observes.

Beneath identical roots like tendencies are perpetuated, manifesting solely by terminations the evolution of thought. Thus, for example, the theological spirit seems to have taken refuge in the theoretical spirit. It is there that Claude Bernard discovers it; he tells us the usefulness and the danger of theories. "One must believe in science," he tells us, "that is to say in determinism, in the absolute and necessary relation of things, in phenomena pertaining to living beings, as well as in all others; but at the same time it is necessary to be thoroughly convinced that we have this relationship only more or less approximately and that our theories are far from representing immutable truths. When we hazard general theories in our sciences, the only thing of which we are certain is that these theories, speaking absolutely, are wrong. They are but partial and provisional truths, which we need like steps upon which to rest in order to advance in the investigation." And furthermore: "After all, theories are only hypotheses verified by a more or less considerable number of facts; those which are verified by the greatest number of facts are the best, but they are still never definitive and should never be credited in an absolute fashion."

Finally he clearly opposes the pure science of Cognition, which considers subjective, that is to say formal relations, and engenders immutable truths, to science proper, which considers objective relations and applies to that content of Knowledge we call the universe. Without circumlocution he assigns ignorance as an aim for this science and, in the following fine formulas, he sets it up as dogma: "The mind of the experimenter," he says, "is distinguished from that of the metaphysician and the scholastic by modesty, because experience is continually making him aware of his relative and absolute ignorance. By instructing man experimental science has the effect of diminishing his pride more and more by proving to him every day that first causes, as well as the objective reality of things, will forever be hidden from him and that he can only perceive relations. That, indeed, is the unique aim of all the sciences, as we shall see farther on."

The unique aim of all the sciences, Claude Bernard says plainly. This declaration of a scientist comes to the support of the philosophical conclusions that have just been accepted. One must detach from them the following two essential propositions, which comprise and distinguish Knowledge in its two aspects: the object of the formal science of Cognition is truth. This object cannot fail to be attained, nor is it susceptible of confusion with any other; it is unique. Conversely, the object of the science of the Universe is to make us sensible of our essential ignorance. Mystery is the keystone of the whole phenomenal edifice; it is this keystone that we are to discover by science in its final effort. Men's idolatry consists expressly in assigning as its object to the science of the content of Knowledge, that is to say, to the science of the Universe, the object pursued and naturally attained by the science of the forms of Cognition.

Therefore the notions of science and of Truth are mutually exclusive. Science never proposes Truth to itself as an object: it is a view, our natural view prolonged, and one which can be extended indefinitely, because it will never lack for space beyond the horizons temporarily limiting it. Science never does anything but interweave chains of phenomena linked together by the relation of cause to effect. At times it ties these chains to a theory chiseled into finality by means of hypothesis, in order to give repose to our astonished curiosity and, by that artifice, to bring out the harmonious beauty of this fragment detached from the immeasurable. But it knows that there is no ultimate finality, that beyond the furthest end there are others, indefinitely, which, once they have been disclosed, will manifest the relativity, the defects and the errors of this theory, the harmony of which now seems complete.

III.

As soon as the intellect, through the apparatus of Cognition, assumes the rôle of a subject before an object and sees some phenomenon appear, all the conditions are immediately realized which must assure the inviolability of the non-true, guarantee its permanence and render impossible any accident of a nature to make the spectacle cease by the intrusion of truth. This fact of scientific uncertainty based on the non-existence of first causes, this essential fact is revealed and affirmed in an absolute fashion in the simplest and most perfect sciences of observation. Thus astronomy, whose investigations have nevertheless succeeded in going beyond the phenomena perceptible to our senses, shows us its impotence and the very source of that impotence.

Founded, as it is, on mechanics astronomy constructs the world on almost exclusively rational data, which fact accounts for the precision of its results and the strange obedience of celestial bodies to its laws. However, this science considers celestial phenomena only for a period of duration, which is preceded by other periods. Moreover, it does not know the relation and the hierarchy of cause to effect, which can exist between the different states of matter and the forces animating it, like heat, electricity, motion. So, from not being able to assign an immediate cause to the cosmic movement, it takes it as given, restricts itself to studying it in its manifestations and, renouncing knowing its origin, withdraws it in a wholly artificial manner from the evolutionary cycle, on which it depends and in which it is in reality lost in the causality of becoming, in the perspectives of that rational law, which compels us to be forever seeking the explanation of a given state in an antecedent one. By this restriction, which it imposes upon itself, astronomy confesses the relative character of its researches and its laws.

Besides, it makes a similar avowal under another form, for it attains and commands but a small fragment of space which, for purposes of study, it isolates from all the rest, on which it depends. Under the name of solar astronomy it considers only the heavenly bodies subject to the attraction of our sun. It leaves to stellar astronomy the task of collecting partial information on more distant fragments of space, and it has not been possible to build a bridge between those two extremities of one and the same science. Newton's laws account for the orbits of the planets around an identical sun, provided the movement is granted, but are of no avail to explain to us the equilibrium of the stellar worlds among one another. From a precise conception astronomical science precipitates us into the incommensurable: it teaches us that the star nearest to our solar system is situated at such a distance from it that the law of attraction could no longer, from such a distance, have any efficacy. Yet the relation of our Universe thus circumscribed with the Universe surrounding it is none the less certain. This dependence, whose law remains unknown, limits the certainty of our observations and implies a principle of error. The unknown Universe embracing us allows, with respect to our little world, a power of causality able to break the partial determinism we have decreed; a miracle ever remains suspended over our previsions. The impossibility of supporting our sun immediately on Centaurus or Sirius compels us to imagine, beyond the known celestial bodies, nameless stars or systems of orbs of an incalculable weight and volume on which to suspend our universe, or rather to assume, beyond the laws of attraction, new laws of which those of Newton would be but a distant corollary. Subject, as we are, to the causality of space we must perpetually extend the unknown Universe in order to balance the known universe and find props for it. Thus the impossibility of circumscribing the Universe and relying on a definite ensemble, in order to deduce real laws therefrom, does not proceed from the impotence of our minds, which we could suppose to be surmounted, but from the very form of the laws of representation. The impossibility of limiting the universe in space and in becoming and, consequently, the impossibility of measuring it, of knowing the veritable laws of its dance comes from the nature of things; it is insurmountable and rational laws here prove to be the means of instituting illusion with a metaphysical art.

IV.

Astronomy has shown us how a principle of uncertainty is introduced into Cognition with the first empirical datum taken as its object. So we must conclude from the inquiry made under the auspices of this science, the least complex regarding the object it considers, that uncertainty is not a particular, accidental and transitory instance of phenomenal Cognition, but rather its law.

Nevertheless, once this demonstration has been made from a theoretical and absolute standpoint, it must be acknowledged that the phenomena studied by astronomy, if the mystery of their origins is disregarded, offer us a sequence of laws so well interconnected that this assemblage of truths could suggest the illusion of Absolute Truth. The study of chemistry would also offer us an analogous spectacle. By means of these phenomena the mind observes the cosmic mirage in its most elementary aspect: organic bodies represent a purely objective reality in the world; they are eternal objects. Therefore, among the relatively simple combinations of matter, the mind is able to attain a cause so distant that it embraces and rigorously commands the succession of phenomena for a period of duration and in a part of space both vast enough to inform us with an exactitude even exceeding practical interest.

But things present a very different aspect when science, abandoning the study of these elementary and purely objective states of matter, considers more complex states. On that path the uncertainty of its results tends to increase with the growing difficulty of distinguishing the cause from the effect and in proportion as it observes more and more specific phenomena, after those of chemistry biological ones, such as physiology and medicine, and finally those we have professed to distinguish from all the others under the name of psychological and moral phenomena.

In this latter world chaos seems to follow the beautiful order presented by the series of physical phenomena. However, it is not as if there were not revealed resemblances and a certain parallelism between the latter and the former; in fact, while chemical repulsions and affinities are resolved in actions and reactions, mixtures and conflagrations, the same conflicts and the same affinities are manifested in higher physiology by formations and oppositions of peoples and countries, religions, moral systems, customs and legislations and, by way of consequences, by treaties of alliance, wars, persecutions and penalties, whose ensemble institutes the entire historical scene. But, while the laws in virtue of which chemical bodies combine or repel each other are known to us to the point where we can foresee with certainty the results of the joining of two or more of them under determined conditions, to the point that we are able

99

to produce the whole variety of compound bodies in our laboratories, it is on the contrary very difficult for us to predict with any accuracy the facts to which the conjunction of two or several groups of men will give rise. The knowledge of prophets is dubious and great men of politics do not, except for brief periods, manage to have a share in historical causality: the succession of events never fails, by unforeseen deviations, to belie the horoscope they had formed and to alter the reality of which they had pretended to prove the instigators. If statistics do reveal to us among the facts of the moral world the persistence of a determinism in hidden regions where we no longer follow it, it gives us only very distant points of reference between which diversity is multiplied and escapes our grasp.

Thus, while the study of the physical sciences forcibly suggests the hypothesis and the illusion of an absolute and initial truth communicating its certainty to all the facts it unites, the spectacle of moral phenomena, sociological facts and beliefs of human mentality gives at first blush the impression of a labyrinth in which masked personages, crossing or interweaving, contribute to misleading one another by false words or by the deceptive aspect of their appearance.

It is natural for it to be so, since it is amid the complexity of the moral world that the apparatus for producing the phenomenon attains its perfection and employs all its means of illusion. To the intervention of time and space, linked by the infinitely fertile intrigues of causality, there is added here in its highest expression the distinction between object and subject, which lies at the core of the moral world and there plays its rôle of supreme magician. But even if we were to neglect this cause of mystification and envisaged the facts of the moral world in their physiological aspect alone, they already show themselves to be situated at the extremities of the phenomenal world so that their positive determination would presuppose a perfect knowledge of all physical and chemical phenomena and their most minute concatenation. Now among the sciences treating of the divers fragments of the Universe, the mind has not succeeded so far in casting the causal cables, which, fastening them to the ring of an identical principle, would connect them among themselves and unite them in a single sheaf.

Between mechanics, astronomy, physics, chemistry and physiology there are breaches of continuity showing abysses, which have as yet been neither filled nor traversed: consequently morality, the last and the most complex of these sciences, the one having the most numerous causal system as antecedent, finds itself isolated from its origin by a greater number of those dangerous intervals over which the fragile flight of hypothesis alone ventures. Morality, then, is the most uncertain, the most dubious of all the sciences, the one lending itself least to a general construction; it proves the most incompatible with that unique law that has already been evaded by the preceding sciences.

Chemistry distinguishes seventy-three different elements each of which has its law, its peculiar morality, which must be respected. In ethics proper, if a scientific method were to be applied to that science, instead of those seventy-three elements forming as many initial causes and commanding all the complexity of material substances, one is, for the sake of rendering deductions possible, obliged to establish as first principles phenomena so specific that they are to be found in infinite number and of equal value. Each individual temperament, with the unknown factor of its different chemical composition, must really be considered as the principle of a series of ways of being constitutive of a morality, the only one valid for this temperament. Besides, each one of these particular moralities can only be determined in the vaguest manner; this is because the individual temperament upon which it is founded, so little known itself in its intimacy, enters into action and reaction with manifold and changing circumstances, were it only, to cite but one, with the composition of the atmosphere constantly modified by meteorology, whose sovereign influence on physiology would require the formation of a special science, one as yet scarcely outlined. Ethics considered from a positive standpoint and as a science qualified to determine the laws of human actions, hence permitting them to be foreseen and experimentally produced, shows itself to be at once the most complex of the sciences and the least advanced, the one whose results are the most doubtful, the one admitting of the shortest truths, little truths without atavism and in infinite number, diverse to the point of seeming contradictory because of the ignorance we represent concerning them as to the too remote causes, from which they are descended and have come down to us, while ceaselessly diverging from one another.

V

Hence it is not the spectacle of the moral world that could ever in a disinterested mind have begotten the illusion of a primal, general and absolute truth governing phenomena, if that illusory idea had not been formed elsewhere through the consideration of the fixed laws, which regulate the form of Cognition. Now, once that concept was formed, it was precisely upon the phenomena of the moral world, those least compatible with it, that men were resolved to impose it. This is what happened: to the most complex empiricism there was applied with the greatest rigor and conviction the law of what is situated on this side of any empiricism.

102

That is explained by the direct interest, which men joined in society have in knowing the laws regulating their associations and their mutual relations. Caught between the need of this immediate knowledge and the impossibility of possessing it, they imagined it. Renouncing a scientific method they had recourse to a theological method, that is to say, to the procedures of the Vital Instinct: they exalted their attitudes of utility and their desires to the status of moral laws. Scientific observation yielded precedence to what Nietzsche terms the will to power. It was not perceived that there are as many particular moralities as there are individual temperaments and that all are equally legitimate. But each individual temperament *established its particular law as universal law* and fought to impose it.

The existence of individual resemblances manifested by similar attitudes of utility drew coalitions together and determined the formation of moral rules approximately common to a group, a people, a race: it is in this way that the different religions and moralities, which extended the struggle for power from individuals to more numerous collectivities, were formed. Every one of these moralities deduced, as it was, from a particular and different temperament, really differs from the neighboring one and, with respect to all the like temperaments it governs, may be said to have an equally legitimate value. It is the equivalent of an element with its laws, which are good solely for it and for it alone. But, in order to augment its power, each morality employs an expedient that is a fiction and this fiction, a means of power, is at the same time the sign of power, for it asserts itself so much the more forcibly as the temperament formulating it is more energetic. It consists in a substitution and a confusion of original causes: that which is an attitude of utility for a certain temperament, a real, empirical and comprehensible principle of all morality, implying the diversity of all moral systems, becomes transformed into a universal law borrowed by turns from revelation or from the *a priori* forms of reason, this law implying that there exists a unique morality, a single form of the notion of goodness decreed by divinity or by a categorical imperative.

VI.

This compromise is the pedestal upon which, in the moral world, the idol Truth is erected. Each morality, different from its neighbor and deeming itself the only true one, is bound to deny the truth of all the others and to hate them. The idea of Absolute Truth, an illusion forged by the Vital Instinct, here divulges its vital rôle; this fiction shows itself here as the instigator of Life, the conception of the non-true, considered by Nietzsche a condition of life, here proving its efficacy.

What, then, is Truth? It is a war-machine. Enthroned in the sanctuary of all religions, irrespective of whether they are secular or revealed, it is a principle of fanaticism and of combat. It is thereby that it is vital, that it shows itself as a cause of acts and communicates movement to the phenomenal apparatus. For phenomenal Life, being diversity, is in its origin differentiation, and differentiation in the moral world is antagonism and hostility. For the distinctions *good* and *evil* formulated by the ancient theological morality, a scientific morality will be induced to substitute other categories: it will distinguish in Life attitudes for living and attitudes for dying, a flow and an ebb. All those will represent attitudes for living which tend to differentiate individuals from one another, attitudes of combat struggling for power, egoism, conceit, contempt of others, ferments of individualism. All those regarding individual differences as illusory will appear as attitudes for dying, those assimilating men to one another and reducing them to a parity of homogeneous and indiscernible elements, all those which tend to reconstitute unity, to suppress the phenomenon, such as fraternity, self-renunciation, justice. Since we are submerged in phenomenal Life, we are aware of it alone and do not know its opposite. Thus all these regressive attitudes tending to evade the phenomenon may have a meaning and attain their aim. But we cannot further that result and in our phenomenal world we are constantly seeing them vanquished by vital and combative attitudes, either vanquished or slyly utilized by the latter.

The principle, which differentiates all things and diversifies beings, is the one we always find triumphant.

The idea of Truth in morality is the mask and the substitute for this principle of differentiation, which engenders Life. This is the way it will be so long as moral facts have not undergone an empirical method of observation and been assembled into a true science, while the system ramified by causes and effects has not been found, by virtue of which all these particular phenomena, all these individual temperaments, the only really legitimate causes of a morality, will show themselves to be involved in a more remote cause, in some cosmic cause inherent in the course of the heavenly bodies or in the composition of matter.

It is permissible to imagine that science will some day succeed in filling in the intervals now separating ethics from its origins, in creating means of communication—methods of mental navigation or aerostation—between the diverse fragments of the Universe at present severed for the mind, that the plurality of the sciences—mechanics, astronomy, chemisty, physics, physiology, psychology and ethics—will be reduced to a single science. The final propositions of moral science would then entail the practical certainty from which the truths of astronomy have benefited; one could no longer impute to them theoretical uncertainty alone, the relativity essential to all phenomenal knowledge, whose necessary character was recognized above.

Would this marvellous result bring some change to the course of Life and more particularly to matters of ethics? It behooves us to doubt it: the diverse moralities now vying among themselves for supremacy and denouncing one another with maledictions would then, to be sure, appear with an equal character of necessity, with equal titles, and would seem different branches sprung from one and the same stock, but it would be hazardous to conclude therefrom that such an ascertainment would dispose them to tolerate one another. Chemistry determined the laws according to which its elements attract and repel each other; it prescribed according to what proportions they combine to form compounds, but the knowledge of these laws in no wise impedes their efficacy. Quite the contrary: it is in the name of these laws that elements continue, according to the hazard of encounters, to blend, to mix or, by sudden explosions, to manifest their irreconcilable hatred. There is no reason for supposing that moral systems, once derived from physiology and chemistry, would yield another spectacle. But rather does the analogy induce us to think that, were they divested of the presumption that some represent Truth more perfectly than others, they would in order to combat one another argue frankly from their unlikeness alone.

Besides, we are far from those frank antipathies and as long as scientific unification, which has been imagined as a hypothesis, is not accomplished, the idol Truth will mask the real and only reason for aversion among men: difference. Men hating one another, because they are different and unequal, will think that they do so in the name and in the interest of Truth, which each group pretends to possess in its camp and sees as its duty to make triumph. Hence the idol Truth appears as the mythological, hypocritical and false representation of a real cause, namely the principle of enmity involved in the idea of difference; but it impels men to the same acts as would this real cause, for men, like all natural bodies, always do what they have to do.

CHAPTER IV

IDOLS OF THE LOGICAL HEAVEN
LIBERTY

"Free will" really means nothing more than an absence of feeling new chains.[1] *Nietzsche*

All living things are obeying things.[2] *Nietzsche*

    I. Liberty, in the positive sense: a state, which accompanies the supremacy of one force over another or several others.

    II. Liberty in the metaphysical sense: a case of the necessary or a negative concept.

   III. The effort of the philosophy of the Vital Instinct to establish the existence in the world of a principle of liberty: its presumption in describing and naming the unknowable.

   IV. Contingency: that this concept is applicable only to phenomena, whose causes we can know.

    V. Free Will.

   VI. Its source in the illusion of personality.

Men, like all other natural bodies, always do what they must do. But they do not believe it. For true causes making them act with necessity they substitute other principles of action, of which they show themselves to be dupes. It is in this way that they profess to be free.

These mythological principles, to which men refer, are of value only to the extent one can see in them representatives of and substitutes for realities, which, in order to live and prosper, have an interest in disguising themselves. We established that Truth, a ferment of ardor and fanaticism, has for its object to increase and legitimatize, by the character of universality it confers, the power of particular instincts and to stimulate the frenzy through which men, distinguishing themselves and opposing one another, accomplish the work of differentiation of which Life consists. Now, while Truth is a means of rendering Life more intense, Liberty, with which men believe themselves endowed, is the very sign of the energy of their activity.

It seems as if those two illusory modes were indispensable to the maintenance of moral being and as if no human existence were possible without their intervention. So it is perhaps necessary for men to be dupes of those waving flags and that martial music leading them. But the Instinct of Knowledge, which does not propose to maintain and fortify Life and whose sole object is to undo its mechanism, does not assume the duty of undergoing the same illusion. In those divinized terms, in so far as it considers them in themselves and independently of the realities they dissimulate, it sees only assemblages of words ill adapted to any meaning, inaccessible to any intellect. It is its pleasure and its task to reveal their emptiness.

We have shown that the idol Truth, considered in the light of a first principle, by means of which Being is to be constructed and defined, is shattered by the form of the laws of causality in time and in space. Liberty is going to prove refractory to any definition. Hence we shall not resuscitate here the ancient quibbles for or against the hypothesis of free will, but show that the word Liberty, taken in the sense in which philosophy uses it, is not intelligible, that it represents nothing apprehensible by any intellect.

I.

Before inquiring whether a thing is or is not, one must really first try to find out if it is possible and, with that end in view, state precisely what one means by its name. Now the word liberty has a very clear meaning from a relative standpoint. One says of a force that it is free, whenever it is not hindered by any other force or any obstacle from producing its entire effect or from realizing itself according to its inner will. As between two forces opposing each other that one is called free which constrains the other and through this constraint, develops its inner tendency; it is free in the measure in which it develops this tendency, its liberty being bounded by the degree of resistance shown by the force it is oppressing.

If we take it in this sense the word liberty has a perfectly intelligible meaning and one that is valid for phenomena of all kinds: it is a meter, which evaluates a relation of dependence between two or several phenomena. A body in the gaseous state is free to expand to the extent that surrounding bodies do not hinder its expansion. A ship is free to pursue its course in the measure in which the force of the motor activating it surpasses the force of the water which resists it. A people is free in the presence of another to the extent the latter does not hinder the different modes of its activity,—the ability to govern itself, to conquer new territories and to develop its industry and its commerce.—Every individual is free within the social group of which he is a part, in the degree in which he is not prevented by power—an expression of the will of one individual or by collective will,—from accomplishing the acts of his choice.

In any case the notion of liberty is clearly discernible: inasmuch as it denotes the consequences of a relation of intensity between two competing forces, it establishes a supremacy. Now, at any rate, two elements at least intervene, two elements or a considerably greater number of elements. Thus we are here in the domain of plurality, in the phenomenal domain in which rational laws hold despotic sway and impose an irreducible determinism. Every time that two or a greater number of given forces are face to face, those which are stronger gain their liberty to the detriment of the others, and it is quite impossible for the mind to conceive it to be otherwise. Just as the whole is larger than the part, so the stronger dominates the weaker and is, in comparison with it, in a relation of free to non-free.

In seeking to ascertain how the word liberty came to be conceived, one observes that it corresponds to a mental construction of the same nature as the word majority and that it satisfies an equivalent logical need. Majority signifies that between two groups one surpasses the other in quantity; liberty that one excels the other in force. It expresses an evaluation of a greater against a lesser without any notation of degree. Now such a meaning of the word *liberty*, which is perfectly consistent with the laws of the intellect, bears no resemblance whatever to the philosophers' liberty in the sense of free will: it should be said that this ordinary and intelligible meaning is diametrically opposed to the philosophical notion, if it were possible to conceive any reality in the latter, to see in it anything but an hysterical aspiration outside of mental reality, an attempt to explain the inexplicable doomed from the start.

II.

Spinoza, however, gave a definition of freedom. But in defining liberty he really suppresses it, for he subjects it to necessity and thus shows that from the metaphysical, as well as from the physical standpoint, this term has no independent value of its own. "A thing is free," he says, "when it exists by the necessity of its nature alone and is impelled to act by itself; a thing is necessary, or rather, constrained, when it is determined by something else to exist and to act according to a certain definite law." [3] We easily comprehend the second part of this definition, for it applies to the order of things in the *world as representation*. Necessity is the law of the phenomenon. "Everything living is an obedient thing." As for that free thing described by the philosopher, we see that there was no need for a new word with which to designate it, that it is but a case of necessity and that Spinoza formed his concept of liberty within the concept of the necessary.

Besides, we do not apprehend in the world anything that is determined to act by the necessity of its nature alone, for we could not reduce to this positive formula our ignorance of the causes, by virtue of which such things exist, operate and become. Neither would we be able with Spinoza to use the concept of necessity in order to make of it the law of Being in itself, which, from the Kantian point of view, corresponds to substance, to the God of the Ethics. The concept of necessity is given us only in phenomenal interrelation and it would be a kind of rational anthropomorphism to apply this phenomenal

112

law to that which, by our hypothesis, we situate outside of the phenomenon. If everything that appears within the framework traced by the distinction between object and subject, on the fabric of time and space and through the meshes of causality and the transparency of the principles of reason is subject to necessity and exists for the mind only by virtue of a determinism, then it is not permissible to say anything of that to which we attribute existence outside of time, space, cause and the distinction between object and subject. Of what is formed by means of negative concepts alone we cannot affirm anything positive.

Hence one will not agree here with Spinoza that God or the Universal Being is a free cause subject solely to the necessity of its nature, for Spinoza makes of liberty, and rightly, a case of necessity; now the concept of necessity is valid only in the domain of the relative, whereas the Universal Being, *that outside of which nothing exists* forms a unity exclusive of any relation and leaves room for no substance whatever, with which it could enter into a relation. For the same reason one could not say of the Universal Being that it is free in the usual sense of that term and in so far as it implies the supremacy of one force over another. All that is left as a resource for metaphysicians is to oppose the *free* to the *necessary* by definition and to make of it the quality of Being in itself, of that which is situated outside of the phenomenon. But this term will then be denuded of all content, for it is not putting sense into a word to affirm of it that it does not mean this, so that the word "free" would here express only our ignorance. Any other word or any other assemblage of syllables would be able to do as much, but this one would, among all the others, have this grave disadvantage that it would then be employed to express two different things, since it already has a customary and

113

perfectly defined meaning in the phenomenal domain as far as it proclaims the supremacy of one force over another, or rather the consequence of this supremacy.

III.

Thus, from whichever side we may ascertain our position, it is impossible to attribute any other real sense to the term liberty than this latter usual meaning, which does not lend itself to any transcendental application. However, the effort of the entire official philosophy goes toward establishing that there is in the world a principle of liberty. That arises from the situation adopted by minds, who are deceived by the principle of causality and need to feel that Being is determined in its essence. Causal necessity, which admits of no first cause, does not permit them to complete the construction they are obstinately bent upon realizing. They are deaf to the warnings of criticism, to the sincere declarations of the laws of the mind which give themselves for what they are, namely means able to institute the cosmic panorama; they cannot persuade themselves to consider the phenomenal world an illusory system, inasmuch as they wish it to represent reality and to afford an explanation. They are set on knowing beyond the limits of Cognition and cannot resign themselves to thinking that the genesis of the knowable Universe is lost in the Unknowable. That is why they seek, outside of scientific laws, a different principle offering phenomenal reality the support which it does not find in reason.

But, while they are going beyond scientific laws to imagine this singular principle fit to govern and explain the real, it is actually in vacuity, outside of the laws of the intellect, outside of the laws of any possible representation that they are instituting their research. What is more, they forget that this reality, to which they wish to assign laws differing from those of the mind, exists only for the mind. In fact, as soon as the mind abstracts itself in order to allow only the object to remain, its attempt fails; in suppressing itself it suppresses the object, all reality vanishes and the world as representation is dissipated and gives place to a state which, allowing no subject, admits of no explanation and is incomprehensible to any intelligence. This state, unknowable in itself, philosophers are relentlessly determined to examine; it is between this state and the world as representation that they pretend to establish a phenomenal bond.

The words *liberty, truth* in the sense in which they are used by these philosophers, defy any definition, because they aim to describe in positive terms what is situated outside of the laws of Cognition, that before which there is no other posture than to establish ignorance as dogma and, by a final effort of the mind grasping its limits, to conceive, along with the antinomy between *existence in itself* and *knowledge,* the impenetrability of one for the other of these two states.

In truth the intellect does not apprehend any existing thing without attributing its existence to another thing or to a law. When, having come to the confines of time, space and cause, it strikes states of being of which it does not know the antecedents, such as the very fact of existence or, in a particular domain, the irreducibility of elements, it formulates, with Spinoza, that these things obey the necessity of their nature, which amounts to saying more simply that they are thus. But submitting them to necessity is its way of assimilating them, for necessity is the term to which the Intellect reduces as to a mental unit everything that has to do with being. When it cannot make that reduction, it no longer apprehends anything, it is ignorant.

It is in the place of this ignorance that philosophers put words. Just as they exclaim *eternity, infinity* in order to mask their inability to limit Being in time and in space, they cry *liberty* when causal necessity ceases to justify the existence of phenomena and fails to account for some reality. Now, this word adds nothing to their ignorance but confusion. For, when we cease understanding by causes, we do not know whether this inability comes from the present weakness of our minds or from the nature of things: in the first case necessity continues to operate in a region in which we lose sight of it; in the second case we do not know anything of what replaces it and can pronounce no opinion of it, but rather it must be maintained that the word *liberty* is the most unsuitable for designating that unknown state, since, as we have expressly noted, it has a positive sense and since in that sense it implies the conflict of two forces and indicates the supremacy of one over the other. Now, who could fail to see that it is impossible to affirm of a thing having no discernible connection with any other that it was victorious in a struggle for which phenomenal existence was the reward, and if the fact of Being itself is in question, is not the absolute contradiction implied in such an hypothesis obvious?

IV.

Nevertheless the philosophers of the Vital Instinct, charged with invigorating the illusion necessary to Life, did not relinquish their task. They sought in a roundabout way to introduce liberty into the world of concepts and to give it the appearance of a meaning under cover of *contingency*. But it is easy to show that the term contingency was for this purpose deflected from its legitimate use and that what we have here is a game of dialectics, of which the artifice is manifest.

The contingent has no signification except in the domain of the possible. It is, according to the dictum of philosophers, that whose existence implies neither, on the one hand, contradiction nor, on the other, necessity. Now, such a thing exists only for the mind, for the mind, that is to say, when it is unaware of a part of the causes which will determine a phenomenon. The contingent is not a quality of the phenomenon: it characterizes an attitude of a given mind with respect to a given phenomenon, whether this phenomenon be hidden from the mind by time, if it is situated in the future, or by space, if it is situated in the past, but at a distance from the mind that speed —couriers, postal service or telegraph—has not yet surpassed. In both cases, whether it be a question of a fact that has already occurred, but is still unknown, or of a future event, the situation of the mind is the same: either it knows all the causes likely to produce the phenomenon and then the latter is called necessary, or it is ignorant of a part of these causes, so that sundry conjectures may be hazarded as to the precise form of this phenomenon and the latter is said to be contingent. But it is apparent that we are dealing with an abusive term and that the phenomenon in itself is never contingent.

Contingency exists only for the mind, by reason of its ignorance of the succession of causes, which determined the phenomenon or will with necessity determine it. As soon as the latter is known, it is apprehended by the mind in its frame of necessity constituted by relations of forces and circumstances: it becomes real and can no longer be termed contingent except in an inexact way and in remembrance of the state of ignorance, in which the mind was regarding it. So it is with blindman's buff. The player who, with his eyes bandaged, seeks with the indications furnished solely by touch, to recognize the prisoner he has seized, the player with the headband hesitates to pronounce a name. If he guessed right, he will, remembering his uncertainty, be able to say afterwards: It could have been someone else. But the one concerned knows well that it couldn't have been anyone but himself.

On the one hand, then, contingency does not express anything real and things in themselves are not contingent. But there is more. For a fact to be contingent with regard to the mind it is indeed necessary, we have said, for the mind to be ignorant of a part of the causes producing it, but another condition is no less requisite: the mind must also know a part of these causes, for it is on this condition alone that it can hesitate between diverse solutions. Thus, neither in the hypothesis of total knowledge, nor in that of total ignorance of the causes of a phenomenon is there room for contingency. Now, philosophers pretend to apply contingency to things of which by definition we do not know the antecedent causes, to the fact of Being itself, or to its diverse and primordial manifestations, such as the laws of nature, in so far as they present themselves to us without justification of origin and without relations among themselves.

In this domain contingency loses all its right to mean anything whatever. For it is impossible for us to imagine of phenomena, all of whose antecedents are unknown to us, that they could have been other than they are. The law directing the evolution of Being, the differentiation of its parts, as well as their correlation, is unknown to us; but does it follow from the fact of our inability to deduce it with necessity from a unique principle, that it is contingent? Has our mind ever been in a position with respect to the fact of existence to imagine contradictory or even diverse hypotheses and to construct other possible ones? Can the notion of possibility apply to a reality, which causes all the others, but whose cause we do not know and of which we say that it exists by itself, or, by reason of a bad mental habit, that it is *causa sui*? Is it not perfectly obvious that with the notion of possibility that of contingency must also disappear?

If, on the other hand, one withdraws from the term contingency the positive meaning it has been granted, what other sense can be substituted for the latter? Our ignorance could hardly endow things with new properties or create in our minds categories unknown until then. Now, as soon as we cease understanding by causes and through the framework of necessity, we are ignorant and it is futile to create, beyond the limits of causality, words with positive pretensions to designate negative concepts. The introduction of a new word into philosophical language does not have the power to bring forth a new mode of mentality, nor does it render intelligible that which wasn't before.

Nevertheless, philosophy in the service of the Vital Instinct is reduced to reliance upon a miracle of this sort and does its best to persuade itself of the accomplishment of this miracle. With this aim it seizes upon terms which have a definite meaning in phenomenal relation, transports them into the absolute and maintains their old meaning as long as dialectics does not intervene. When confronted with an objection as to the arbitrariness of the procedure, it empties the word of its former meaning, just as a scent bottle is emptied of the perfume it contains; but it conserves that empty word as a label of the undefinable, counting, in order to create and sustain an ambiguity, on the persistence of the quondam meaning, which has remained in the contour of the syllables like the aroma of the vanished perfume on the sides of the glass.

In a book [4] in which a fine intelligence and a great ingenuity are put in the service of a thesis, which was only too patently chosen by the preconceived opinion of a will, M. Boutroux subjected the concept of contingency to a treatment of that sort. He sought to induce belief in the miraculous. He believed he could base the contingency of the laws of nature on this fact that Being does not admit of a unique principle, from which the entire series of phenomena is deducible according to a system of relations necessarily linking these phenomena among themselves. So M. Boutroux proposed to establish that the Universe manifests itself to the Intellect as a composite of several distinct worlds superposed and irreducible to one another, that between these worlds there exist intervals between which there hangs, broken, the chain of the causes. Therefore it is impossible to explain the concept of bodies, that is to say, of physical and chemical essences, solely by the concepts of matter and movement, to explain physiological life by the mere properties of chemical bodies and thought by physiology alone. Thus it is that each one of these worlds, material, chemical, physiological and psychological, begins a series and has a spontaneous virtue of its own, whose existence cannot be justified by the properties of inferior worlds.

That such is the case in the actual state of Knowledge could not be subject to any doubt: that it is that way absolutely by reason of the nature of things must be granted without examination, in order to establish forthwith that such a state of fact does not confer upon the term "contingent" a valid sense and one apt to qualify it metaphysically.

Indeed, whether the Universe eludes the grasp of our understanding on but one point, or whether the mystery has several foci of origin, appearing at several points athwart the perforated fabric of the phenomenon, that does not change in any way the attitude of our mind with regard to the incomprehensible. To say that the laws of nature are contingent, because they cannot be systematized into an ensemble of laws all necessitating one another, or to say that the mere fact of Being is contingent because we cannot attribute any cause to it, is the same and, in one case, as in the other, amounts to withdrawing its ordinary sense from the word contingent without substituting any other for it. For the contingency of a phenomenon, as has been said and as it is well to repeat, supposes that at a given moment the mind could hesitate between the phenomenon destined to be realized and several other possible ones. Now, as regards the unique fact of Being or those laws of nature in which Being expresses itself, the mind was never in a position to ask itself if Being would be, or what its laws would be, nor yet to imagine other analogous, closely similar or different ones. For of those laws we only know the descending series of their effects and they themselves, as has been granted, are without any knowable cause. Thus the mind, which understands only through the mechanism of causality, is incapable of imagining them; for it those laws are outside of the category of the possible. It comes into shattering conflict with them in the simple fact of *existence*, which is contradictory with *understanding*. It establishes them, submits to them and can say nothing about them except that they are. All the names by which one characterizes them or with which one claims to describe their nature are no more than sterile pretense, vain attempts to break the seal of an enigma, efforts to violate the mystery, in which nothing but impotence is displayed.

This inanity of metaphysical terminology created to describe the nature of these incomprehensible laws is, moreover, manifest in that for such an undertaking, terms deemed contradictory prove to be equally good and thereby confess to being equally bad. Whether one takes the unique fact of Being or one of its particular laws, the law in virtue of which every part of hydrogen combining with another body necessarily supposes two atoms of hydrogen, it is equally permissible for us to see in either case the fact of liberty or that of necessity. Being, we shall say, is provided with liberty, because no force can limit it. The property of hydrogen just set forth evidences the liberty of this element, since no different power, no chemical agent can compel it to behave otherwise. But the word necessity characterizes just as aptly these two phenomena. Being necessarily exists, since we cannot conceive anything outside of it, since it cannot fail to be. Hydrogen obeys the necessity of its nature, since it is not free to be other than it is, since it is not free ever to enter into a combination with another body through the intervention of a single one of its atoms and must always commit two of them together.

Accordingly, as applied to Being or its laws, the term contingent does not admit of any sense. The contingent, like the free, is a case of the necessary and is comprehensible only in the measure in which we can restore it to this mental unity. M. Boutroux demonstrates that, with respect to our mind, the determinism of the Universe is destroyed in several places. The science of Knowledge which considers the Universe in its essence as precisely escaping all determination, does not have to reject these conclusions which it, nevertheless, does not need: for the indeterminate character of a single phenomenon, if all the others depend upon it, entails the relativity of all the rest. But what one could not repeat with too much insistence, is that the fact of a phenomenon being indeterminate in principle does not establish for it any presumption other than this, namely that it is indeterminate. A thing, which does not appear necessary to us, is a thing, of which we do not know the cause, and nothing more. If that cause is later discovered, the phenomenon will then take its place in our understanding under the category of necessity. If, on the contrary, one goes so far as to concede that this phenomenon by its nature escapes all causality, the result will be that our mind is condemned to remain forever and absolutely ignorant as to its genesis, but certainly not that this phenomenon is free or contingent. If it were contingent, then our mind, far from being ignorant of this genesis, should have been in a position to imagine several versions thereof; were it free, in the only intelligible sense of the word, one would have to admit that this phenomenon which, hypothetically, is unconnected with any other, had arisen before our mind following a victorious struggle with other powers, which would be contradictory.

V.

That hypothesis of absolute contingency constructed in the void of terminology was imagined with but one aim, namely to permit the introduction of Liberty and that phantom palace can indeed contain this inconsistent guest. But the very zeal, with which philosophers strive to demonstrate that a principle of liberty exists in the world, indicates the far more urgent concern to establish that a like principle exists in man; the immediate practical and vital interest of metaphysical liberty is to engender free will in psychology and in ethics. "In order to realize mandatory good, in order to follow the attraction of the beautiful man is endowed with an intelligent spontaneity, whose highest form is free will or the faculty of choosing between good and evil, between actions that bring one nearer to God and those which alienate one from him." [5] Such is the natural and instinctively logical conclusion at which M. Boutroux' treatise arrives, that in which he sums up the utilitarian tendency of every philosophy of State.

One could abide by what has been said above on the subject of liberty and refuse to accord free will any intelligible value. But the belief in the freedom of the will is the essential mechanism of phenomenal life and the Instinct of Knowledge could not become indifferent to the modes, according to which the Vital Instinct constructs its illusion and gives it a practical value. Nor yet could it weary of exposing the inanity of this illusion and the inconsistency of the stuff of which it is constructed. That is peculiarly the work of Knowledge—certainly not a work of propaganda: by taking to pieces the springs of Life in humanity one does not mean to suppress them, even less to replace them with others; wishing to extirpate belief in liberty in men's hearts would amount to a cessation of knowledge and serve the Vital Instinct directly. It would mean becoming a dupe and believing oneself free. To know is, among other things, to be aware that, wherever there is human life, there is belief in liberty. But that is also why it is of such great interest to study the delusive ruse of Life here at its source and to be enraptured with its power to deceive and to intoxicate.

Thus the entirely empty conception of a metaphysical liberty will, under the influence of that rapture, behave like a living thing: it will multiply, reproduce itself and engender other illusory conceptions arrayed with verbal appearances; it is going to create all that fictional vocabulary able to express the error of men, the error of these spectators, who are at the same time actors and figurants of the cosmic panorama.

May we recall here that the mind can adopt but two attitudes towards every existent thing: it either knows the immediate causes of this thing or is ignorant of them. Now, it conceives under the category of *necessity* all the phenomena it knows by their causes; the others, which are known to it only by their effects and which, by their extremity, fall into the unknown, range themselves under the category of *ignorance*. Within the concept of necessity, in order to make distinctions and classifications among the phenomena known by their causes and linked by more or less direct relations, the intellect also forms various secondary concepts which are valid only in the domain of relation, such as, among others, those of contingency and of liberty. It is needful that this latter one be kept in mind and that we remember what it is: as we have said, it characterizes the state naturally resulting from the supremacy of one force over another or over an aggregate of forces. We intend to show that the fictitious terms created by the metaphysics of the Vital Instinct, terms for which this metaphysics would like to establish a new meaning, are all brought back to one of these two categories, *necessity, ignorance,* or to the secondary concept of *liberty,* taken as a case of *necessity.*

Thus it is with the term free. Given an intelligent will which, after having wavered between two or more acts seeming equally possible to it, executes one of them, in what way can one say that this act is free and that it constitutes a choice?

Now, on the one hand, one can suppose the will, which has commanded the act, to be a simple thing not admitting of analysis, independent of any extraneous influence; in this case only one will be possible for it, hence no choice, or the word *choice* will here signify the *necessity* for this will to accomplish a certain act to the exclusion of all others. One cannot say of this will that it is free, because it hasn't been connected with any other force over which to establish its supremacy, or if one says that it is free, one infers a liberty like that of the God of Spinoza and this valuation will have to be completed by declaring that the will is free, possessed of a freedom subject to the necessity of its nature, so that these two terms *liberty, necessity,* contradictory according to their metaphysical value, unite to characterize one and the same thing and thus show their nothingness. All that remains to be done, then, is to confess our *ignorance* as to the mode of action of this will.

If, in the hypothesis just postulated of a simple, indecomposable will, independent of extraneous influence, one nevertheless sees the resolution commanding the act preceded by a contest if, before the decision contrary motives appear in the field of consciousness, one must suppose that this contest exists only for the spectacle, that it is a game and a vicissitude without any effect on the result,—that the will itself has disposed these motives with the solicitude of assuring supremacy to the one representing its law. Thus in the booths of itinerant traders professional wrestlers sometimes plan in advance the vicissitudes of the struggle up to the triumph of the designated victor who, in the semblance of a great effort, throws the two shoulders of the complacent adversary on the hard ground.

Are the philosophers of the Vital Instinct going to try to mask our continuing ignorance of this mysterious why of the will by a new positive term? Will they proceed to decree that the will is *spontaneous?* "That," Nietzsche would say, "is as if the silkworm sought freedom of will in spinning." [6] Is there, indeed, anything more contradictory to the idea of liberty, in the sense of free will, than this concept of spontaneity? A spontaneity either is or is not, it admits of a more or of a less; no premeditated design can develop it where it isn't, and as soon as it appears, it supposes no conflict between motives, no hesitation, no choice. It amounts within humanity to the type of laws, which govern the most elementary activities: it is in man the same power which in the magnet attracts iron, the same unknown force, which directs the sprouting of the seed, the growth of the plant. It is precisely one of those things which, by their manifestations, are enchained in necessity and, by their origins, plunged in mystery, so that, owing to their unknown genesis, they are classed in our minds under the category of *ignorance*. .....

If now, in a second hypothesis, volition is considered as a power of the same nature as the motives, with which it is contending, if it is one motive among others, the act will obviously be determined by the stronger motive, so that the will is to be regarded as *free* in the positive rather than the metaphysical sense of the word, when it is the stronger; it will be constrained in all cases where a motive, which it has not approved, prevails against it. Here again, therefore, the act cannot be considered the result of a choice of the will. The will has never wished but one single thing, but, according to circumstances, it either has or has not been strong enough to impose that thing.

Accordingly these words liberty and choice, taken in the metaphysical sense, envelop nothing real nor even imaginable; both betray the temporary state of ignorance of the human being either, in the first hypothesis we formed, as to what his will really is, or, in the second hypothesis, as to the degree of strength of the motives in conflict and consequently the outcome of the contest involved.

Hence the word liberty which, in the sense of the metaphysics of the Vital Instinct, allowed no possible construction and admitted of no definition, maintains this vacuity when one tries to apply it to man. So one need not inquire here into the question of whether man is or is not free, but should rather maintain that a research of that sort has no object. Between the two preceding hypotheses relating to volition in the human self there is no room for anything intelligible. One must either consider the self as simple, or else say that it is made up of several parts. In the first case it is comprehended in that category of things which, like Being, like the elements of chemistry, cannot be other than they are and whose liberty is con-

127

founded with fatality. It must be said that, despite appearances, despite inner struggles, despite remorse, the self wishes all it accomplishes, wishes its crimes and its heroisms. In the second hypothesis the single self disappears and yields to a multiplicity of distinct selves: these, like all things in nature that are in competition, combat one another and struggle among themselves for supremacy, so that by turns some of them are, with respect to the others, free or oppressed in the relative and perfectly clear sense, which these words denote.

VI.

After having established the absolute nothingness of the term liberty it still behooves the Science of Knowledge to investigate how such a word comes to be formed, to account, if that is possible, for the artifice which constitutes that natural illusion of liberty.

We have said that the complexity of the moral world had its cause in the distinction of Being into object and subject and in the uniting in one and the same phenomenon, the human phenomenon, of object and subject. In every man, in fact, there is realized the miracle of unique Being representing itself to itself in diversity, situating itself as an object for its own contemplation. This miracle appears clearly in the fact of consciousness, whose singular rôle is to witness as a spectator the actions and gestures of the divers actors of the representation, and consciousness is possible only by means of the illusion of personality, which consists in making a presumption of unity reappear in the heart of phenomenal multiplicity. "Our body," says Nietzsche, "is but an association, a colony of souls." [7] Every human being, indeed, is composed of a multitude of distinct entities, which appear alternately in the field of experience, some perceiving the external world, others acting as centers and points of departure of impulses in all directions, still others making valuations and judgments: the conscious entity completes them by saying *I* of each one of them.

This is its unique rôle, and when these different forces, instead of agreeing, conflict, consciousness says *I* by turns to each of the combatants; it says *I* once again when, after the termination of the contest, one of them has gained the advantage and has been able to accomplish the action. Inasmuch as it says *I* when the command is given, it necessarily believes that it delivered the order. Having identified itself alternately with each one of the entities in conflict, it again identifies itself with the victorious one. Whereas it had but one function during the struggle, namely to receive information, to record accomplished facts, to group these facts into an illusory unity by means of synthesis, assembling them as if by means of a single thread, it came by dint of this constantly repeated *I* to believe it was giving advice. It attributed an active rôle to itself.

In reality things happened just as if there had been no consciousness and as they occur in some chemical combination. But, while the other entities, which alone really act, succeed one another in time and only appear separately one after the other, the conscious entity is always in the arena. Thus it believes itself to be alone and is, consequently, unable to imagine that it is constrained. Besides, it isn't; it couldn't be, for it has neither will nor desire and enters into no conflict with other elements, but merely adds itself, lends itself to all. Therefore it could not, as it thinks, be the author of the accomplished act either: this act is the result of a struggle between combatants, all of whom are now dead or moaning except for the victor, who alone is able to call himself free in the true sense of the word, in the sense of the supremacy he has secured for himself over the others.

Thus the belief in free will has its source in the

fact of consciousness and in the illusion of personality, which has originated from this fact. The effect of this illusion is to give the appearance of unity to what is multiple and thus the semblance of action to that which merely records. Under the sway of this illusion this conscious self, which absorbs in itself alone the individuality of all the combatants, who reflect themselves in it, assumes the responsibility for the act commanded by the strongest. It never presents itself until the acts have been committed, but is always there to claim their paternity. Don Juan sings the serenade under Elvire's balcony and then slips away; Leporello remains to receive the caning or the declarations of love. Thus the entire series of moral sentiments originates from a substitution of persons. One sees them emerge, rouged and painted, from this trap of personality set by the machine for instituting the phenomenon, wrought by the distinction between object and subject, this trap in which is caught the vanity of consciousness ever ready to attribute to itself alone everything that happens within its purview. If free the human person is responsible; if responsible it can be punished or rewarded; it is *right* for it to be punished and rewarded and it will feel remorse or satisfaction according to whether the acts accomplished were at variance or in accord with the acts desired by the impellent entities, which the valuing entity approves and favors. This entity, which appraises, will more often than not be the convention as to what is good and evil established by social interest. For this social interest has its representative among the instincts, whose personality is usurped by consciousness and it is this representative that education, by a continuous action, strives to render preponderant.

It is in this way that the sovereign illusion of freedom implants in minds caught in the snare of consciousness the whole monstrous mythology of morality. In the shadow of the idols Truth, Liberty one finds extolled the ideas of Good and of Evil and, between them, the ironical conception of Justice, which, applying like measures to unequal entities, solemnly hallows, supports and multiplies inequality and injustice, which are the conditions of phenomenal life.

CHAPTER V

THE PHILOSOPHICAL REGRESSION

Moral faith is as fanatical

as religious faith [1]—*Max Stirner.*

I. Kantism of practical reason.
II. The critical philosophy of M. Renouvier.
III. German Neo-Kantism.

An interpretation of the CRITIQUE OF PURE REASON according to its extreme logic showed us the Instinct of Knowledge suppressing the springs of Life in humanity. We indicated the following: the idea of a God outside of the world, useless in itself and incapable of accounting for the Universe, employed, when rationalism comes upon the stage, for the purpose of luring the spirit of examination on a false trail and, thereby protecting for a time the rational fictions, which alone are indispensable to the maintenance of Life. Indeed, while philosophers attack the divine idea, they remain attached to these fictions and even think they are reestablishing their hegemony by detaching them from their state of dependence with regard to theology. In reality they uncover them and expose them to the attention of the mind. Thus, in its latest ascertainments, the Science of Knowledge no longer had to be preoccupied with the ancient God; it now drew into the light of its analysis the new little idols, which philosophical devotion was in a position to divinize, and showed their inanity.

Whether there be a God or not, that is a question of only mediocre interest for humanity. But that the ideas of truth and of finality, with their power to create the idea of the Good and their ability to direct effort, should be vain, that liberty through which man believed himself capable of aiming at and attaining his destiny, should be deceptive and a mere error of perspective, this is a great disaster. Man needs to feel Life determined in its principle and in its end: that is his secret desire, that is the hope which, even unavowed, endures in the hearts of philosophers and, under the dryness of formulas, influences and falsifies their inductions. Now the science of Knowledge shows us the knowable Universe as essentially indeterminate: from it we learn that it is forever indiscernible by virtue of the laws of Cognition themselves. It is absolutely impossible for a given whole to represent itself to itself in its total reality, because the spectator subject, invariably and necessarily retrenching himself from the spectacle to be contemplated, mutilates it and, as often and as fast as he removes himself, always carries away with him an element of the whole. The indefinite forms of time, space and cause only render this impossibility apparent. Projecting, as they do, an interrogation and a condition beyond every spectacle seen, they apprise us that this spectacle is not of a complete Whole and that an essential element is lacking.

Beside the impossibility of determining the Universe, of discovering an absolute truth and proposing

it as an aim for effort, the science of Knowledge proclaims the impossibility for man to direct his activity;
it reveals the illusion of liberty. Either, it says, man
acts by virtue of a universal determinism and is not
free, or a spontaneity develops in him imposing ways
of being and acts, whose cause is indiscernible, and
in that case he is still not free, since this spontaneity
either is or is not in him independently of any intervention on his part. And the science of Knowledge
logically infers the absolute emptiness of the concept
of liberty outside of its positive meaning where, as
a particular instance of determinism, it expresses the
supremacy of one force over another.

Does such a body of doctrine admit of the possibility of a moral philosophy? Yes, if by a moral philosophy one means the ensemble of the modes of being
which, determined by a particular conception of existence, logically accompany this conception. What, in
this sense, will this moral philosophy be? An intellectualism pure and simple. What could this meaning
of the Universe be for minds, who are conscious of
the impossibility for them of really forming an idea
of the world or of exerting any influence on its development? That of a spectacle, of which they are
the spectators and which they consider solely from
the standpoint of its visibility. They will abstain from
passing judgments of good and of evil on things and
actions which cannot be otherwise than they are. They
will never ask themselves what they are to do and
what society is to do; at the most they can be dis-
tracted from the pure and simple contemplation of
what is by searching with curiosity into *what will be,*
into what a human society, its antecedents being
given, will be compelled to do.

If one admits that things may be seen from the
point of view of their beauty when one ceases considering them from the utilitarian or the moral position—it is all one,—then it can be said that the only

sentiment to which such minds will be susceptible and which will still determine in them the subject needful for any spectacle, will be an aesthetic sentiment. Where other men will propose to modify Life in a direction of utility or morality, they will make it a law not to intervene and to contemplate the sequence of events, the result of the play of forces engaged. They will be able to consider that Life thus realizes in them its final wish, that by instituting a succession of phenomena to which it is impossible to assigne a goal, Life has no other desire than to give itself a representation, so that by witnessing it they are piously accomplishing its will. Such an hypothesis could plausibly be made by way of a metaphysical conclusion from a pure science of Knowledge. An explanation of the Universe from the viewpoint of the Genius of Knowledge could well be something of that sort.

But, in taking this very point of view, one is forced to concede that this aesthetic morality could not prevail, that it could be the appanage of only a very few: for, supposing it became general, actors would in time be wanting and the spectacle would cease; that would be contrary to the desire which one attributes to Life. Besides, one should reflect that this appetite for pure knowledeg appears only in some beings and toward the last stages of their phenomenal evolution, in races, in families and in individuals approaching their extinction. On the contrary, the individuals destined, by living and perpetuating themselves, to prolong the spectacle, are incapable of admitting the conclusions of the science of Knowledge such as they have just been set forth. Whatever may be the acuteness, sagacity or range of their intelligence they will elude the evidence, because physiology requires it and opposes their *knowing* in an absolute sense, because the Vital Instinct animating them gives them the force to create the necessary fictions. Like a sergeant charged with enlisting recruits, Life dispenses the wine to them that makes them believe in promises.

To believe and to induce belief, this then is what will be the aim of the greater number of philosophers, after as before the CRITIQUE OF PURE REASON. Bacon of Verulam [2] was substantiating the fact that in the Universities of his day people were taught to believe. That is still true in ours. But it is not only in universities that this teaching is lavished, but in every book capable of finding a public of readers. What men ask of philosophy is to give them something in which to believe, to give them a first principle by which to determine their conduct, an aim toward which they can have the illusion of orienting themselves, inasmuch as, for the reasons that have just been stated, the number of minds for whom the joy of comprehending suffices in itself, can never be but insignificant and negligible. If we, nevertheless, take the point of view of those minds, who in Life have the part of the genius of Knowledge, it will be of some interest to make a rapid survey of the systems which, in the broad daylight of the *Critique,* have, from Kant to Nietzsche, sought to rehabilitate the ancient illusions or to disguise them under new aspects.

Among these systems some, like Kantism and French Critical Philosophy, without counting the survivors of the old spiritualism, represent nothing more than a return to the *petitiones principii* of metaphysics and theology; others, like positivism in France and in England, endeavor to deduce a principle of obligation from the data of experience alone. Besides, in these latter schools the term obligation admits of a less rigorous meaning than it had in the metaphysical systems: perhaps this elasticity will suffice to render possible a derivation from some of these doctrines of

136

guiding principles susceptible of being approved by humanity.

It is the rôle of the Science of Knowledge to be equally critical of all of them, for, in so far as they strive to give themselves out as true, they are all equally false, but the force and the verisimilitude, with which each imposes its fiction, decide their chances of success. No ethical system is viable unless it leaves room for the development of that power of illusion, which discloses in men the real presence of the Vital Instinct and its energy. This is what one should remember, but if recourse to fiction is inherent in morality, this appeal still has to be made with enough ingenuity, pertinence and dissimulation, in what might be called a sufficiently contemporaneous manner, for it to be illusional in its effect and beget faith in some form. That is whereby it might be possible, by way of prognostication, to distinguish, among the more recent systems, those whose chances of being applied seem the most probable.

I.

Among the systems of regressive philosophy which, after the work of mental sanitation accomplished by the CRITIQUE OF PURE REASON, tried to restore theological ideas, it is expedient to cite in the first place the one formulated by Kant in the CRITIQUE OF PRACTICAL REASON, the FOUNDATIONS OF THE METAPHYSICS OF MORALITY and the METAPHYSICAL PRINCIPLES OF MORAL PHILOSOPHY. To Kant it is Kant himself, whom one must first of all oppose and immolate. It has to be done without reservation and anything like deference omitted because of the momentous influence exerted on many minds by the false rationalism which he restored.

It is to the credit of M. Maurice Barrès that it should today be impossible to treat such a subject without citing his name and recalling that, as a novelist and as a sociologist, in a work of analysis and imagination of the highest psychological value, he pointed out the Kantian ethics as a national peril.[3] Kantism, on the moral side, is a peril for the Mind, for this general state of intellectualism, which the CRITIQUE OF PURE REASON is made to found theoretically and which has spontaneously attained in our country, by virtue of a gift of clarity peculiar to the race, its most perfect practical expression. This intellectualism is above all a state of disinterestedness concerning faith; it excludes every absolute doctrine and evinces a delicate repugnance toward whatever lays claim to a principle or to a presumption of universal truth. Such a state presupposes a race that has attained to maturity of mind; this is the case with the French people, which, having consummated its crisis of religious puberty under the form of Roman Catholicism in the early centuries of our era, has since shown itself refractory, for the most part, and disinclined to become impassioned again for such interests and no longer feels religious sentiment except as an attitude of usefulness transmitted by ancestors. They are very different therein from neighboring peoples, who but yesterday, so to speak, in the middle of the sixteenth century, were close enough to barbarian credulity to exchange their religion for another one.

This difference is of considerable importance: Catholicism in France in its authoritarian aspect no longer exercises on consciences but an action restricted to customary observances, social utility, the sentimental and traditional attitude belonging to the race. It no longer inspires fanaticism. The believers themselves, more convinced of believing than is actually the case, content themselves with external demonstrations and customary gestures, in which they find their satisfaction. As for the greater part of the nation, it is entirely freed from faith and draws from the religious décor amid which it evolves, no more than an etiquette and immediate principles of conduct by which each is inclined to the manners of being that are the most compatible with communal interests. Indeed, one of the traits throwing the most vivid light on the French mind and informing us the best as to its quality is this very fact of a religion, which has passed the time of its fermentation. By the rarity of this privilege the French people is at present best prepared to see the most intellectual modalities of Life come forth, that is to say social states in which the Vital Instinct shows the widest tolerance with respect to Knowledge and seems almost to be reconciled with it by requiring less in the way of fiction to preserve itself.

Nothing is more destructive of such a state than Kantism. Kantism, in ethics, is a religion and it is a religion in the midst of a crisis of fermentation. It attracts to itself all those, whom religious disquietude continues to anguish beyond ordinary limits. It is for this reason that Kant alone, among all the great men comprised in the modern spirit, found grace in Tolstoy's spiritual tribunal. In the manner of a religion Kantism engenders an observance. In the manner of a religion it persuades its adherents that they are possessors of the one and only truth. "We are fully convinced," says M. J. Tissot [4] "that any moral philosophy diverging from the principles so well stated by Kant would, by that very fact, be stamped with error." And it is the same author, who, having to characterize "the morality of Kant," adds this fervent rectification: "I mean *morality* in an absolute sense." This *absolute* morality is the very principle of fanaticism.

In reality Kantism is confounded with Christianity.

139

Yet there is an essential difference between these two forms of an identical religion: One, Christianity, is founded on revelation; the other is based on reason, or at least makes that claim. One is an attitude of utility identified with a purely voluntary act of faith, the other an attitude of utility referring to a hybrid principle, a rational act of faith.

The former has with us this advantage of having been offered to the race in the time of its infancy, when the all-powerful Vital Instinct created for it the illusion necessary for living and prescribed for it the formula of its needs. The latter requires an even more violent intervention of the Vital Instinct, a still more complete illusion,—for it is a question of falsifying reason in the name of reason itself and of begetting the phantoms of the night in the broad light of midday. Now, the race is far from its infancy; the Vital Instinct no longer has enough power over it to constrain it to such a point of absurdity. It has found its definitive form as a species and does not vary any more. It can derive its moral life only from traditional attitudes ingrained by custom and by heredity, attitudes which with it have become ways of being independent of the faith that they presupposed at the beginning. This ensemble of ideas we find embraced and circumscribed in M. Barrès' conception. When it is applied to a race having arrived at the precise point of its evolution, where ours finds itself today, the Kantism of pure reason can have the power to dry up the ancient roots, but the Kantism of practical reason is powerless to create a new plant, to impose its graft in a useful manner, because it lacks the connivance of the Vital Instinct.

The triumph of Kantism in morality would, therefore, be a peril for the race, in that it would tend to make it sterile and would signify the seizure of the national spirit by an alien group. In reality Kantism is Protestantism. Forcibly dominated by the Vital Instinct and near their puberty, the Protestant peoples are at present still undergoing that illusion, which accompanies the epochs of religious fermentation; they are and show themselves to be capable of an adherence —monstrous from the intellectual point of view—to rationalist dogma. They are already prepared for it, inasmuch as the categorical imperative harmonizes perfectly with the belief in a natural revelation, which is the doctrine of the most emancipated Protestantism. It is, moreover, what partisans of Kantian ethics in our country have positively felt and it is thus that, not long since, M. Renouvier, in order to assure the triumph of his ideas, inferred the necessity of "protestantizing France." With us that triumph would mean the decadence of the indigenous race and the supremacy of a minority which, by placing itself always and by all the means created by circumstances in opposition to the attitudes of the greater part of the nation, showed that it belonged from the ethnic point of view to other groupings and was linked to this one by no more than the hazard of fortune.

Such a triumph would, if it came to pass, also have disastrous consequences of a more general sort. From the standpoint of intellectual freedom it would sanction in humanity a retreat of several centuries. A religion like Protestantism, however free it may seem to be and whatever progress it may have realized in its time and in certain milieus beyond other religious forms, such a religion, by the mere fact of its being in the period of its virulence and inspiring an active faith, naturally entails an obscuration of the intellect and realizes a far less pure state of Knowledge in a people than the one seen to be compatible with an ancient religion entirely relinquished, whose bonds no longer enchain. By its mental qualities, by the antiquity of its religious system, the French people is now the only one in which one may hope to see endure, for perhaps a period of several centuries, that state of practical intellectualism not tolerated by the Vital Instinct except at rare turning-points in history. On these grounds, therefore, the triumph of Kantian Protestantism would, by making the French people lose the intellectual benefits of its maturity, not only be a national peril, but also in a general way dangerous for the mind, because it would retard the reign of one of its purest manifestations and defeat something rare, whose success requires not only particular conditions, but also long centuries of preparation. Hence it is as a principle of possible fanaticism or, in any case, as a religious and regressive state in comparison with the more intellectual state realized by the evolution in this country that we shall here, without indulgence, envisage the Kantian dogma of *Practical Reason.*

§

Kant established in his first Critique that pure speculative reason is powerless to attain the ideas of liberty, soul, supreme good and divinity and, consequently, unable to demonstrate their existence. He verified that experience alone, by furnishing concepts with a content, shows them to be provided with an objective reality and permits one to affirm that an existence animates them. Now, by their supersensible character, the concepts God, soul, liberty and good escape any possibility of seeing their existence revealed through experience. Kant will never retract this verdict of impotence pronounced against pure speculative reason. He will maintain it on every occasion with an entire assurance and in his treatise relating to THE FAILURE OF ALL PHILOSOPHICAL ESSAYS OF THEODICY he is so insistent, in order to show the nothingness of all the old proofs concerning metaphysical ideas and in order to thoroughly establish the inability of speculative reason to justify divine sanctity, justice and goodness, that in this work belonging to the period of reconstruction, the nihilism of the Critique appears in its best light and with all its force.

On what irrefutable proof solid enough to permit him to dispense with all the others will Kant, then, found the reality of those theological ideas which he revives one after the other? On the existence of the moral law discovered in a new faculty of human mentality, which appears here under the name of *practical reason.* It is practical reason which, *a priori,* signifies an imperative to the will, a "You must" to human activity. From this fact Kant is going to deduce the existence of all the metaphysical ideas relegated by *pure reason* to the domain of the Unknowable. A command supposes, in the one receiving it, the freedom to obey and here we have liberty, which pure reason was unable to attain and which, besides, remains incomprehensible for us,—Kant with good reason wishes it thus,—liberty postulated by moral law, which could not be practised without it, so that we must consider its existence assured. Liberty, said Kant in the FOUNDATIONS OF THE METAPHYSICS OF ETHICS, must be regarded as a property inherent in the will of every rational being. But man's will, apprised by the *imperative* of the existence of moral law, is solicited besides by sensible motives the power of which does not permit him to accomplish entirely and immediately the orders transmitted by the *law,* to attain the sovereign good. Holiness, that is to say, perfect conformity to moral law, cannot be realized by man, a rational being plunged into the sensible world, except by progress conceived as infinite. Now this progress without end implies for this same rational being an existence and a personality equally prolonged to infinity, that is to say, the immortality of the soul.

The existence of God is in its turn postulated, ac-

143

cording to Kant, by this fact that a cause endowed with intelligence and volition is alone able to associate happiness and morality in the idea of sovereign good. In order to disengage his doctrine from anything like eudaemonism Kant really desires man to fulfill the moral law for itself, independently of any appetite for happiness. But *sovereign good* would not be *sovereign good,* if with an ideal of virtue it did not include an ideal of felicity. The fact of a being, who deserved happiness, not obtaining it would offer the spectacle of a defect of harmony incompatible with the very idea of *sovereign good.* The synthesis of these two elements: morality, happiness, which cannot be in a relation between themselves of cause and effect or of principle and conclusion, therefore requires the intervention of a perfect being: this being is God; having reached this point in the development of his thought Kant connects the bundle of metaphysical ideas, which he has just gathered, with Christianity and thus, after the detour of the CRITIQUE OF PURE REASON, he restores a theological and moral system just like the one that existed before his critical enterprise. But he thinks that he has in that way, by founding his aspiration on reason and by giving revelation a rational dogma as support, rendered a great service to the metaphysical and religious need of humanity.

In reality the CRITIQUE OF PRACTICAL REASON is the most scornful defiance that the Vital Instinct has ever hurled at the Instinct of Knowledge: to compel a great philosophical mind like Kant's to such a complete blindness is, on the part of the Vital Instinct, the token of the most patent ascendancy and of the most disdainful sort for the mind. One sees therein something like a shameful punishment inflicted by the very high dispenser of Illusion and of Life upon the perspicacious hero of Knowledge, who had until then divulged the means of Illusion and of

Life more than all the others. Kant here finds himself exhibited as an example like some Nebuchadnezzar, not of temporal power but of the mind, metamorphosed into the most complete antithesis of the mind and expiating a dangerous lucidity by the humility of his new language.

The CRITIQUE OF PRACTICAL REASON is grounded entirely on the most naïve begging of the question conceivable, purely and simply on a substitution of verbal designations and, finally, on the most radical negation of the principle of THE CRITIQUE and of the laws of all criticism. The entire theological system restored by Kant rests on this single fact, the existence of a universal moral law, a categorical imperative. Now Kant regards the existence of this moral law as a fact given *a priori* by practical reason, a fact in which one must believe without examination. Whereas the ideas of pure reason are forms, which prove themselves to be objective only to the extent that empirical material comes to fill them, the moral law is a form, whose reality is not revealed by any experience and in whose objectivity Kant requires us to believe. The artifice, then, consists in comprehending belief under one of the categories of reason, in pronouncing the word "faith," as if it were to be spelled *practical reason.*

Kant himself recognized, and M. Fouillée verifies it in his excellent book, CRITICISM OF ALL THE SYSTEMS OF CONTEMPORARY ETHICS,—Kant acknowledged "that there are no other bases for the metaphysics of morals than a criticism of practical pure reason." Now, neither in the FOUNDATIONS OF THE METAPHYSICS OF ETHICS nor in the CRITIQUE OF PRACTICAL REASON did Kant make this criticism of practical pure reason. "It follows," says M. Fouillée, "that Kant's morality lacks a foundation." This does not prevent M. Fouillée from devoting, after this statement, a hundred pages of his volume to showing how Kant is at variance with himself on all the secondary points of his doctrine, on all the deductions made from this first principle, which rests on vacuity. To be sure, this criticism gives evidence of the most subtle, the best and the most unerring qualities of the analytical mind: it remains clear in obscure regions and patiently penetrates into the most minute details, to which it is applied. In view of the actual state of philosophical mores this criticism had to be made. But what is one to think of a philosophical custom making philosophy consist in discoursing so patiently on a theory, whose absolute lack of foundation was recognized in the first place? If it is so in truth, if this theory really lacks a foundation, and if it is not a vain formula conveying no sense at all, what remains to be done except to severely condemn such an idle theory without consideration? The opinion which a disinterested reader, one free from scholastic reverence, would form of Kant's moral theory, after reading M. Fouillée, can only be summarized as follows: an inexcusable begging of the question powerless to unify and render coherent a sequence of subtleties and quibbles, for which dishonesty or religious fanaticism in its moral form, with the blindness ensuing therefrom, can alone furnish the explanation. Will it not seem strange to such a reader to find M. Fouillée himself, the creator of this opinion, concluding with eulogies?

Those, one will say, are games of philosophers, but they are of the sort to disturb all those, who approach philosophical questions with a serious conscience and see in metaphysical research something besides a vain dialectical sport. If the science of knowing offers some interest, even though it were but for a small number, we put ourselves on record here to the effect that anyone flouting it deserves to be stigmatized and that more rigor is in order when the author of the affront, bearing a greater name, puts knowledge in greater jeopardy by that very prestige. Hence the moral preoccupation, which made Kant's intelligence deviate, will elicit no respect from us. Morality for a philosopher means to follow the mind wherever it leads him and were they the most perilous paths, to hold nothing sacred in comparison with the integrity of the intellect. That requires an asceticism, which we shall find again in Nietzsche, but which was totally lacking in the aged Kant.

Here, then, the few mental defects, that disqualify Kantian morality in principle, will be pointed out. The fact of these having been ascertained will impose upon us the duty of ceasing to go any further out of our way in pursuit of deductions which, moreover, do nothing but resuscitate all the irreconcilable contradictions of ancient theology.

*

We have shown above how the inadequate conclusions of the CRITIQUE OF PURE REASON and the illegitimate hypotheses hazarded in that work had alone rendered possible the pretensions of the Imperative. Pure speculative reason, said Kant, cannot attain the metaphysical ideas God, soul, liberty; but it does not prove that these ideas are unreal. It is true that in the phenomenal world, the only one given us, we do not know any simple substance, nor a first cause, and that necessity is the law of things. But, from the fact of our knowing things only as they appear to us, we are justified in supposing that outside of the world of appearances there exists another world, that of things in themselves or noumena so that, if by a different means than that of speculative reason, the existence of metaphysical ideas were revealed, we would be able to grant this existence in the noumenal world, which Kant also terms the intelligible world, without their incompatibility with the laws of the sensible or phenomenal world implying contradiction. Now, in order to remain on the ground of pure criticism, the following should have been stated: pure speculative reason exhausts the faculty of knowing in its entirety; there is no method of knowledge outside of the faculty of knowing and everything that the faculty of knowing fails to attain remains unknowable. Besides, not only does pure speculative reason not attain metaphysical ideas, but it declares their existence to be impossible or refuses to conceive anything under the names by which they are designated, so that, in following Kant on the singular terrain of his dialectical hypotheses, one would have to say this: *if by a way external to our faculty of knowing* it were given us *to know* the existence of those ideas, we would not be able to accept that revelation without renouncing the use of our reason.

To treat here of only one of the metaphysical ideas placed by Kant in the intelligible world, we bring to the remembrance of the reader that the absolute hollowness of the term *liberty* outside of its use in the world of phenomenal relation was demonstrated in a preceding chapter. It was established that liberty, far from being the opposite of necessity, is in the phenomenal world a case of the necessary and expresses the state, which is determined with fatality by the supremacy of a force over one or several others. If by "free" one means to designate what is not determined by a cause, that is a negative concept which only expresses our ignorance and inside of which it is improper to situate anything positive, upon which it would be possible to speculate. When forces manifest themselves to us of such a character that they appear to us to be without causes, we are reduced to thinking either that they have a cause unknown to us, or that they are what they are by reason of the fatality of their nature. On that one must insist, because neither of these two hypotheses permits us to grasp a new notion, that notion of free will so indispensable to Kant, if his moral law is to have a meaning.

The contrary of what has a cause is that which is without cause. There we have the negative concept which it is permissible to form on the occasion of the concept of what has a cause; now this negative concept is wholly unintelligible. To give a name to what is unintelligible, to state that what is without cause is *free* amounts to saying nothing or forming a word without any sense. Could what has no meaning in the phenomenal world, which is for us, by Kant's testimony, the only knowable world, take on a meaning in the unknowable one?

The question of free will only appears so complex, because it does not exist: what does not exist is necessarily inexplicable. Every human being is a bundle of instincts disposed among themselves according to a more or less elastic and variable relationship —but of a given and fixed elasticity,—by virtue of which the hierarchy among these instincts is susceptible of greater or lesser modification according to the unknown virtuality belonging to each of them. These possible modifications are produced under the influence of the exterior: circumstances, education,—but within the absolutely determined limits that are assigned to them. We do not and we cannot know the exact hierarchical relation which exists among instincts, nor the measure in which this hierarchy is susceptible of being reversed, that is to say we do not know the different combinations with which one and the same person complies; but this particular disposition and subordination of the instincts in each person, the intensity of every one of these instincts, the chances of supremacy of each one of them, the revolutions which will make the power pass from one to the other, all this ensemble constitutes what we call the character of the human personality. All the acts committed by the latter are the necessary result of the conjunction of his character with the external forces. And we say that it is so, because we have no other principle of explanation. We can only conceive the act as committed under the category of necessity, although we never know and can never know all the causes determining this necessity.

Hence it is not the question of a universal determinism that is involved here. There is not, there cannot be a universal and absolute determinism, because the idea of a first principle is contrary to the very essence of causality, the foundation of determinism, the formal law of the mind and the principle of the magic of the Universe. But every act appears to us as necessarily determined by a conflict between known causes and unknown causes. At the origin of each causal series there is always a force, whose cause we do not grasp and which thereby arises for us from the unknowable and of whose quantum and virtuality we are ignorant. But if we do not know the intensity of this force, the degree and the possible modes of its virtuality, it is absolutely impossible for us to conceive that these elements do not exist, for no existence can be apprehended by the mind outside of the categories of quantity and quality. Now, since these elements exist, we cannot imagine their not concurring to determining the act according to the stringent relationship which exists between them and the elements of causality known to us. Thus the intervention of the unknown and the unknowable in every act emanating from the human personality has no other effect than to introduce into the conditions of the act a principle of ignorance for the mind, by which this act escapes the possibility of being foreseen mathematically, but by which it could by no means escape the character of necessity that determines its accomplishment.

Every human act, furthermore, has a double origin; on the one hand it implies a sequence of the thoughts and reflections able to enlighten the person as to what is most advisable for it to do and, besides, whatever the principle, interest, duty or sentiment to which it may be resolved or accustomed to subordinate its conduct; on the other hand it implies a power of its own to exercise volition, that is to say, to execute what has been judged to be the better course, were it contrary to instincts which might impel it to act differently. Now, as Nietzsche has said, "a thought comes when it wishes, not when I wish." A thought such as arises in Caesar's brain does not appear in Caliban's. It is the same with willing. The faculty of willing either exists in me, or it doesn't, and that is independent of my intervention. No more does it depend on me to form a resolution to will or not to form it. Where one proves to have an efficacious will, another shows himself incapable of anything like volition. With the same fatality and in virtue of his absolutely determined character one will perform an act of volition and another, for all his desire to do so, will fall short of achieving it. If man were free to will as he likes and to carry into effect always what, in his opinion, he has judged to be the best, what possible motive could prevent his availing himself of this power? Likewise, were man free to have the best thoughts in order to determine the best purposes for himself, would anything keep him from always making use of this privilege? But, "a thought comes when it wishes." A will appears in the service of an instinct when that instinct is the stronger, and man is free neither to will nor to think outside of the precise limits and individual modes of his faculty of willing and thinking.

One is, therefore, constrained to recognize that in the acts of the human being there is room only for *necessity*, for a necessity determined by a double current of causality: one of an intellectual and the other of a voluntary order. Now, liberty is the first postulate of the moral law, of the categorical imperative imagined by Kant. Without liberty the imperative crumbles carrying away in its fall, according to the expressed feeling of Kant, the ideas of duty, the soul and God, which were supported like a hazardous pyramid on that bandy-legged foundation.

*

Man escapes necessary ignorance only by falling into absurdity. In order to make room for the inconceivable concept of liberty Kant imagined a noumenal world. It has already been established that the hypothesis of the noumena is inadmissible and that it constitutes one of the most palpable defects of the CRITIQUE OF PURE REASON. We said that outside of space, time and cause, whose intervention immediately brings into being the phenomenal world, with the rigorous apparatus of its laws, there is room only for the hypothesis of the *thing in itself*, of which we cannot prejudge anything except that it is situated on the outside of any state of knowledge. A noumenal world implying laws, hence distinction between object and subject, hence diversity, would be absolutely confounded with the phenomenal world, so that such a hypothesis does not even come to be constructed. Besides, it results only in resuscitating the theological extravagances and in creating antinomies, for which the human mind in its worst aberrations is alone responsible and which do not exist in the nature of things. Thus it is evidently no more possible to reconcile phenomenal necessity with noumenal liberty, than it was in theology to reconcile human liberty with divine prescience and omnipotence.

Consequently one must proclaim in no uncertain terms that if Kant, with the best part of the CRI-

TIQUE OF PURE REASON, where he sets up the relativity of knowledge as dogma, endowed the philosophical spirit with the most potent thought of modern times, he also, with the CRITIQUE OF PRACTICAL REASON, by endeavoring to deduce the absolute from the relative, begot the most unfortunate mental monstrosity ever produced by the imagination as a prey to the suggestions of the Vital Instinct. We realize, in this connection too, the rôle of illusion as a necessary form of every manifestation of Life and that no epoch can avoid this necessity; however, this illusion must be in rapport with the intellectual development of the period to which it proposes itself. The old theological illusion offered to naïve peoples had the modesty to justify the contradictions it implied by means of a "credo quia absurdum" which remained respectful of the laws of the mind and at least compromised only volition. The Kantian illusion, which, nevertheless, offers itself in a period reputed to be less coarse, substituted for that formula this unforeseen challenge: an "intellego quia absurdum" which, to tell the truth, has become the motto of all contemporay rationalism.

§

Before abandoning definitively this fabric of intellectual monsters represented by the work of the second Kant, we must still point out that the very title of his last critique, if one takes into account the meaning given it, implies a confusion between existence and knowledge, which was the theological means of all spiritualistic metaphysics both in Greece and in the Middle Ages, and a begging of the question on which every moral philosophy of duty is founded, namely the following: the power attributed to man of choosing his acts and of directing his activity. Kant, as we have already said, seems in the

153

CRITIQUE OF PURE REASON to have examined the value of our entire faculty of knowing. Now this new title, CRITIQUE OF PRACTICAL REASON, supposes that we possess a new faculty of knowing and that this faculty is volition, the faculty of producing acts; for it is of this faculty that Kant is going to treat. But, to consider volition which, by the acts in which it is manifested, is an *object* of knowledge, as a new and particular means of knowing, amounts to settling the question at issue, the very one that needs to be examined, and to creating a confusion in consequence of which those irreconcilable antinomies are engendered, for which one would like to hold reason responsible, whereas they proceed only from the improper use made of it.

Beside the CRITIQUE OF PURE REASON there was room for another work, for a *Critique of Pure Will.* Anyone, who had undertaken it with a spirit unscathed by moral bias, would have been led to conceive Will in the manner of Schopenhauer—outside of man as well as in man—as the matter and the content of Life. He would have established that man possesses the faculty of taking cognizance of this content on phenomenal grounds, according to the forms of Cognition already described. Proceeding then to criticism of volition, as it is manifested in man, he would have endeavored to discern in each act which is the part of Will and which of Knowledge. He would have been compelled to reduce the rôle of Knowledge to the single act by which the subject takes cognizance of all the modifications of the object. He would have seen that in every inner struggle which precedes the accomplishment of a visible act, the Will performs a series of invisible acts rigorously determined by the state of complexity and perfection of the cerebral organism, and that all these acts, *once accomplished,* are reflected in consciousness where they become objects of knowledge under the mythological name of *motives*. He would also have seen that Knowledge never intervenes in the determination of acts, but that the latter succeed one another in man, as they do outside of man, according to the laws of natural causality, unrolling before the regard of Knowledge the indefinite fabric of the Universe of perceptions and sensations. He would have seen that it cannot be otherwise, because the fact of taking cognizance of something necessarily supposes that something exists, inasmuch as this very fact of becoming aware is subordinated to a molecular movement in the organism, a movement that belongs to the series of causal necessity.

Such a conception, founded on the respect of natural distinctions, no longer demands attempts at an impossible conciliation between a noumenal free will and a phenomenal fatality, between liberty and divine omnipotence, because such questions are no longer posed. No longer is there a law that can be violated like that singular categorical imperative which it is easier to infringe than observe. But, on the one hand, a world as the object of knowledge offered to one's view and unfolding itself before the curiosity of the mind like a panorama in motion, a world employed by means of which we do not know the principle; on the other the subject of knowledge witnessing this spectacle in the *self* and outside of the *self* through the optical apparatus formed by the laws of phenomenal representation.

Having arrived at this point of view the author would have been intent on seeking to explain this double aspect presented by the objective world, according to whether the manifestations of its activity appear within the self or outside of the self. The point where sensation changes into perception would have shown the close union of these two modes simultaneously with the principle of their distinction. The method would then have required setting aside, in order to study them better, the manifestations of the will inside of the self and investigating the particular forms through which this will appears. For it goes without saying that this criticism would, like the other one, have been purely *formal* and would have decided nothing as to the substance of the will, which is unattainable and comes from the unknowable. Pleasure and pain could have been regarded as the forms of volition, imposing on desire its realization in action. But there would have been reason to ask oneself, if there do not exist on this side of these forms of sensibility, and by analogy with mineral affinities which, independently of all pleasure and all pain, determine the motions demanded by the law, purer forms of volition in man, primordial suggestions plunging, underneath the flowering of psychological appearances, into the deep world of chemistry and of which pleasure and pain would be but the most ordinary interpretation. Thus one would attain a veritable imperative armed with the chains of necessity and assuring the drama of the Universe a representation conforming in every respect to the text.

Moreover, whatever these pure forms of the will may be, once disengaged by criticism they would certify their legitimacy in that, contrary to the Kantian imperative, they would exercise a really universal dominion and that an act would no more be able to come about outside of them than an object could appear to the mind outside of space, time, causality and the categories of the intellect.

This criticism of volition is a work that remains to be undertaken and one the object of which the CRITIQUE OF PRACTICAL REASON, a mere religious and social petitio principii, did not even approach. By searching into the question of what men ought to do, instead of investigating the laws in conformity with which men necessarily perform acts,

Kant may be said, from the viewpoint of knowledge, to have propounded a problem analogous to that which would consist in investigating what the molecules of a liter of water heated to one hundred degrees *ought* to do, as if the concern to choose could be attributed to them.

II.

What has just been said of the concept of liberty in reference to Kantian ethics, conjointly with the special analysis which was made of that idea, considered as an idol of the logical heaven in a preceding chapter, dispenses us from criticizing henceforward the philosophical systems one sees arising from Kant to Nietzsche, systems which, contrary to the principles of pure speculative reason, all presuppose liberty and give way without it. It is, then, only a question of enumerating them as briefly as possible, naming them one by one in a rapid survey, like troops in the pay of the Vital Instinct, provided moreover with old-fashioned weapons whose range, it would seem, ought no longer to be effectual.

Among these systems, however, the critical philosophy of M. Renouvier is distinguished by this peculiarity that he attempted to substitute for the concept of liberty itself the psychological fact of a presumption of liberty with which men are undeniably equipped, a presumption which seemed sufficient to him for founding the moral law. This presumption of liberty is, in fact, the deceptive appearance, which, in practise, originates the diverse moral philosophies that are seen historically to govern men. For a legislator of peoples—benevolent or tyrannical—it can be a means of imposing laws and of modeling a social state. But a philosopher, who knows the falsity of that deceptive appearance and that there is no liberty, cannot think seriously of founding a real law upon that appearance. By attempting it he substitutes a means of government for a philosophical theory, accomplishing what until now all philosophies in the service of the Vital Instinct have accomplished; he forcibly converts a principle of utility into a principle of truth. Moreover, this illegitimate procedure is indeed the only one which justifies any rationalistic system promulgating an imperative. One discovers it at the core of the Protestant dogma which M. Renouvier would have liked to impose on this country, a dogma which from its beginning lays down the belief in the existence of God by virtue of a natural revelation (practical reason), because it is convenient and useful to have at one's disposal, in reality, such a being in order to regulate moral, individual and social life. But this power, which surpasses hypocrisy, to deceive or dupe oneself as a measure of utility, this power that is the privilege of peoples in the service of the Vital Instinct, such as the Anglo-Saxon peoples are now, does not seem to be the appanage of an intellectual race like our own, whether it has this clarity of mind from native qualities, or whether it must be explained by the state of its maturity. It may be deduced from this consideration that the theories of M. Renouvier, estimated as a system and a social danger, will not succeed in obscuring the national mentality, however menacing they may appear at present through their alliance with the Protestantism of the university of whose tendencies and compromising acts M. Goyau informs us in a recent and very carefully documented book.[5]

On philosophical grounds it goes without saying that such a system admits of no discussion and that, by its appeals to faith, it ranges itself outside of the science of knowledge. But it is of an extraordinary interest that a philosopher of the value of M. Renouvier should not have been afraid to formulate it. That gives the measure of the all-powerful control which

158

the Vital Instinct can exert on good minds, and we gain some conception of the circumference within whose scope they are enclosed and where for them all logic fails.

This compass is built with the materials which are—or at least these philosophers declare them to be—indispensable to the maintenance of existence. No reasoning prevails against this supposed interest: it is on this interest and on no other argument that the dogma of the primacy of morality is founded, the one by which the faculty of understanding is subordinated to the faculty of believing even in the concerns of the Intellect. It is the fact of being animated by the zeal of so powerful an interest that makes M. Renouvier *à propos* of Kantism exclaim with that accent of Polyeucte acknowledging the true God, so shocking to a philosophical ear: "And what is extraordinary, is that metaphysical dogma is reestablished even in the CRITIQUE OF PURE REASON, a work of demolition, and that the great novelty, affirmative critical philosophy, *ethics taking precedence of doctrines, in short real criticism* belongs to other works." [6] And in a note the author again affirms his faith in these terms: "The conclusions of M. Secrétan are not entirely different from our own, for, if he continues to hold with metaphysics, he at least admits the preeminence of *ethics and that is the essential point.*" Finally, one could not resist citing here that other passage which, under the cover of an illustrious name, is apt to idealize that entire class of minds, servants of the Vital Instinct, and to show, simply by recording their avowal, the order of considerations biased according to desire and unconcerned in any logic, upon which their philosophy is confidently founded. The philosopher, who is here made to appear, is Aristotle himself, translated by M. Renouvier and whose declaration we have here by way of a conclusion to a theory on future contingencies: "This future is truly uncertain in some cases. Otherwise there would no longer be any liberty; everything would be necessary and men's deliberations would be futile, which is not tolerable." [7]

"Which is not tolerable!" In that manner was the father of philosophy reasoning *ab irato* two thousand and some three hundred years ago. Such is typical intolerance, such the wilful act which is required at its origin by every philosophical system concerned with formulating an authoritative moral philosophy and this same intolerance is still, in our day, the sole justification for this doctrine of the primacy of ethics, which fanaticizes critical philosophy in France and incites it to range itself as a positive religion.

*

However, M. Renouvier did not content himself with this presumption of liberty whose virtue risked seeming really too wavering. He tried to make room in philosophy for the concept of a real liberty and, in order to attain this end, he proceeded in a round-about way and did an excellent piece of work. It is known that M. Renouvier rejects, among other things in Kantism, the entire theory of the noumena: that induces him to deny all reality to the ideas of infinitude and substance which, according to Kant himself, could lay claim to no more than a noumenal existence. Faithful to this conception M. Renouvier undertook a general criticism of those concepts through philosophy of the different ages, a criticism of the greatest interest and of a grand solidity. But does one know for what purpose the philosopher undertook to ruin those concepts? M. Renouvier thought he could impair the concept of necessity with the same stroke; at the very least he hoped to make a breach in that inexorable idea, one through which liberty, or so he flattered himself, could be introduced into the world

160

of phenomena. If the infinite can be conceived as a substantial, full and continuous whole, it also follows that "everything is solidary," that "all is interconnected and indissolubly linked in the substance of the plenum." [8] Nothing can escape necessity. Therefore it is, in the philosopher's judgment, indispensable, in order to make room for liberty, to destroy the ideas of the infinite and of substance. Without the Infinite "material Substance disintegrates, the eternal series of phenomena (a parte ante), then any prevision or antecedent determination whatever (a parte post) lacks a foundation and one must admit beginnings, first beginnings for every thing and for all things." [9]

Here then, introduced by M. Renouvier, is this conception of the beginnings of series and of the hiatuses between causal sequences, which was already encountered in the course of this study on the occasion of M. Boutroux' book LA CONTINGENCE DES LOIS DE LA NATURE. Here, then, one can only object once more that liberty is not the contrary of necessity, that liberty, outside of the relative sense in current usage, is a concept destitute of all meaning, that causal necessity is for the mind the only principle explanatory of phenomena, that the domain of ignorance begins for us wherever we cannot apply this principle and that there is no room for any concept in this domain, not even for liberty, however great a need may be felt for this lever by philosophers desirous of transforming themselves into priests or politicians and of engraving the law on the tables of conscience. It is not proven that the concept of an indefinite, refractory to all determination, substituted for the concept of an infinite embracing the totality of conditions, would necessarily bring about solutions of continuity in the chain of phenomena; but if this proof were made, it would lead to nothing more than an extension of the domain of ignorance and an impoverishment of scientific hope. However

161

considerable one might imagine the number of commencements of series to be, it would never happen that, from the shock of these multiplied enigmas, there would burst forth in the mind anything at all like liberty in the metaphysical nonsense of the word.

§

Beside M. Renouvier one could not forget M. Pillon, the founder of that *Année philosophique*, who was and still remains the fortress of critical philosophy. The doctrine of M. Pillon is identical with that of M. Renouvier: primacy of morality, integral acceptance of the CRITIQUE OF PRACTICAL REASON and of the imperative as indisputable dogma and as a principle of explanation of Knowledge, rejection of noumena and a like pretension of setting aside all metaphysics. This similarity is rare among philosophers, but it is explained precisely by the act of faith that is hidden under the dialectical appearances of the system and, as M. Pillon tells us, "makes of critical philosophy a really positive doctrine." What should have been said is a positive religion.

The critical philosophy of M. Renouvier seems to have been the most important manifestation of Kant's dogmatic rationalism, although it is at the same time its most heterodox expression by the rejection of the noumenal world. But, in addition to philosophers of this school, many others, being inspired by the Kantian *peripeteia* judged it to be possible to conciliate these two instincts, to believe and to understand, which are mutually exclusive. Among these philosophers, of whom some sacrificed more to religious faith, while others set a higher value upon criticism, one must group around Messrs. Renouvier and Pillon and in the train of M. J. Tissot, who was a fervent observer of the rational religion, names such as that of M. Lachelier, who tried to confer upon the principle of finality, a logical form of Cognition, a noumenal reality, such as those of M. Dauriac and M. Boutroux, in short those of numerous independent, spiritualistic or Christian philosophers, who did not escape the strong influence of Kant and sought to find in the arsenal of his dialectics weapons with which to defend ideas dear to them and pretexts only to emerge always, after appearances of emancipation, with some restoration of imperative morality. For all of these, by virtue of some secret pact of instinct, the moral law, a theological vestige, the chosen bell-tower, remained and continued to be the aim of every journey across the realm of ideas. In this category one may rank, in the train of Messrs. V. Cousin, Jouffroy and the eclectic group, Messrs. Ravaisson, Secrétan, Janet, Franck, Caro, Jules Simon and also M. Vacherot,— although he claims to disengage morality from its dependence on religion and metaphysics and to ground it solely on psychology. The systems of all these philosophers suppose an imperative moral law and liberty: thereby they pertain to previous criticisms and testify to this philosophical regression of which Kant, after the CRITIQUE OF PURE REASON, has given the most illustrious example.

III.

Whereas French critical philosophy, if one considers it in its most authorized representative, rejects Kant's noumenal theory and is founded upon the CRITIQUE OF PRACTICAL REASON, on the categorical imperative, in order to persuade itself that it is attaining the absolute, the German philosophers, who undertook to speculate in the train of Kant, employed an entirely different procedure to attain the same end. The spectacle remains one of a beautiful and complete irony: scarcely has the Instinct of Knowledge, as manifested in the critical genius of

Kant, shown the impossibility for the mind of attaining anything but what is relative, scarcely has the word *unknowable* been inscribed on the confines of the phenomenal world, than presently the same man of genius, by whom this clear discovery was promulgated, rushes upon that closed door of the unknowable and employs all his old powers to weaken it, and everyone in the world pretending to philosophize invents false keys, paralogisms and sophisms in order to penetrate into that inaccessible domain in the belief that he is bringing the absolute back from it in some form.

In Germany, through the agency of men like Hegel, Fichte and Schelling, the noumenon is going to become incarnate in the phenomenon, unless the phenomenon is raised to the noumenon. Both are drawn close and blend, while from the subject confounded with the object there emerges the absolute. With Hegel the phenomenon is no longer the subjective appearance which Kant had determined; it is endowed with an immediate existence, necessarily engendered by the logical development of the idea. Fichte and Schelling will deal with the critical laws with the same liberty and these different systems are but designs ascribed to the absolute, descriptions copied, like tracings of historical and scientific data, from the modalities of Being which, at the end of its evolution, always takes cognizance of itself in sovereign fashion. Such theoretical views could have some merit as hypotheses and conjectures hazarded on the destinies of the Universe: on this basis they could be philosophical novels offering to metaphysical avidity an aliment or sundry aliments according to the will of predilections. Still, in order to be acceptable in this mode, they should be constructed in such a way as not to violate the laws of reason and refrain from showing us an absolute state of knowledge and consciousness in a confusion of object and subject, which leaves no room whatever for any state of cognition. Such conclusions, common to all these systems, reveal them to be in contradiction with the critical principles to which they lay claim.

After that one could not really blame them for admitting among the number of their elements this concept of liberty, which was always the cement of metaphysical hypotheses, not that this concept should not be represented in them, but because it figures in them without any usefulness whatever and does not really constitute a part of the edifice. In a system which asigns to the world a spontaneous, mechanical development in the manner of Hegel's philosophy, one searches in vain for the place of liberty. Nevertheless Hegel introduced it, because it has its place in all the old theological edifices and the disposition of men is seen to be attached to it and because it implies responsibility, and modern sentimentality, like that of ancient times, requires this condition in order to warrant morality, justice and the right to punish. Besides, isn't introducing liberty into the world of necessity the old philosophical procedure productive of antinomies, which one posits as irreconcilable and then resolves with ease, and whose presence, driving reason from its function, assures the perpetuity of the metaphysical game?

One would not be able to deny that Hegel with his dialectical form produced a method of proceeding very qualified to systematize, an industrial procedure in some sort, in this sense that, once it is employed by the most mediocre intelligence, it works by itself on the material confided to it, without there being required on the part of the author any new original effort of thought. Parallelism of the rational and the real, confusion of being and thought in the idea, which unfolds these modes by turns only to reabsorb them, dialectical movement of the idea—thesis, antithesis, synthesis—by which the latter itself engenders its successive forms, counteracting and dividing itself only to be reconciled and become united in a higher unity, such are the wheels of this dialectic.

Under the direction of Hegel this ideological engineering produced, in its developments susceptible of practical application, the political system of absolute government which, by chance, happened to be the Prussian ideal around 1828, an epoch to which the philosopher dispensed his teaching in Berlin with sovereign authority. Hegelianism has since become democratic. With Karl Marx and generally with all the builders of future Salentes,[10] it gave rise to a great many social theories in which the most vulgar optimism flourishes. For, thanks to synthesis, everything is always arranged: if life shows antagonisms anywhere, the author rejoices and humanity has only to congratulate itself with him on the conflicts in which it is rent; for this antagonism, by showing us that the idea grows and evolves, that life gains in complexity, announces to us coming solutions in a more perfect order. Everything in nature is coordinated, conspires toward unity, concurs toward harmony. Through the arduous modern toil humanity is proceeding toward an era of felicity. As in bad novels everything ends well: synthesis promises the world a Messiah and, whereas the present time is fulfilled amid the customary struggles, we catch a glimpse of an Eden in the vistas of the future, a disquieting Eden, the happiness and tedium of which can only be imagined through the ancient Catholic paradise. For, in the matter of happiness, as in any other order of conception, the metaphysical pretension of creating something absolute clashes with the laws of our faculty of understanding, whose indeterminate forms engender only what is relative. The secret sensibility of human nature rejects the insipidity of that perfect felicity. In harmony with the curiosity of the Intellect, which anything in the way of satisfaction excites to a more anxious search, it knows itself to be insatiable. Goethe's Faust knows this law; he speculates on this form of human sensibility in order to dupe Mephistopheles when concluding the pact with him subject to this condition under which he insists "If you can entice me to the point where I please myself, if you can beguile me amidst the gratifications of pleasure, may this be for me the last day! I offer you the bargain . . . If I ever say to the moment: Linger, thou art so beautiful! Then you can cumber me with fetters."

CHAPTER VI

THE PHILOSOPHICAL TRANSFORMATION

"Of Hazard"—that is the oldest nobility in the world;
that gave I back to all things; I emancipated them
from bondage under purpose.—ZARATHUSTRA [1]

With the Kantism of *Practical Reason* and the critical philosophy of M. Renouvier, with the German metaphysical systems of Hegel, Fichte and Schelling, with the different spiritualist or frankly theological schools which have been previously enumerated, the nomenclature is exhausted of the systems which, after the CRITIQUE OF PURE REASON, continued to speculate outside of the limits and against the laws of the Intellect.

Positive philosophy is born: Auguste Comte names it and, despite the systematic apparatus with a superfluity of his ideas, despite his pretension of founding a new spiritual power, he must not be despoiled of the honor of having been the first to formulate with clarity the importance and the character of this advent. He was also the first to recognize the necessity of circumscribing and arranging this positive domain of the mind by instituting a classification of the sciences, by tracing outlines in which to distribute the more or less advanced sketches of intellectual labor and effort. Retrospectively he did from a sound point of view totally embrace and delimit the rôle of the critical science of Knowledge, destined to destroy the dominion of theology and of metaphysical ideas, but powerless to create new forms of life. Finally his work exhibits foresight: he called attention forcefully to the danger with which the positive spirit was threatened by the false Kantian rationalism, by this compromise, for which Kant furnished the model and which consists in reestablishing, counter to the solutions of reason, by virtue of a moral and political interest held superior, the authority of the ancient beliefs. "This systematic compromise," he remarks on this subject, "is by no means peculiar to the Jesuits, although it constitutes the essential basis of their tactics; the Protestant spirit also gave it in its way an even more intimate, more extensive and especially a more dogmatic imprint of consecration: metaphysicians in a strict sense adopt it just as much as do theologians themselves; the greatest among them, although his high morality was truly worthy of his eminent intelligence, was induced to sanction it essentially by establishing, on the one hand, that theological opinions of whatever sort do not admit of any real demonstration and, on the other, that social necessity makes it obligatory to maintain their ascendancy indefinitely." [2]

So accurate an estimate of the precise moment of evolution, this knowledge and this premonition of the peril still threatening the mind assign to Auguste Comte a rank of the first order in the history of thought. One can reproach him for the character of religiosity with which he stamped scientific ideas and condemn his pretension in resolving the moral problem by a new dogmatism founded on a presumption of finality. But it will be seen that this presumption is the ultimate metaphysical fault which still characterizes all positivistic systems. Accordingly Comte remains, on these grounds also, the most typical representative of the new spirit, offering both its qualities and its defects with a sort of striking relief.

Before unveiling this last metaphysical vestige, which has persisted in positivistic philosophy, like an organ giving evidence of an anterior mental state, it is important first of all to establish the unprecedented progress that has been realized with this new conception by the science of Knowledge.

Positivism in France, England or Germany is the practical consecration, the immediate and logical application of the deductions of the CRITIQUE OF PURE REASON. Henceforth philosophical science may be said to comprise two distinct sections: in the first the mind proceeds to a critique of cognition and determines what is and what isn't knowable; in the other the mind undertakes the study of all that is knowable. Philosophy considered in this double aspect thus recovers the rank of a science of the universal, to which it had aspired in the first place. But if one reflects that the critique of cognition has been made once and for all, then, clearly, there no longer remains any matter upon which to philosophize, that is to say none to know outside of the science of the phenomenon and the true philosopher, properly speaking, is the scientist, whatever kind of phenomena, moreover, he may observe.

Thus the system of metaphysical illusionism, toward which the Critique converges, has for its counterpart in the phenomenal world the most rigorous determinism. If in effect the laws of the mind are of such a nature as to conceal from us how the universe is constituted and what it is in its essence, so that, according to the rigour of a mechanism, we witness a spectacle without end, then nothing remains for us but to contemplate this given spectacle, to try to see it better, with a closer and a more distinct view by means of all the optical instruments invented by science.

Inasmuch as the metaphysical questions of first cause, of the origin or essence of the world, of the soul or of liberty are relegated to the domain of the unknowable and that of pure impossibility, any effort of the intellect applied to such objects is henceforward condemned. The mental activity which, for centuries, was consumed in vain efforts to resolve these problems situated outside of cognition is thus brought back to its real object, which will have to be studied so much the more thoroughly and better. It may, then, be claimed that, since the great event of the Critique, the best philosophers are those, who refrain with the greatest care from any metaphysical speculation and confine themselves most strictly to the realm of observation. From this point of view the absence in this country of great philosophical systems like those beyond the Rhine and our silence as to metaphysics during this century could no longer be imputed to us as a deficiency. Quite to the contrary, one must see in it the manifestation of the critical instinct of the race, the privilege of a naturally clear and sound view, especially when one compares with this dearth the extraordinary productiveness in the same period of the scientific mind represented by such giants as Lamarck, Lavoisier, Laplace, Geoffroy-Saint-Hilaire, Cuvier, Claude Bernard, Pasteur. It is a fine quality of the unconscious of a race, the one which consists in producing, at such a precise hour of evolution, the very men required by this moment of duration.

Within the compass of philosophy itself M. Taine proved a faithful observer of this metaphysical abstention. By showing, in his fine book DE L'INTELLIGENCE, the parallelism between the series of psychological facts and the series of physiological facts which, without ever being able to join, correspond across the enigmatic abyss of conscious representation, he outlined for philosophical research its useful task in the duplicate path open to it. Identifying himself with the part which could be saved from the sensualistic philosophy of the Eighteenth Century, he excelled in resolving individual or ethnic mentalities, entire systems of abstract ideas into their elements by means of associations of images. From the same point of view one should also consider as the mark of a splendid intellectual discipline and of a wholly scientific disinterestedness the existence of a documentary school like that of M. Ribot: confined within the strict domain of psychological studies and preparing excellent materials for future constructions, it knows how to abstain from premature undertakings, whose aim would be to connect orders of phenomena between which bridges are still lacking and which will perhaps never be established.

II.

The positivist systems, properly speaking, in France as well as in England, those of Auguste Comte and Littré, those of Darwin, Spencer, Stuart Mill and Bain do not always evince the same scrupulousness in their authors and it is going to become apparent that the metaphysical spirit of adventure has slipped into the most vital part of their speculations, namely moral science. Considered as purely and simply a science of observation, ethics must be, as Nietzsche characterized it, a chapter of natural history. It is evident that the modes of men can be the object of a scientific observation by the same right as the customs and manners of being of the different animal species, which are amenable to determination with an almost rigorous precision. But here the matter to be studied is more complex. Likewise it seems that, if animal species are for the most part and henceforth fixed, the human species may through its highest organs, the brain and superior nervous centers, still be in evolution. From this fact, while observation is rendered more difficult, the temptation grows to investigate what will be the direction of this movement forward, to determine how it will be accomplished, in short to prejudge the course of Life. From there to deciding what men must do and to reestablishing the idea of duty there is a logical enticement, which the new philosophers have not resisted.

Having at first studied, as required by positive science, the past and present modes of men, they ventured to investigate by induction what these modes will be in the future, what they will become in virtue of a necessary development. Thus they came to sub-

173

stitute for the former conception of a moral type properly so called, subject to an imperative, the conception of a normal type, one in harmony with the direction of evolution. This induction not only supposes that the principle of finality has an objective virtue and pertains to a Universe in itself, but also that the end of this Universe is determined and known. Therefore the knowledge of this end entails the conception of a universal and positive Good. The Good becomes the ensemble of the tendencies and the acts most apt to realize the aim of the Universe. The accomplishment of this purpose, being fatally assured by natural selection, gains an imperative character. On the other hand, since man has become conscious of the aim of the Universe in humanity and of the path leading to this aim, it is his duty to further natural selection by a voluntary and parallel intervention. At least humanity's share contributing to this assistance must be called good and virtuous, seeing that it proves to be in harmony with the tendency of the Universe.

Such are the conclusions reached by most positivist systems. One sees that in them the concept of finality revives the idea of a sovereign Good and that artificial selection discharges the function of duty. Now this conception of purpose is really no more than an intellectual presumption substituted for the former moral presumption. What philosophers take for a divination—by means of a scientific induction,—of what the future will be, actually always allows an element of personal valuation, by which their theory ceases to be scientific and becomes, according to Nietzsche's expression, "a dispute about taste and tasting." [3] Thereby it enters into competition with other different theories, undergoes the chances of combat and has no other virtue than its strength. It is not permissible to assign aims to life; rational laws deprive us of the possession of the first causes, in which would be found recorded the quality and the virtuality of the forces, whose evolution constitutes Life. With that unknown quantity at the beginning of the causal series it is impossible to determine its course otherwise than by a sort of wager and game of chance. The particular tastes and instincts characterizing each man and each group of men, these tastes and these instincts, in which desire assumes its force as a lever, are the only legitimate source of an idea of finality; consequently this idea is quite relative. Positivistic philosophy, by assigning to humanity in its entirety and to Life an ultimate finality and one determined as to quality, dogmatizes in the manner of ancient philosophy. It exceeds the limits of cognition and enters the service of the Vital Instinct, using the old theological procedure, which consists in transforming attitudes of particular utility, *petitiones principii* of individual or ethnic temperament into the idea of truth for the purpose of acting on imaginations. In that way it reestablishes the notion of a supreme good and of a universal morality: it creates a falsehood, a vital fiction.

*

What is this fiction? In very truth it differs little from the preceding ones, inasmuch as it is still Christian in form. It consists in posing the existence of a natural law which, after having led the individual to the realization of his own good, then compels him with necessity to realize the common good, so that in the course of evolution egoism is fatally transformed into altruism and the final harmony of all the instances of happiness is the aim of evolution.—It goes without saying that justice is not being done here to all that is excellent and scientific in the first principles upon which positivist philosophy is based in order to found its ethics, all that is ingenious and conclusive in its analyses, all the very considerable part of renewal it permits, when we retain at the bar of this critique only that vestige of the ancient metaphysical spirit, that presumption of finality which has just been formulated.—

"Love thy neighbor as thyself," says Christ. "Love your neighbor, love humanity more than yourself," exclaims Auguste Comte. M. Littré abides by this formula; he predicts the necessity of the final reign of equality and justice, and the mind of Mr. Spencer, scientific as it is, subscribes to these principles. Now, if it is permissible to express oneself mildly on the score of old metaphysical ideas and old religious forms, because they are very much dead and if one must leave to political philosophers, speculating on the chronic stupidity of the populace, the easy and lucrative task of attacking those inoffensive ruins, one could not without pusillanimity observe the same attitude with respect to an idolatry, which has in our day just completed its growth and attained the height of its greatest force. The religion of Progress realizing Equality, Justice and universal Happiness, a scientific error on the part of philosophers, serves as the text and, in its practical realizations, gives occasion for the lowest forms of sycophancy toward the masses through the fear or the ruse of an adventitious aristocracy inferior to its fortune. Such a religion represents the most humiliating ideal that can be offered to humanity and to a sound democracy, pregnant with potentialities for the future and the promise of an élite.

We are concerned here only with the error of philosophers. It consists, we have said, in the presumption of assigning aims to Life: it constitutes an anthropomorphism in rational form. Positivist philosophers, like rationalists, still regulate the progress of evolution by the rhythm of human desire. In proposing as an aim to Life the realization of a blissful harmony, the reign of fraternity and of universal

176

Justice, they are in reality only obeying their Christian atavism. But they have recourse to other reasons. M. Littré founds moral life entirely on a struggle between egoism and altruism, of which he derives the first physiologically from the instinct of nutrition and the second from the instinct of reproduction, and he infers a final preponderance of altruism by reason of that biological law which grants supremacy to the complex over the simple. Now M. Littré considers nutrition and generation as sources, respectively, of egoism and altruism in the light of phenomena irreducible to each other. Therefore, how is one to decide whether one is more complex than the other? Wherein can the act of nutrition be regarded as more simple than that of reproduction? The act of nutrition consists in converting foreign substances into one's own substance, the act of generation in propagating a like substance out of one's own substance. In truth, what criterion other than a theoretical need or a dialectical interest could decide between the two from the standpoint of complexity?

With Mr. Spencer and the philosophers of the evolutionist school it is different. The latter do not consider egoism and altruism as two distinct phenomena; instead they rightly, and by clear analogies, reduce the one to the other. For them egoism is the unique mode, whose substitutes engender moral activity in its entirety. Consequently, if one says that altruism is the aim of evolution, it must not be forgotten that altruism is here no more than a name given to egoism in one of its phases, and that in any altruistic act, under whatever aspect it may present itself, there must be found on analysis the elements of pure egoism composing it. The biological law previously invoked will, therefore, have to be applied directly to egoism without any substitution of terms. It will have to be said merely that the most perfect forms of egoism are the most complex and one will fall again under the dominion of the laws of the mind by establishing that this complexity can grow indefinitely, so that it is really impossible to assign to evolution any qualitative aim whatsoever.

Thus altruism will no longer be opposed to egoism, but rather it will be discerned that altruism represents a refinement and really an augmentation of primitive egoism. The English school directed its analyses along this course. Man, it observes, lives in society. Now, social life requires from each individual a partial renunciation of his immediate egoism acquiesced in to the extent this egoism would be irreconcilable with that of others. Here, then, is an act having an altruistic appearance. But social life is also for man a condition of strength; it enhances his wellbeing, so that this immediate renunciation which has just been established has, upon analysis, no other motive or purpose than to obtain indirectly an extension of egoistic power. Thus it constitutes a calculation of self-interest requiring a certain cerebral complexity: this calculation operates in the individuals of all human groups destined to live and the chances of triumph of a group in its competition with others is determined by the degree of its perfection. Natural selection eliminates the collections of individuals in whom this calculation is not made, the groups in which this foresight and this power of selfish disinterestedness are not exercised. Hence all the altruistic virtues, that is to say all those in which one takes into account the interest of one's neighbor (sincerity, faithfulness to the plighted word, charity) appear here in the clearest fashion as means of egoism. Logically that is what gives them their value. That is their title to nobility, one which is intellectual in nature.

*

It is the same with the sentiments of justice, brotherhood and equality of which M. Littré makes a

178

category of superior aspirations and which he implicates in a mental tendency toward identity. The sentiment of justice, which epitomizes the others in their common results and in virtue of which, by a transference of egoism, an individual comes to suffer from the fact of another not possessing the same advantages as himself, the sentiment of justice permeating a society is one of the means best qualified to assure the conciliation of individual egoisms and to render social life possible. But the usefulness of the sentiment of justice and its very possibility presupposes the existence of a matter to which it applies, that is to say of an intense egoism, the true substance of life, whose excess it tempers in order to control its manifestations.

Justice, in effect, could be no more than a means of regulating egoism, of rendering it possible and assuring its triumph. It cannot be an aim in itself. We stated above that a new and free analysis of the elements of human activity would result in their being ranged in two great general classes: one would include all the attitudes for living, the other all the attitudes for dying. It would be inadmissible to place all altruistic sentiments in this second category; it will become clear later that they can have another origin and we have already shown how their roots are immersed in egoism, but the sentiment of justice, considered as a distinct entity, is the prototype of those attitudes making for death and can only be interpreted as a manifestation of lassitude and exhaustion aiming directly at the suppression of all evolution and the annihilation of all phenomenal life.

Justice must in truth be conceived here, apart from all confused sentimentality, in the positive manner of M. Littré, as *a tendency to identity*. Such is justice in its essence and it is only in this intellectual form that a comprehensible meaning can be attached to it; but presently it shows itself to be in direct opposition to the tendency of Life, which demands diversity. The appetite for justice can only be assuaged through the complete abolition of all difference between individuals, logically by the abolition of the individual, for it could not be admitted that the reduction of all beings to a qualitative likeness satisfies the exigencies of absolute justice; since beings, however alike they may be in relation to one another, are nevertheless distinct, they are distributed in different places and this difference of situation engenders inevitable inequalities which, according to the formula of Aristotle, *could not be tolerated.* Justice, such as it is in itself, realizes its will to identity only in absolute Unity, in a nirvana outside of phenomenal life, the latter being, in its essence and in principle, differentiation.

If justice is not supposed to consist in levelling either, nor in effacing differences established by nature among beings, but in respecting them, if we regard it as right that the one, who ought to command, commands and the one, who ought to obey, obeys; if we view the reign of justice as a hierarchic coordination of all beings creating a harmony of the Universe,—who is going to determine these hierarchic relations among beings? It could only be struggle, which weighs the forces in order to bring them into equilibrium. Therefore justice would simply amount to the consecration of the triumph of the stronger and the acceptance of their authority by the weaker.

If this interpretation of the idea of justice is relinquished as being here distorted from its true meaning, can one at least assume that such a harmony of the Universe, without considering the means by which it is realized and which would tend to disqualify it in the eyes of humanitarian philosophers, is the goal toward which evolution tends? This pretension is still tainted with metaphysical presumption, for it supposes the world to be a given whole susceptible of being embraced by the mind. Now, the world as we know it, is not for us a given whole: we are ignorant of its principle and the sources of Being are forever disappearing before our explorations in the desert of unknowable regions. It follows, as was said before, that, inasmuch as we do not know the nature and the power of the cause, it is impossible for us to determine the direction of the phenomenon it engenders or to foresee the conditions of its fulfilment, that, in short, any pretension to assign a finality to Being is doomed.

Deprived of the knowledge of the end, evolutionist philosophy proves to be vulnerable in its pretension of formulating a universal morality, since the principles constituting this morality were nothing more than the means best suited to attain the end and since the existence of the end was alone a guaranty for the legitimacy of the means, while at the same time sanctioning their authority and assuring the triumph of the law.

III.

We have seen Kant, with the CRITIQUE OF PRACTICAL REASON, subordinate the whole sheaf of metaphysical ideas to the existence of a moral law, the reality of which neither he nor his disciples were able to establish. Now, if one recapitulates the different transformations of philosophy, from the CRITIQUE OF PURE REASON to the most recent conclusions of the positivist schools, it is to be observed that, through the fact of Kant's great authority, this manner of posing the problem has prevailed.

Abandoning, for the purpose of founding moral law, *a priori* dogmatic means and recourse to faith disguised as a special category of reason, positivist philosophy has nevertheless sought to establish the existence of a moral law. It gave as a support for this moral law, as we have just disclosed, the metaphysical idea of finality. This pretension of assigning purposes to the Universe was condemned as an instance of rational anthropomorphism as unsound as the *petitiones principii* of preceding dogmatisms. Accordingly we remain confronted with this conclusion: there is no universal moral law. No revelation, no rational axiom bids man do what he ought to do. Nothing is good in itself, nothing evil in itself.

If, that being well established, one turns toward life, this fact based on observation affirms itself at once: that there are systems of morals everywhere, that, from the standpoint of these ethical systems, there exists a good and an evil, and that it is even the characteristic fact and the unique function of every morality to create a good and an evil, in consideration of which are to be promulgated a "Thou shalt" and "Thou shalt not." In the presence of this unique function of all moral systems and if one considers, in contrast, how much these notions of good and evil in the interior of each morality differ among themselves, the evidence of this conclusion blinds the mind, rendering it unable to know that the moral fact, with its corollary, good and evil, is subordinate to an anterior principle imposing its form upon it, that, like all other phenomena, it is situated in the world of relation, that it is an effect of a certain cause.

Where, then, is this cause to be sought, unless it be in human activity where the acts appear, to which the designations of *good* and *evil* apply? Where shall we look for the cause of the diversity of ethical systems except in the diversity of the temperaments in which their roots are implanted? Therefore, we shall say that it is activity itself which creates its law and reveals it to the mind, instead of it being the mind that commands it.

This is the end of the metaphysical fog: here we have, dissipated and melted away in the whiteness of the air, the last little bit of mist which still adhered to the speculations of the positivist school. It is also the end of nocturnal hallucination; it is the crowing of the cock; the light of day restores to the things of nature their true contour; phantasmal trees, hedges set at the side of roads, thatched roofs with disquieting forms are seen clearly. It is the dawn and such is the symbolic title given by Nietzsche to the book in which he salutes this matinal awakening and the light it sheds upon the landscapes of the Intellect. A halt is indispensable here: it is a changed scene and one must see and touch these veridical and innocent things which, in the darkness of the night, terrified us.

Thus the principle underlying the whole ancient apparatus of morality with its Procrustes bed, in which energies of all dimensions had to be equalized, was a wilful inversion of cause and effect, of principle and consequence. In the notions of *good* and of *evil*, consequences of a given manner of being, forms of an attitude determined by some will, one wished to situate the principle of these manners of being, the law of this will. Consequently, what it is now important to show is how and by what artifice this ancient misunderstanding originates, the manner in which the quid pro quo of morality is formed. That will become evident in the course of the analysis about to be made, an analysis whose aim it will be to investigate at what precise moment of its evolution activity engenders moral law.

*

All activity is at the beginning and for the first time entirely spontaneous. Under the action of necessity and without any intervention of conscience movements are projected towards an end. This end is either attained or not attained: if it isn't, new movements are essayed until in the living substance which is the source of these trials, the series of movements least suited to attaining the end are eliminated, until through mechanical memory the series of movements most apt to attain this purpose is registered, conserved and integrated. In case of success here are constituted, by the fact of the adaptation of a means to an end, an individual, an organism, a function. At the same time this individual, this organism, this function find themselves in the possession of a method. Every innovation, every invention, every change which, prior to this success and this adaptation, involved a chance of realization and accordingly had to be considered elements of progress, would now be a sign of deterioration. Henceforth there is no more room except for acts of repetition. The most perfect sequence of movements, which created an organism, also marks the limits of its evolution. It is a model and this model will be repeated indefinitely, with perfection as long as the organism is in the period of its vigor, or maladroitly when this organism tends toward its decline. This procedure finds its application from the top to the bottom of the biological scale: it occurs in the formation of the simplest cellular aggregates, as well as in the formation of the most complex organisms, such as the apparatuses of mentality. This definitive process, which perfectly adapts need to its satisfaction, while at the same time creating for the organism its power, its means of living, realizes it and gives it its particular form, determining its functional, individual or specific finality. It is by virtue of these accumulated processes that, through the obscure work of cellular associations, all animal species, all varieties of races within the same species, all the individual varieties within the same race were realized in the course of evolution. These processes have always and everywhere involved the fixation of a species, a race, a type; they have simultaneously realized and created aims. As realizers of aims they emanate, as far as we can determine, from that focus of unknown causality where life forges diversity. As creators they are models for every living substance, of the same species, to imitate. They comprise a group and they define it and whoever, among the individuals of a group, imitates them with perfection prospers, whoever imitates them badly declines.

If, upon this biological process, everywhere identical, one superimposes consciousness, behold the moral world with the illusion so soon arisen of liberty which, under new names, is going to reflect faithfully the circumstances and vicissitudes of physiology. Isn't it apparent now at what moment of physiological evolution it is proper to place the formation of an imperative, of a moral law? It is at the precise moment which follows the invention by the organism of the perfect process, by means of which it realizes itself and determines its finality. Hence this organism, which was constituted in the fashion just described and whose origins are lost in unknown causality, now carries its destiny within itself. A more or less harmonious coordination has been established among the different nervous centers composing it and among the diverse tendencies soliciting it. With more or less good fortune it vibrated, in the period of its greatest power, according to the most harmonious rhythm which it was in its power to realize. This rhythm will serve as a model to all subsequent rhythms; according as organic memory is more or less good, it will be more or less faithfully reproduced and the individual will have more or less of power at his disposal. But, at the same time, through the intervention of the mirage of conscience, this model rhythm is going to appear, in mental representation, under the form of an ensemble of imperative precepts, whose clarity and authority will be in proportion to the more or less perfect coordination realized in the organism. Likewise the fictions of merit and demerit are going to be the faithful representations and the shadows produced by the more or less efficaceous energy developed in the physical phenomenon. Every time the organism proves inapt to reproduce the useful process, this failure will be evinced in consciousness by the sense of guilt, by remorse. Each success will be manifested by inner contentment, by the feeling of a good conscience. Good and evil will be that which realizes or fails to realize the determinate end of the organism.

*

Evidently, individual moralities which, one would be inclined to think, should be very numerous are, on the contrary, very rare. Temperaments which, having become conscious of their modes of being, accept them whatever they may be, recognizing as good what favors their tendencies and as evil what oppresses them, are exceptional. For each individual is born amidst a group, which already has its morality and which, through education, imposes it upon the newcomer. It is in this sense that Nietzsche was able to say: the pleasure of the thou is anterior to the pleasure of the ego. In every human group some stronger temperaments have prevailed and, by the fascination of example, have imposed upon all the others their own ways of being and their valuations on things; they are those whom Nietzsche will call creators of values: it is they who affix on acts the labels "good" and "evil." They are the authors of social ethics, of moralities properly so called, of those that are common to an entire group.

What, then, is a social morality? It is, one will say, the formula of a temperament which has prevailed. In what epoch of the evolution of a human group must the source of the social morality peculiar to this group be situated? In what men ought one to seek the principle of that morality and its legitimate claim? In those who, in an epoch usually prehistoric, spontaneously realize the attitudes most apt to secure for the organism, which is searching and fashioning itself with their help, its greatest power. In consequence of this adaptation of a means to an end, by the shortest line, through this success proceeding from a law of the unconscious or springing from chance they have realized according to its perfection an ethnic type and have created for a race its destiny. They have furnished the model activity. It is according to the curve of their gestures that legislators, coming afterwards, design the moral law. Hence the codification of ethics and its promulgation are not characteristic of the greatest period of strength and health of a human group. The men of that perfect period require neither methods nor moralities, since they accomplish naturally the gestures best suited to them, those which procure the greatest power for them. But the men of the following period commence to imitate their ways of being. They imitate them, because they procure power, because they are the most fit to coordinate their activity and to collect all its elements into a group.

It is in this epoch that the legislator or the priest appears; it is appropriate to place here and following his intervention that substitution of consequence for principle, which afterwards blinds men and marks the historical genesis of all morality. For the legislator selects in the models, that he still has before his mind, what in them were attitudes of utility, that is to say means of power. These attitudes of utility he does not give simply for what they are; but rather, in order to augment their force and consecrate their prestige, so that they may restrain the race on the slope of decadence when the latter has lost its instincts, he makes of them commandments, assigns a divine origin to them and imposes them upon credulity by fear and promises,—immediate or future punishments and rewards.—Thus these rules, which derive their value merely from the fact of their being transferred from the modalities of an activity, these designations "good" and "evil," which represent no more than specific purposes sought or avoided by that activity, these rules and these valuations are situated for subsequent activities, for which they are proposed, in a region anterior to all activity, in a superterrestrial region which is invented and has appeared by turns as divinity and reason. By consequence Good and Evil, removed from the causal series, are converted into those rational idols which have taken the place of the old theological ideas.

Everything considered, the fate of moralities is seen to be tied to the fortune of the activities, which served them as models. Among the latter it is the best endowed, the most qualified, in a word the strongest that have succeeded in living, in enduring, in imposing their modalities, that is to say their Good and their Evil. That which was favorable to these activities, what was for them a means of power and nothing else has in consequence become the Good. The Good is therefore a sometime form of Power. As a shell attests that a living animal once formed it in order to create a dwelling and a fortress for itself in it, every concept of the Good proves that a strong activity delighted in it not long ago, finding therein its joy and its strength. Power alone decides as to what is the Good. The concept of the Good is within the concept of Force; it is plainly subject to it and derives from it all that it has in the way of value. Force is the ancestor transmitting to the Good the heritage of its nobility, the title it was able to acquire. Such are the conclusions that will have to be accepted as soon as one's gaze has been elevated above the metaphysical fog, howsoever they may contradict the rationalistic sentimentality so highly esteemed at present.

IV.

These conclusions will find their perfect expression in the work of Nietzsche.

However, with respect to this special point, but one of supreme importance, of the subjective origin and the purely relative character of morality, it is impossible to pass over in silence the contribution of Carlyle to the new solution of this problem and one could not, without injustice, either contest or belittle his rôle as a precursor.

What is remarkable in Carlyle is the sureness of mind with which he imagines a new procedure of inquiry and how, with a clear and eminent good sense, he searches for the moral fact where it is concealed, like ore in the rock of the mountain, in the concrete substance of human activity. This is a notable fact as one leaves metaphysics. To this question: Who created morality? Carlyle instinctively replies: Man, the hero. At a single stroke he reestablishes the true order of the relationship reversed by theology, dissipating the quid pro quo; henceforth it will be possible to gain a clear understanding. Carlyle is fully aware of the following, namely that the moral fact consists in a principle of coordination distributing the elements of activity according to a hierarchy in such a way as to determine for a man or a group of men their several destinies. This directive principle appears in man without his intervention; it is an impulse of the Unconscious, coming from nature, from the unknown. Indeed M. Barthélemy, in his fine study on the Scottish master,[4] rightly compares the conception of conscience in Carlyle to that of the Unconscious in Eduard von Hartmann. If Carlyle values conscience so highly, it is because it appears to him the means of grasping that principle of coordination, which gives its true meaning to every specific entity and brings with it a revelation of the content of Life. Carlyle proclaims the necessity of silence; conscience is for him a thing of solitude: closing all the openings of the soul which give access to the outside world, shutting oneself up inside of oneself, directing one's gaze and concentrating one's attention solely within, witnessing the mysterious opening of one's own self and gathering its orders, here is the genesis of every individual morality. Therefore it seems to have as its condition a constraint exerted upon oneself, a constraint which permits one to hear the command of the governing instinct imposing its supremacy upon all the others and signifying to each of them their task. But this constraint exerted upon oneself, apparently a means, is in reality but a consequence of the power of this governing instinct and does no more than reveal its existence. It is because this instinct exists that a constraint is exercised by it on all the others: that is the first act of its authority; it imposes silence before presenting distinct commands. At the origin of individual morality, as at the origin of social morality one finds *a fact of domination;* in both cases it means the triumph of a force imposing its manners of being upon either a group of nervous centers or a group of men.

This quite positivistic conception of the moral fact is revealed in many a passage of Carlyle's work. Thus he admired in the ancient Norsemen "that wild sea-roving and battling, through so many generations. It needed to be ascertained," he says, "which was the *strongest* kind of men; who were to be rulers over whom?" [5] and he recognizes that the triumph of an idea or of a man determines the value, the goodness of the one and of the other. "I say sometimes, that all goes by wager-of-battle in this world; that *strength,* well understood, is the measure of all worth. Give a thing time; if it can succeed, it is a right thing." [6] Here we have what is excellent in Carlyle, here is the novelty that came out of his Unconscious. Not in vain did he isolate himself from the noises of the external world and painfully strain his entire attention in order to catch the words of that voice without a mouth, which arises for some from the inner abyss. What that voice babbled in indistinct sounds, he made articulate in clear formulas.

Nevertheless it seems that, beside this purely intellectual attitude, Carlyle also showed some weaknesses, that he did not entirely escape the influence of his environment, inasmuch as he allowed himself to be hindered by ways of thinking which, as far as he was concerned, should have been surpassed, that he failed to express with the rigor they deserved the consequences of the principles he had brought to light. According to M. Barthèlemy, whose discerning and conscientious study gives evidence of a profound knowledge of his author, the characteristic feature of Carlyle's conception is the following one: "The sentiment of the identity of Force and of Right, of moral Value and Intelligence." [7] Now, identity is not saying enough. To metaphysical theology formulating with Kant the primacy of morality, one must oppose without circumlocution the primacy of Force. Indeed there is an apparent identity between Force and the Good only in so far as Force remains static. Wherever Force evolves and expands, it substitutes new forms for the old forms of the Good and the Right. The Good, then, assumes various aspects; there exist very diverse conceptions of it: wherever an activity having Force at its disposal has established itself for a while, it has created a form of the Good and made the Good inhere in certain qualities. Thus the idea of the Good receives the impress of Force, recognizes its ascendance and undergoes the metamorphoses imposed upon it thereby. Force, on the contrary, always remains identical with itself: it varies only in quantity. Hence it is the venerable ancestor from whom all virtue proceeds, and what actually happens is that, long after having lost all efficacy, the Good still derives some credit from this genealogy, just as a title of nobility still evokes in the presence of the one bearing it the memory of the ancestor, who merited it.

This *identity* between the idea of the Good and the idea of Force granted by Carlyle, when the priority and the supremacy of Force should have been proclaimed, therefore constitutes a first concession to the old conception of morality. It will induce him to concede others. The notion of duty seems implicit in this maxim, in which a presumption of finality is revealed: "Man first puts himself in relation with Nature and her Powers, wonders and worships over those; not till a later epoch does he discern that all Power is Moral, that the grand point is the distinction for him of Good and Evil, of *Thou shalt* and *Thou shalt not.*" [8] Everything that is right is implied in this fact of cooperating with the real tendency of the world; you will succeed by this fact (the tendency of the world will succeed), you are good and on the right path. Yet it is difficult to assign to this phrase the true sense it permits: words are but symbols of thought, symbols in several degrees; according to the level of the Intelligence using them to express itself, they must be transposed by one or two tones. We already established that the moral world was, with new names, only the reflection in consciousness, in the illusory light of liberty, of the real phenomena which evolve in the organism. Every organism, it was also said, admits of a model process assuring its best functioning, which it repeats with more or less perfection, according to whether it is itself in the period of its energy or its decadence, and which gives the ideal measure of its force. This dynamic ideal conveys in conscience the conception of *Obligation* and of *Duty*. Consequently the accomplishment of Duty really corresponds to the state of strength and health of the organism and the mythological idea of Duty here signifies the real fact of Force. It is, therefore, true to say that, for the or-

192

ganized being man represents, the great point is to distinguish his Good and his Evil, what he *ought* and what he *ought not* to do, if by that is understood that the power of making such a distinction and of acting accordingly denotes a state of strength and harmony in this organized being. The whole difficulty is in deciding to what extent the words used by Carlyle must be transposed in order to be reduced to confessing his true thought, in knowing whether or not he is a dupe of the mirage of conscience.

According to the more or less strong tendency impelling everyone to reduce the thought of others to his own or to distinguish it therefrom, one will grant Carlyle the benefit of the symbol or contest it. Certain valuations expressed in *Heroes* or in *Sartor Resartus* establish that, at some moment of his evolution, his thought was largely opened to a world of pure fatality, to which morality has no access. "Wiser were it," according to the pronouncement of Teufelsdröckh, that we yielded to the Inevitable and Inexorable and accounted even this the best." [9] If one takes into account this strong conception of the *fatum*, which appears in his work at times, it seems as if one ought to interpret as images and appearances the words *duty* and *good* and *evil* used by him and which, outside of a theology, are irreconcilable with the fatalistic point of view. On the other hand, in order to remain as objective as possible, it seems that one would also have to take into consideration the atavism, the puritanical milieu, the race of which, after all, Carlyle recapitulates the ideal in himself according to its best meaning and with an extraordinary intensity. Such factors gave him the taste for asceticism, for constraint, for the cult of effort. Those are exercises in the course of which the inner activity elaborates Force. They betoken the presence of Force. Carlyle probably placed liberty where the fatality of his nature dominated him with the most inflexible violence, where his character manifested itself with the most entire autonomy, in that power to exert himself in him developed to a high degree, a power given like all the rest and for which he was not responsible, but whose purely representative rôle he may have forgotten, so that the illusion of liberty, with the moral consequences it carries with it, remained for him attached to that power.

However that may be, by this cult of Force and of Effort, which seems to him to be its means, Carlyle offers a new point of resemblance with Nietzsche. His conception of life is clearly immune from any eudaemonism; it does not aim at man's happiness, but rather his greatness. It is this same viewpoint that Nietzsche will develop with an incomparable beauty, when he defines Life as: ". . . *that which must ever surpass itself,*" when he enjoins man to tend toward the superhuman and gives as the sole basis for morality the will to power.

Before considering this conception of morality in the work of the German philosopher, it was important to render to Carlyle the justice due him and to show that on this point, at least, he was a precursor. Carlyle did not interpret according to all its rigor the conception which germinated in his mind. Nevertheless, he expressed it in terms sufficiently clear to admit of its being translated by other minds according to its inviolable signification. Perhaps it is the way of great thoughts to burst forth from the depths of Instinct, mysterious and veiled from the one who produced them, and then to flower in the hour of their maturity, refulgent and fully revealed, in consciousnesses more distant.

CHAPTER VII

FRIEDRICH NIETZSCHE

Amor fati *—*Nietzsche*

I. Of the sources of philosophical thought.
—Every philosophy is the objectivation
of a temperamental state.—The philosophy of Knowledge is the objectivation of
the Instinct of Knowledge.—Nietzsche
brings to the truths of the *Critique* the
consecration of a sensibility.—The evolution of the Instinct of Knowledge toward supremacy. The character of this
evolution in Nietzsche. Its means: the
Instinct of Grandeur under the appearance of Christian asceticism.—Ancient
moral virtue as a principle of philosophical transformation.—The immediate and concrete value of Nietzsche's
work.—

II. The philosophy of the Instinct of
Knowledge.—Negation of the ideas of
God, the thing in itself.—There is no

first cause, no universal end, but ignorance at the origin and the issue of
the phenomenon.—The illusion of the
self as a foundation of the illusion of
free will.—The impossibility of a universal moral law. The purely formal
value of truth.

III. The morality proper to the philosophy
of Knowledge: aesthetics.—The world
justified as a phenomenon of beauty:
Schopenhauer and Nietzsche.—Apollinic
art and Dionysiac art.—The vain and
the wicked, good actors of Life.—The
virtuous one is the spectator.—

IV. The philosophy of the Instinct of Grandeur: the superhuman taken as a symbol.—Cruelty toward oneself is the
unique practise. — The circumstantial
morality adopted by Nietzsche: condemnation of the aesthetic attitude.—
Condemnation of Christianity.—Opposition to eudaemonism.—The morality of
masters and the morality of slaves.—
The more general character of the doctrine: its efficacy.

I.

Every philosophical system is the objectivation in
the mentality of a temperament taking cognizance of
its modes of being, its desires and its aversions, establishing as good what favors it, as evil what is adverse
to it.—This idea dominates and illumines Nietzsche's
entire philosophy, besides having a controlling influence over every valid estimation of this philosophy.

Nietzsche expressed this salient idea in many a
place in his work, but developed it with peculiar dis-
tinctness in the first pages of BEYOND GOOD AND

EVIL. "It has gradually become clear to me what every great philosophy up till now has consisted of—namely the confession of its originator, and a species of involuntary and unconscious autobiography; and moreover that the moral (or immoral) purpose in every philosophy has constituted the true vital germ out of which the entire plant has always grown." [2]

He adds with insistence: ". . . In the philosopher, . . . , there is absolutely nothing impersonal; and above all, his morality furnishes a decided and decisive testimony as to *who he is*,—that is to say, in what order the deepest impulses of his nature stand to each other." [1] Thus a person's fundamental instincts are fathers of philosophy. ". . . every impulse is imperious, and as *such,* attempts to philosophize." [2] At the source of every philosophy there is to be found "a suggestion," a desire of a heart, and Nietzsche denounces the lack of honesty in philosophers, who do not admit this to themselves, who all lay claim to a rigorous dialectic and the procedures of the Instinct of Knowledge alone in order to set up their prejudices as truths. Then he perceives that this is a ruse of the particular instinct leading them, a means for that instinct to gain power and impose its sway. Men have, indeed, attached a great importance to the decrees of the Instinct of Knowledge, which have been distinguished under the name of *truths* from the *petitiones principii* of all the other instincts. Each particular tendency, as soon as it aspires to domination, therefore resolves first and foremost to enslave the Instinct of Knowledge in order to compel it to promulgate its own wish, so that its innermost desire may be consecrated as truth. "Your will and your valuations have ye put on the river of becoming; . . . It was ye, ye wisest ones, who put such guests in this boat, and gave them pomp and proud names, ye and your ruling will!" [3]

Thus there are in the world only instincts, whose

joint relationships produce states of temperament. There is no philosophy that does not have one of these states of temperament as a prop or buttress.

§

A first consequence of this principle is that the philosophy of pure knowledge itself has as a condition for its existence a particular state of sensibility, to which it is indissolubly bound. Like any other philosophy it is the objectivation of an instinct that has become preponderant; it is the objectivation of the Instinct of Knowledge. "And even thou, discerning one, art only a path and footstep of my will: verily, my Will to Power walketh even on the feet of thy Will to Truth!" [4]

That does not imply that the principles of the Science of Knowledge are purely subjective, but that they are not visible, that they acquire imperative force only to the extent a sensibility having an interest in discovering them through the pleasure they afford it, materializes them and renders them concrete. It is one thing to deduce a philosophy in the manner of Kant, by means of abstract analyses and procedures in some degree algebraic, in which the brain alone is employed, and it is another to carry it impressed upon the sensibility in the rôle of intuition and instinct, as was the case for Nietzsche. The first method determines scientific truth, but does not establish it, since it is valid only for minds devoid of passions concerned with contradicting its verdicts. The earth continues immobile after Galileo's discovery until a new form of sensibility, prevailing over the ancient biblical conception, tolerates its course.

Moreover, truth does not have the importance that men have attributed to it since it became the object of their idolatry. If men are to agree, they must adopt similar interpretations regarding phenomena, but

198

whether or not they concur on truth or on error is inconsequential; that is why by universal consent they were able to live and to die for thousands of years on an immobile earth without inconvenience. In his variations on the nature of certitude M. Remy de Gourmont [5] remarks that there is no such thing as historical truth, that only indifferent facts are uncontested. If one of these facts once considered certain ceases being unimportant, it immediately becomes an object of controversy and is divested of its character of truth. With certain limits this ascertainment may be extended to the axioms of reason. In order not to be contested and to appear incontrovertible, rational realities must have been able to move a sensibility cogently enough for the latter to make them its own and, by elucidating them, make them apparent. Before a reality can pass as truth it must gain the assent of human belief. Even mathematical truths could not be appreciated by the intellect until they were revealed as indispensable for the solution of some practical interest. Intangible as to their reality, their truth could not become evident without recourse to the sanction of minds and this sanction had to be partial in principle. The necessity of dividing lands doubtless gave rise to the discovery of the laws, which apply to the measurement of surfaces, but in all probability these laws were not rigorously determined until the day when two joint heirs of equal strength were compelled, because of neither being able to gain an advantage over the other, to accept the arbitration of the Intellect alone.

At least one would like to believe that, once revealed, these mathematical truths were thereafter immediately patent to all. But it would be rash to affirm it, considering that the negative truths of philosophical criticism, so close to the preceding ones, did not enjoy this privilege. The example of Kant, so near to us, was of a sort to enlighten us. The CRITIQUE

OF PURE REASON did indeed make us witness that singular fortuity of a philosophy in opposition with the dominant sensibility of the philosopher formulating it. The same can be said of the truths of criticism as of the discovery of Galileo: they are justified as a phenomenon of somnambulism. In order to explain their premature appearance one must imagine the Instinct of Knowledge, still in the time of its servitude, remaining, during some lethargic sleep of the other instincts, alone vigilant, and surreptitiously achieving mastery, celebrating its rites, promulgating its laws and anticipating the epoch of its supremacy. But, whereas Galileo persists in his dream and whereas the discovery he brings, disavowed by the men of his day, finds a refuge in his consciousness as a connoisseur. Kant, as soon as he has awakened from the somnambulistic state, in which he played the rôle of medium of the Genius of Knowledge, hastens to deflect the enterprise initiated without his knowledge from the object toward which it was being directed. This is what had happened: not only had Kant's sensibility not participated in the elaboration of this philosophy, but its conclusions were in absolute antagonism with the modes of his sensibility. The first act of Kant restored to himself, once more subject to his normal *suggestion* and obeying *the wish of the heart* guiding him, is, as we have seen, to overturn this scaffolding erected in his name, but actually without his concurrence. He imagines noumena. Presently he becomes again the ideal professor of that scholastic philosophy, to which Mephistopheles, concealed under the robe of Doctor Faust, refers the young student in the following ironic terms: "And then you must, above all things, devote yourself to metaphysics. There you see fathomed what is not within the scope of man's brain."

We have seen how, in the wake of Kant, this teaching continued to be in favor for a century. However, immediately subsequent to the secret work of the Instinct of Knowledge impressing its law on the tables of the Critique, the principles of pure reason possess the same scientific value that one accords them today. What, then, do they lack in order to reign? The consecration of a temperament, which adopts them and confers physiological life upon them. Nietzsche is this temperament. The fact he denotes is the acceptance and the consecration by a sensibility of the metaphysical nihilism created unintentionally by Kant with his CRITIQUE OF PURE REASON. From the viewpoint dominating this study, in which one has taken the part of the Instinct of Knowledge in its long revolt against the tyranny of the Vital Instinct, that is the most important event consummated by the appearance of the new philosopher. With Nietzsche the Instinct of Knowledge became in its turn master and tyrant.

*

From its very dawn Life has appeared to us provided with an Instinct of Knowledge, for the Instinct of Knowledge is the principle of phenomenal life itself. Without it there is no representation, since there is no spectator. Thus it gives evidence that the activity of the Universe interests itself in the representation of its own exuberance, that joy is attendant on the mere fact of knowing. Nevertheless, originally and during the greater part of physiological evolution, the Instinct of Knowledge proves subordinate to all the others. It is a serf; the intellect is a *means* at the service of the other instincts. It is trained to apprise them of the dangers to be avoided and the good strokes to attempt. It speaks and lies at their fancy and is silent at their behest; at the same time it is the mirror in which they proudly enjoy the reflection of their power. It is also a scribe and composes philosophies, religions and moralities for their use, methods of hygiene and remedies designed to prolong their strength; it is not yet its own end inherent within itself. But simultaneously we find it acquiring little by little a growing importance, so that biological evolution seems to proceed from a lesser state of knowledge to a greater state of knowledge. Thus, to cite but one example taken from the origins of physiology and the first stages of phenomenal life, the action of light on cellular tegument, which is at first revealed only as agreeable or painful sensation, changes and becomes fixed in representations of colors differing according to the degree of intensity of the primitive sensation. In that way sensation is transformed into perception and the external becomes sharply defined. One part of the unique activity diffused through the Universe becomes, for the other, a spectacle. While it is going to continue to be diversified into the succession of phenomena according to the virtuality of the cause multiplying and shattering itself in its effects, the Instinct of Knowledge, deserting the scene where the play pursues its course, will appear in its superior function under the form of spectator activity which gives a *raison d'être* to the spectacle.

Every state of knowledge is nothing more than a relation of position and quantity between these two modes of activity, in the Universe and in man, according to whether one takes a metaphysical or a psychological point of view. If we take this second standpoint, it appears that evolution toward the most perfect Knowledge is accomplished by a tendency of the *self* to retrench from itself and situate outside of itself as an intangible spectacle an ever greater part of the sensational world. In the same way as the eye has converted luminous sensation into a perception, into a fact of knowledge, the *self*, in the measure in which the Instinct of Knowledge has managed to dominate it, retrenches from itself and situates as a spectacle the emotions, the desires and the fears of all the other instincts. At the end of this evolution there has supervened a complete inversion, a displacement of power. The unique energy of Being, which animated the diverse multitude of the instincts with so abundant a life, has withdrawn from them in order to center in the single instinct of Knowledge. Thenceforth the whilom victors are no longer able to impose their interpretation of existence: deprived of movement, inert and congealed, they are powerless to dissimulate, by the rapidity of their gestures, the feints and fictions by whose means they deceived. Hereafter it is the Instinct of Knowledge that gives the Universe its meaning, and the Universe, with regard to it, is nothing more than a fact of perception. The other instincts, while they were masters, invented purposes which they revered and, for these purposes, means which they sanctioned. These means and these ends are for the Instinct of Knowledge a cause for interest, but it does not see anything else in them than the fictions and stratagems qualified to institute the representation, which it is its rôle to witness and whose rational ground for existence it professes to be. God, Truth, Liberty, all the finalities imagined by the instincts seem to it just so many perspectives and décors able to create the scenic illusion and to satisfy it. Since the time when it has no longer been subjected to appearing on the stage beside the other instincts, it has acquired a clear view of all that sorcery practised by hallucinated actors. It is its peculiar joy and its function, while lending itself to the game of the spectacle, to know its artificies and to describe them; it is at the price of this knowledge that it is a good spectator and that, informed as to what the spectacle allows in the way of what is unreal and expedient in principle, it does not risk becoming indignant ineptly and deranging the representation by an ill-timed intervention. The principles of this superior initiation are contained in the philosophy of pure

Knowledge, in that philosophy which, according to Nietzsche's expression, "dares range morality itself under the world of appearances . . . among 'the illusions' as simulacrum, conjecture, prejudice, interpretation, art." [6]

*

The intellectual temperament giving rise to the philosophy of Knowledge has just been described. It remains for us to investigate how this temperament was formed in Nietzsche, to reconstitute, if possible, the phases of its evolution and to determine its genealogy. The accession of the Instinct of Knowledge to the sovereignty of the *self* does, in fact, admit of several interpretations; perhaps it also admits of several origins.

The conception of the world peculiar to Schopenhauer, like the one just expounded, gives way at some moment to the preeminence of the Instinct of Knowledge. But this reign of Knowledge is here only the sign announcing the decline of Life. Life, evil in itself according to Schopenhauer, evolves from a state of intensity characterized by a blinding of the Instinct of Knowledge and an exuberance of all the other instincts toward a diminution of itself. In the course of this evolution and this decline the total activity of the Universe is dissipated; at the same time the instincts which it animated dim and, as in the mental landscape just described, appear immobilized by the torpor that overcomes them before the clear gaze of Knowledge. This gaze abolishes the illusion that was creating belief in the reality of appearances and, in this perfect cognizance it takes of its fictitious character, phenomenal Life, weary of its dolorous course, finds the supreme motive determining it to deny itself. The last fragment of energy still persisting in the world vanishes and the Instinct of Knowledge, itself a phantom and an appearance, which has done no more than survive all the other instincts, determines, by shutting off its gaze, the fall of the phenomenal universe into the nirvana desired by the yogi and by the saint. Thus the reign of Knowledge supervenes here, not because the Instinct of Knowledge has grown stronger, but because the other instincts have been impaired. It marks the last stage of phenomenal life and, from the standpoint of the pessimist, the awakening from the bad dream of Life.

Nietzsche's conception is different. The total energy of the Universe does not, in his view, evolve from a state of intensity toward a state of diminution, and then toward a denial of itself; it evolves from one of its modes toward the other, from action to knowledge. No fragment of the energy diffused through the Universe is dissipated, but all energy relinquished by activity in action is retrieved integrally by spectator activity. The life-phenomenon is in some sort the flow of the *unique activity* from one of its forms to the other. Given this conception of the Universe, what in Nietzsche will be the principle determining the transformation of energy in action into spectator energy?

Life, according to Nietzsche, is instinct of power; it is that which wishes eternally to surmount itself. Now, if every philosophy is indeed a confession of its author and the expression of a physiology, this definition of Life yields us the secret of the tendency which, in Nietzsche, became imperious; it reveals to us the instinct which governs him and in which he situated his *self*. Nietzsche himself, then, one will be inclined to say, is an incarnation of the instinct of power, of the instinct of grandeur; he is the one who finds his joy in the consciousness of his strength and who wishes unceasingly to rise above himself. And, to be sure, it is evidently to this very disposition of mind that one will be obliged to have recourse continually as a principle of explanation of every mental attitude adopted in the course of the evolution of his thought. It is the instinct of power which in him is the generative cause of all movement and which, by a logical process, assures at the desired time the triumph of the Instinct of Knowledge and of a purely intellectual philosophy. This instinct of power invented its own means: cruelty toward oneself. How is its strength to be augmented except by setting it at variance with what one knows to be stronger, and nothing in any man is stronger than his dominating instinct. This instinct, which knows nothing stronger than itself, is therefore going to contradict and torment itself. Having vanquished all the exterior it is going to vie with its own contradiction in order to overcome itself and thus create in its place something higher than itself.

Nietzsche is cognizant of this means of greatness; he has disclosed it and he celebrates, extols and explains it. "Almost everything that we call higher culture is based," he says, "upon the spiritualizing and intensifying of *cruelty*—this is my thesis. . . . That which constitutes the painful delight of tragedy is cruelty; that which operates agreeably in so-called tragic sympathy, and at the basis even of everything sublime, up to the highest and most delicate thrills of metaphysics, obtains its sweetness solely from the intermingled ingredient of cruelty. . . . There is an abundant, superabundant enjoyment even in one's own suffering, in causing one's own suffering—and . . . Finally, let us consider that even the seeker of knowledge operates as an artist and glorifier of cruelty, in that he compels his spirit to perceive *against* its own inclination, and often enough against the wishes of his heart: . . . ,—even in every desire for knowledge there is a drop of cruelty." [7]

This cruelty toward oneself, taken as a means of the Instinct of grandeur, is going to account to us for the bond existing between the moral attitude of Nietzsche and the Christian morality, which seems to have served as a point of departure for his evolution. The asceticism, of which Christian culture sometimes admits, actually bears a great resemblance to this cruelty toward oneself, which is for Nietzsche the means of greatness, so that one might be tempted to attribute this virtue of the philosopher to his Christian atavism. But that would be an inversion of cause and effect, against which one must be on guard, if the Instinct of Grandeur is to render us its entire explanatory force.

Christianity is in its principle absolute renunciation. That is its essential character. It is an oriental religion and, like Buddhism, an attitude for dying, an attitude of immediate utility for wearied activities. It is in this form that it manifests itself in its perfection and in its purity among the drove of slaves assembled by the Roman world and, later, in its ideal form, in the IMITATION OF JESUS CHRIST. It is a denial of life, without hope of return and without calculation. If it includes some asceticism, this asceticism is transitory, without any future and without virtuality. It consists in renouncing impoverished joys, the last bonds which still attach a sick person to existence; it is a means.

Christianity plays a wholly opposite rôle in the barbaric milieu. Here it is no longer its own inherent aim; it is in its turn a means, a tool of the Instinct of Grandeur and of a cruelty toward oneself, whose virtuality far exceeds the Christian form, which can only be considered a phase thereof and again a transient one. For any nature that is excessive and violent in actions, the renunciation of the free play of the instincts or of the exercise of its force presupposes self-constraint. Any force ready to project itself outward, to spend and squander itself in its effects is withheld and turned back against itself: a power of inhibition is thus constituted. The Christian barbarian, who teems with living forces, places his *self* in this power of inhibition alone, since he knows nothing stronger than himself and what emanates from him: consequently it is with himself that he is going to struggle and it is in the victory over himself that he will experience the feeling of his greatest strength, his greatest power. Christianity in the barbaric milieu is only an expedient: wherever, in society or in man, there is found too intense a force of impulsion, always ready to be dissipated, Christian renunciation supposes a constraint and creates a center of inhibition; far from weakening the individual or the social organism it lends it vigor by coordinating it, by ordering the instincts hierarchically under the command of a single one.

But the fact that the barbarian knows how to apply the remedy of this constraint to himself implies as preexisting in him this disposition to cruelty toward oneself, which will be the means of his greatness. Hence it is those things, pride and the love of power for itself, that one must recognize beneath the Christian in the barbarian. This instinct betrays itself by the attitude of the will always set in the direction of the greatest effort, by the quest and the choice of the most difficult path. The renunciation commanded by Christianity does not, then, have any intrinsic value for the barbarian; he finds it alluring only because, at a given moment, it is the most difficult thing. If it ceases being the most difficult thing, it loses its value and represents an obsolete ideal, one that has been surpassed and if, by practise, it has become a natural instinct bringing joy, if it has become the easiest thing, then presently it is contemptible and inimical and it is henceforth well to triumph over the tendency in which it expresses itself. Thus Christianity is, in the barbarian, but one of the transient forms of the instinct of grandeur served by cruelty toward oneself. This instinct of grandeur admits of an elevating power able to lift one to still more rigorous and nobler summits.

By delving in this way until the veritable roots of Christian atavism have been discovered, one is able to account for this heredity in Nietzsche as a characteristic element of the evolution of his thought. Therefore it is interesting for us to learn from M. Lichtenberger that Friedrich Nietzsche, who was born in a Protestant environment, belongs to a priestly line and that, during a part of his childhood, he proposed to himself as an aim the perpetuation of the tradition of his people.[8] In our view this fact of a Christian culture pursued to the stage of perfection marks the point, to which the instinct of greatness has attained in the course of its evolution, when Nietzsche reaps its heritage from the mentality of his ancestors. Beneath the appearance of Christian asceticism it is already the instinct of grandeur peculiar to the western barbarian, which we shall see in Nietzsche evolving toward new destinies.

Equipped with this temperament, which finds its greatest joy in cruelty exerted toward oneself, Nietzsche is, first of all, affected by the atavism closest to him and accepts this Christian religion prescribing to him command over himself, and yields to it his passions to be dominated in order to exercise his strength. He is then in the situation of those priests, whom he is to combat later, but for whom he will retain his admiration, saying of them: "They called God that which opposed and afflicted them: and verily, there was much hero-spirit in their worship!" [9] It is for the heroic attitude which is required of him that Nietzsche loves the Christian God and Christian verities. But behold how presently this attitude has become too easy for him and observe how the acts of renunciation enjoined by the Christian ideal are realized without exertion. The power to restrain oneself, painfully acquired by ancestors, is now employed without effort: the love of the more difficult cannot find gratification any more in this act of domination which no longer encounters any revolt. Thus the same instinct of grandeur, which lately and logically engendered the Christian attitude, is going with an equal logic to engender a contrary attitude. It is going to invent for itself some new agony to surmount and, for the sake of developing itself, will rouse against itself the Instinct of Knowledge, giving it the liberty to distil "that drop of cruelty" which it conceals. In this way it will be induced to analyze its happiness," . . . to deny, where it would like to affirm, love and adore; . . ." [10] In the Christian form it sacrificed in his ancestors and in himself its immediate happiness to a future happiness situated in God. The sacrifice was transformed into joy; by the perfection of its attitude it realizes *immediately* the happiness which was to have consisted in the *future* possession of God. The Instinct of Knowledge is going to establish a new God higher than the old one: Truth. Henceforth Nietzsche will submit all his *former* beliefs to the test of Truth, inasmuch as this new God is alone strong enough to make him feel the agony he covets. "One must never ask if a truth is useful, if it can be a destiny for someone." [11] Here we have the new maxim, to which the philosopher is going to adhere strictly: with its help he will rise from a utilitarian conception in ethics and metaphysics to a purely intellectual conception and it is through it that, in the course of his search for Truth, he will be led to discover and confess the Science of Knowledge.

❋

Thus it is evidently to the intervention of a moral quality that the Science of Cognition owes its consecration. After the explanations whose aim it was to establish its true genealogy for Christian asceticism, cruelty toward oneself and victory over oneself must be considered the highest virtues of Christianity in the Occident. They constitute the principle of inner life, of which Christianity is for a moment the manifestation and the opportune form. Under this Christian form they are called *asceticism*.

Therefore one may note, with M. Lichtenberger, that it is by means of the highest virtue of Christianity that Nietzsche overcomes Christianity, deism and all the postulates of the vital instinct. But, just as it has already been stated,—after the CRITIQUE OF PURE REASON,—it is precisely this moral virtue, which alone is indispensable to bring out the splendor of the principles of the science of Knowledge. The sun of Knowledge has been shining upon the world since Kant, so that all things struck and awakened by this light project shadows where they can take cognizance of themselves. What men lack is the courage or the ascetic virtue to look at these shadows, in which are inscribed images so different from the chimeras which they brought forth during the nocturnal incubus. They resemble those inhabitants of a distant country,[12] whom M. de Gourmont described for us in a conte with so precise a symbol, the inhabitants of that country in which custom requires that the eyes of the newly-born be slit, where the use of the pupils is an infirmity, where the one who has not undergone the liberating operation is despised by his brethren; for he is unable, in the presence of real spectacles, to perceive the phantoms which a traditional covenant renders visible for all the others. Kant made amends for his crime of having evoked the sun of Knowledge by extolling that golden needle of faith which gives back to men, in broad daylight, the blessed blindness. But Nietzsche is, in that singular country, the audacious being who dares to open his eyes and who, despite the initial pain of the retina shocked by the light, travels through the world of phenomena scrutinizing all the shadows in which things are represented, interrogating his own shadow and proving willing, without reticence, to see all that presents itself to his view.

Without reticence, but not at first without asperity and without distress. Until 1881 and principally with HUMAN, ALL-TOO-HUMAN and THE VOYAGER AND HIS SHADOW Nietzsche's attitude is in effect that of a heroic pessimism. He is mounting the steps of that "great ladder of religious cruelty" [13] which he has himself described; he has reached that height where man, having sacrificed his strongest instincts, "his own nature" to God, has nothing more to sacrifice but "all consolation, all saintliness, all hope, all faith in a hidden harmony, in beatitudes and future justices." Specifying the ascetic character of the evolution of his thought Nietzsche concludes: "Was it not necessary to sacrifice God himself and, by way of cruelty toward oneself, to adore the stone, folly, dullness, fate, nothingness?" This pessimistic attitude will, nevertheless, give way later to another one. Nietzsche, having descended to the lowest stage of his vitality, is going, under the dominion of ascetic discipline, to put himself on the defensive against pathological depression and strive to overcome it. "A sick man," he will say, "hasn't the right to be a pessimist" and, considering the truths of criticism with a more intrepid and a colder gaze, he will get inured to this new mental landscape to the point of finding his joy in it. [14]

Hence we shall find Nietzsche declaring himself on all the questions raised by metaphysics. His judgments will be distinguished by a negative character, but that, for the most part, will be mere semblance and his negation will do no more than smite the hazardous affirmations of previous philosophies. If the ensemble of these judgments is regarded even here as the consecration of the nihilism of the CRITIQUE OF PURE

REASON, it is on account of that tendency of the human mind to persuade itself that Life in its entirety is comprehended in the old conception it has formed of it and that, outside of this conception, there is room only for nothingness. From the point of view of that prejudice Nietzsche does, in ruining the former ideal, seem to ruin Life. In reality he destroys affirmations which were themselves smothering under their shadow other forms of reality and of Life, from which only their faith in themselves concealed their tyrannical and destructive character. Is not the idea of *God* a negation of the *man* idea and the idea of a *thing in itself* a negation of the phenomenon? Does not the idea of liberty negate the idea of law? Is there not a tendency for the idea of truth to diminish reality?

*

The professionals of philosophy quarrel with Nietzsche on another score. They even contest his character of a philosopher, because he does not employ the dialectical procedures customary in the school, because he does not force himself to question everything again, to resume, in order to oppose them to one another, the ancient, consecrated and contradictory proofs. These attacks were already evaluated, when it was said that after Kant the science of Knowledge was constituted, that thenceforth the perfection of the philosophical genius consisted in no longer calling it in question. This perfection exists in Nietzsche. His affirmations, postulates of a purely intellectual temperament, are valuable owing to the manner in which they are superimposed, like canopies of light, over scientific analyses. Where Kant deduces, Nietzsche contemplates with a direct view; where Kant does algebra, reasoning on letters which represent sequences of ideas, Nietzsche handles realities, the ideas themselves. His philosophical and genial gift displays itself through the choice of the concepts upon which he poses his affirmations and his negations, by the angle which he opens to vision, inundating ideas with a sudden light. As to structure philosophy, in Nietzsche, is anatomically perfect, but it proves to be covered, as with a quivering flesh, with a lyricism and a concrete phraseology rich in images where the abstract is endued with life and becomes real. And it is also the marvel of this mind, which has plunged to the most profound depths of logical entities, that it has the ability, with chosen arguments, with a few words whose precision acts like a flash of lightning, to show the evidence of an idea or its impossibility according to the procedures of common mentality. Besides, it should not be forgotten that if, thanks to these gifts, a part of his work is accessible to quite a considerable number of readers, it is to minds who are the most accustomed to abstract speculations that it reveals its integral value, because the latter, initiated as they are into the rites of philosophical technique, are alone in a position to appreciate the feat by which Nietzsche transfigures and transposes into the epitome of the phrase, the image and the symbol the most arduous problems of metaphysics.

II.

The ruin of the ancient fictions is symbolized first of all in the death of God. For rationalists, who still think they can disengage from the disaster some of the metaphysical and moral ideas and make them perform the function of the dead God, the death of God leaves room for the reign of the old fictions. It seems to them that nothing has changed in the government of the world, unless it is that the conception of the universe has been purified and spiritualized. To them the moral idea taken in itself and without disguise appears as something nobler than the divine form in which it was contained. They are ready to substitute one superstition for another and to esteem the new prejudice excellent provided it is useful. But a mind like that of Nietzsche has long since interpreted the idea of God according to its most profound, most abstract, most vast and most highly symbolic signification: when a conception of this explanatory value happens to fall under the regard of such a mind, that fall into the abyss takes on an unparalleled importance. So Nietzsche, extraordinarily moved by the greatness of such a catastrophe, concludes, judging by the indifference he discovers on the faces of all, that this formidable event is still unknown. Descending for the first time from the summit of the mountain, where he has for a long time established his retreat, Zarathustra encounters in the valley the pious hermit, who continues to honor the ancient God by his solitude and his fervor. "Could it be possible! This old saint in the forest hath not yet heard of it, that *God is dead!*" [15] In order to account for that general ignorance Nietzsche invents this explanation: in the mental world and with regard to the spirit the grandeur of an event corresponds to the distance of bodies in the world of space in relation to the eyes. "The light of the furthest stars is longest in reaching man; and before it has arrived man *denies*—that there are stars there." [16] That is a standard, "a means of creating rank" for the mind. It is this measure that in JOYFUL SCIENCE is applied by Nietzsche to the death of God. "This formidable event," he says, "is still on the way, it is advancing, it has not as yet come to men's ears. Time is needed for lightning and thunder, for the light of the stars, actions require time, even after they have been accomplished, to be seen and heard." [17] It is only among superior men, among those whom an exaltation of the spirit places on the level of great events, that this news is known, and when Zarathustra meets them on his mountain, drawn to them by the cry of distress which rose to his cave, he addresses with a greater deference the old pope, who was present at God's last moments.

Nevertheless, this reverence does not cover any uncertainty as to the reality of the event. God is indeed dead in the view of Knowledge. "*If* there were gods," cries Zarathustra, "how could I endure not to be a God! *Therefore* there are no gods." [18] And under its ambitious form this reasoning implies all the pantheistic wisdom; it expresses what is inconceivable for the mind in any dualistic hypothesis formed concerning the Universe. It formulates the impossibility of the coexistence of man and God, of the finite and the infinite, from the standpoint of power, of justice and of space, from the point of view of morality and from the point of view of cosmology.

But God is only the symbol of metaphysical ideas, the earliest, sentimental and crude expression of the problem. Nietzsche searches, underneath this popular symbol, for the finer and more subtle manifestations of these ideas. Behind God, who has disappeared, he finds *the thing in itself* and, from the time of his first works, he denies the necessity of believing in a thing in itself. However, until the time of his conception of eternal recurrence, Nietzsche will not find arguments in the arsenal of the mind to deny the possibility of there being one. This conception of eternal recurrence, with the absolute phenomenalism it implies, will even arouse in his mind no more than a strong presumption against the possibility of this existence. But he assails from the beginning the construction put on the *thing in itself* by philosophers, when they not only pretend to pose its existence, but to define, attain and apprehend it. He reproves Schopenhauer for considering the will as the thing in itself, but he reproaches him especially, and that is where his argument becomes very strong, for having believed that the will, taken as a thing in itself, could attain itself.

"Schopenhauer has given us to understand that the will alone is really known to us, absolutely and completely known, without deduction or addition . . ." [19] ". . . as though cognition here got hold of its object purely and simply as "the thing in itself," without any falsification taking place either on the part of the subject or the object. I would repeat it, however, a hundred times, that "immediate certainty," as well as "absolute knowledge" and the "thing in itself" involve a contradiction *in adjecto; . . .*" [20] The conception, which Nietzsche condemns here, is that of a thing in itself which would be knowable for an intellect, so that his thought, based upon the feeling of an essential irreducibility between existence and knowledge, is indeed identical to the one that was set forth here in a preceding chapter and is expressed in this formula: the thing in itself, of which one cannot say whether it is or is not, could not be anything but unknowable for itself. Consequently he places it in that ideological domain, "where indifference is necessary." "What is requisite," he says, "in the presence of these last things, is not knowledge as opposed to belief, but indifference toward belief and pretended knowledge in these matters." [21] Then he thinks of the thing in itself what Zarathustra expresses on the subject of God to his disciples: "God is a conjecture, but I should like your conjecturing restricted to the conceivable.[22] And in proportion as his thought ripens, so also does his distrust of the concept of a thing in itself grow, this distrust the reasons for which were epitomized by Stirner too in the following aphorism: "By the fact of elevating Being one lowers the phenomenal world to a pure illusion."

*

With the negation of the thing in itself, or of the conception of a thing in itself situated beyond knowledge,—from the standpoint of metaphysical logic it

217

amounts to the same thing,—the ideas of first cause and of universal finality vanish. The phenomenal world, which alone remains, rejects these ideas tending to abolish it. Whoever says phenomenal world, also says diversity in time, space and causality, diversity irreducible to unity. Now the imagination of a first cause becoming resorbed in the final purpose, which one assigns to it, presently suppresses all representation in time and in space. Absolute harmony reconstitutes and equals absolute unity. The perfect adaptation of desire to its end suppresses any interval between desire and its realization and allows no evolution. But the phenomenon has as its support a principle of irreducible divergence, a principle of irreconcilable hostility among things, which alone has the power to compel them to remain distinct in time and in space, which alone maintains them in their panoramic place and in their representative rôle.

In this world of the phenomenon the principle of causality reigns in its entirety and, whereas it commands an inflexible determinism toward objects of knowledge, toward things such as they are disposed with regard to the mind, by its two extremities it is lost and leads the mind astray into a realm of ignorance. It informs it of the incompetence of its laws to attain Being in its totality and in its reality. It signifies to it that the notion of law does not gain access to the realm of Being. Thus the phenomenon, which alone is given us, suddenly appears to us in its diversity, in its multiplicity, emanating from a region forbidden to Knowledge. To discover, in the principle of things, that region in which ignorance is the only law of Knowledge, to confess that rational laws do not apply to the concept of the Universe taken as a whole, this is the Unique wisdom of the mind exploring and fixing its limits in the course of philosophical research. This wisdom abounds in Nietzsche. In order to indicate this impossibility for the mind of embracing the Universe in its law he has Zarathustra in his most lyrical song celebrate that realm of ignorance where Being dissimulates itself to itself, that realm situated beyond cause, effect, consequence and necessity. "Verily, it is a blessing and not a blasphemy when I teach that above all things there standeth the heaven of chance, the heaven of innocence, the heaven of hazard, the heaven of wantonness." "Of Hazard"—that is the oldest nobility in the world; that gave I back to all things; I emancipated them from bondage under purpose. This freedom and celestial serenity did I put like an azure bell above all things, when I taught that over them and through them, no "eternal Will"—willeth. This wantonness and folly did I put in place of that Will, when I taught that "In everything there is one thing impossible—rationality!" [23]

It is from this unknown region that there arise creators of values, all things and all beings, who do not tell their why, who do not know their why and for whom it suffices to be affirmations of oneself, realities. Such are the multiple and irreducible properties of elements which foil the analyses of chemistry. Such in man that indecomposable energy signalized by Nietzsche in the following terms: "But at the bottom of our souls, quite 'down below,' there is certainly something unteachable, a granite of spiritual fate, of predetermined decision and answer to predetermined, chosen questions. In each cardinal problem there speaks an unchangeable 'I am this'; . . ." [24]

Every life arose in the past from this unknown region, everything new that appears in life springs from this region. When Nietzsche, in the apologue of the THREE TRANSFORMATIONS OF THE SPIRIT, seeks to characterize the creator of new values with a symbol, it is the child he chooses to play this part, the child that is "Innocence . . . and forgetfulness, a new beginning, a game, a self-rolling wheel, a first movement, a holy Yea." [25] In effect there is in man no more than what he has acquired from education and what he received from the infant he was at birth. Everything he has gained or holds from education is repetition, substance already ruminated and digested an indefinite number of times. But if there is some innovation in him, that, education was not able to give him and he necessarily has it from the selfsame infant he once was. It is a taste, a new appetite, a new gift for seeing colors, for perceiving sonorities, for feeling emotions, which until then have been neither seen, perceived nor felt. Thereby the child creates new aspects of reality, new realities; he originates the phenomenon. This new taste has no purpose and it escapes all causality; but as soon as it is manifested, it creates a causality and sets itself up for a first cause; for, if there is no single first cause, there is an infinity of first causes, of rocks of fatality, of properties indecomposable for the mind, arising from the unknown region anterior to the phenomenon, and each one of these causes creates an inflexible determinism which brings it to its own end, in which it vanishes and is dissipated without either compromising the security of Being or resolving its enigma. Thus every phenomenon arises spontaneously, emerges from the unknown and presently appears distinct in a world, in which there is room only for the multiform, where nought is admitted without a disguise; it appears formed all of one piece, determining and realizing by the act of its opening alone and with an absolute rigor, its essence, its appetite, the object of its appetite and the proper means for attaining this object. creating the world of relation. "Taste: that is weight at the same time, and scales and weigher; . . ." [26] In the world there are only tastes and colors.[27] Tastes and colors, which are Life, surge directly from the unknown region where causality is not exercised, so that Life, being without cause, could have no end. Hence, for phenomenal Life no cause and no end whatever, but within the framework of phenomenal life, a serried fabric of particular causes and ends, a narrow harness of necessity bridling all phenomena and enthralling them to their task.

＊

To such a metaphysics, to such a conception of the Universe, of the macrocosm, Nietzsche juxtaposes a psychology, a conception of man, the microcosm, no less consistent with the laws of knowledge. No more than the Universe is the self apprehensible as a unity and, if we have become accustomed to considering it as a distinct substance, it is by virtue of a fiction, whose only value is linguistic and as a method for constructing thought. "Willing," says Nietzsche, "seems to me to be above all something *complicated,* something that is a unity only in name—and it is precisely in a name that popular prejudice lurks, which has got the mastery over the inadequate precautions of philosophers in all ages." [28] Our body, which we imagine to be subject to the hegemony of the self, is really "a colony of souls": "—indeed, our body is but a social structure composed of many souls—" [29] or, to specify the letter of this definition with an expression that is more usual with Nietzsche, a colony of instincts. The conflict of these instincts, the momentary alliances or the more durable associations they form among themselves in order that each may sustain its particular interests, this conflict is manifested by decisions and by acts. Now, it is in these acts, which constitute a resultant, that popular prejudice situates the *self.* The self, then, is evidently an algebraic formula recapitulating, under a simple term—but provided with only an abstract reality, a whole development the concrete reality of which is dispersed in a very great number of distinct and contrary elements. Popular prejudice accords concrete existence to the abstract unity formed for the convenience of language and of thought. A fact is taken for a substance. Set up as substance and considered as a real entity this fact, which is a resultant and an effect, becomes a cause, the cause of the fact it really is,—*causa sui*. Thus the conception of the *self* in psychology, like the notion of God in metaphysics, consists in a realization of abstractions. An abstract creation of the intellect is regarded as a creation of nature. And that is done by means of an inversion, namely of effect into cause and of consequence into principle, sanctioned by language. "We are still constantly led astray by words and actions, and are induced to think of things as simpler than they are. . . . Language contains a hidden philosophical mythology, which, however careful we may be, breaks out afresh at every moment." [30] In the mind of the populace which, under the unity of the word, can no longer perceive the complexity of the living phenomenon, language thus instills popular superstition. Modern man believes in the reality of the self, a fictitious representation and momentary resolution of the conflict engaged among the multiplicity of the instincts, as the ancient Greek believed in the reality of the god Pan, a symbol of the infinite diversity of the forces of nature.

The quid pro quo, which has just been explained, necessarily engenders, as one may imagine, the entire imbroglio of morality, with the belief in free will, merit, blame, responsibility, with the inner remorse or contentment created by this belief,—all that fable of morality, singular, moving, laughable and pitiful, tragic, droll and dolorous, of which men never tire of being the candid and convinced actors. An initiation of this sort entails a state of knowledge that goes beyond the negation of free will, since it reveals the deception and the misapprehension, by whose means the illusion is naturally formed. Is it not indeed evident that, when an instinct has become master of all those forming a colony in the same body and has accomplished the act of its choice, it takes possession simultaneously, as of the colony's flag, of the *self* which it waves over the accomplished act and its consequences. It is naturally free, since it is the strongest. But liberty has here its usual sense; it is not free will. Liberty is here what it is everywhere, namely the privilege of the stronger, the consequence of a fact of domination. Who or what is free here? It is the particular instinct dominating all the others, not the *self*, ensign or flag, of which this instinct has gained possession and which will soon belong to another instinct, if the preceding tyrant is dethroned by a rival, For this rival will in turn possess itself of the self, the symbol of power. The *self*, always claimed by the strongest instinct, invariably appears as a victor and it is from this circumstance that the illusion of free will originates in the one, who realizes this simulacrum and this token in a substance.

Nietzsche, in DAWN OF DAY, makes us witness this struggle of the instincts contending for supremacy, of which the possession of the self is the symbol. He establishes that the will to curb an instinct, which moralists term command over oneself, does not manifest anything else but the entrance upon the scene of another instinct struggling against the first. "Whereas we think we are complaining of the violence of an instinct, it is in reality an instinct that is complaining of another instinct." [31] And this new instinct attacks the other at the moment expedient to it, with the appropriate weapons of which it disposes and with its particular tactics, so that "the will to combat the violence of an instinct is beyond our power, just as much as the method one hits upon and the success that one may have in the application of this method." [32]

Here, then, we find abolished in Nietzsche's philosophy, in the most radical fashion, the conditions of a universal morality, here indeed hermetically sealed all the fissures through which the moral idea could venture to slip into the science of Knowledge. In metaphysics there is no thing in itself, no finality of the universe informing men as to that toward which they should aim, signifying to them what is good in itself and what is bad; thus, no sovereign good, so that, if men possessed free will, they would not know for what end to use it. In psychology no *self*, but instincts contending among themselves for power; no free will,—the very word being destitute of any meaning, since it would be the property of an imaginary phantom, an abstraction, *the self*, and not of a will— so that, if there existed a sovereign good, men would not be free to attain it, so that men would by no means be responsible for anything they might undertake in opposition to the idea of sovereign good or in favor of that idea.

Nietzsche does not fail to draw from these metaphysical and psychological premises the explicit conclusions they warrant and his entire philosophy rises, now violently, now with irony against the Kantian idea of the Categorical Imperative. "Verily," proclaims Zarathustra, "men have given unto themselves all their good and bad. Verily they took it not, they found it not, it came not unto them as a voice from heaven." [33] And Nietzsche, without the interposition of his hero, expresses in DAWN OF DAY in analytical fashion the same thought, when he says: "Until now the moral law had to be placed above one's pleasure: properly one did not wish to give this law to oneself, one wanted to take it somewhere." [34] That is to say that one pretended to assign an extraneous law to the instincts, one differing from one's own law. Now, the deductions of metaphysics and morality have substantiated that no being exists from whom to request this law or from whom to receive it, and that an instinct does not, outside of a constraint imposed by another instinct, breaking and oppressing it, obey any law other than its own.

What, then, remains standing in the world of human activities? Instincts issuing from an unknown origin, but provided with a form, with a determinate tendency, distinct from one another and endowed with more or less power. Within every human being, every group, every race a colony of instincts. As soon as a race, a group, a man live or persist in duration, they prove thereby that a hierarchy has been formed among the various instincts inhabiting them, which assigns to each instinct its place and its rank among all the others. The description of the hierarchic relationships, which have thus been established among these different instincts, formulates an ensemble of ways of being; it is permissible to designate this description as a morality. But it is clear, on the one hand, that this morality has no efficacy by itself, that it seems imperative only by reason of an equilibrium of forces which contain one another to the extent of their ability. This equilibrium offers a certain historical constancy by which it can deceive, but it does not imply any supernatural character. It is the result of a conflict of activities engaged, rather than a living and imperative cause situated in a region superior to activities which it commands. It is evident, on the other hand, that in lieu of one morality common to all, there exist as many social moralities as there are social groups, as many individual moralities as there are individuals. "He, however," says Zarathustra, "hath discovered himself who saith: This is *my* good and evil: therewith hath he silenced the mole and the dwarf, who say: 'Good for all, evil for all.'" [35] . . . "This—is now *my* way,—where is yours? Thus did I answer those who asked me 'the way.' For *the* way—it doth not exist!" [36]

In the most absolute fashion, no universal morality, no morality at all in the accepted sense of the word, that is the conclusion of the science of Knowledge, such as it is formulated by Nietzsche without reserve. While recording these nihilistic conclusions it is essential that we remember their religious origin. Nietzsche has complete cognizance of that origin: he considers atheism the latest form of the Christian ideal that has appeared. For him the principle of Christianity consists above all things in the notion of sincerity towards oneself. Now what has ruined the Christian God? "*What, . . . has really triumphed* over the Christian God? The answer stands in my JOYFUL WISDOM, Aph. 357: the Christian morality itself, the idea of truth, taken as it was with increasing seriousness, the confessor-subtlety of the Christian conscience translated and sublimated into the scientific conscience, into intellectual cleanness at any price." [37] The same principle that gained the mastery over Christian *dogma* must gain the mastery over Christian morality. "By reason of this attainment of self-consciousness on the part of the will for truth, morality from henceforward—there is no doubt about it—goes *to pieces: . . .*" [38] Thus it is the notion of sincerity contained within Christian morality which gave birth to the present-day, atheistic and denying scientist; it is this scientist who should be considered the most perfect representative of Christian culture. His manifest ties with the ascetic ideal consist in this common trait, namely that, in the manner of the Christian ascetic, who immolated his instincts to God, he created a new God for himself, to whom he immolates all things: this God is Truth.

Nietzsche is going to transcend this new ideal. He subjects to analysis the very concept of *truth* regarded until then, comparably to the manner in which the ancient God was long held, as above all criticism. Under the action of the analysis the concept of truth undergoes a change and dissolves, at least the concept of truth, such as objective scientists envisaged it. The latter took it to be a measure applicable to the substance of things, one able to serve to classify phenomena among themselves, to decide as to their peculiar preeminence and goodness, to attain them in their reality. Now that is precisely the idea toward which Nietzsche instinctively showed himself the most hostile. "The people on their part may think that cognition is knowing all about things, but the philosopher must say to himself . . ." [39] He speaks of his invincible distrust concerning the knowledge of self, a distrust, he says "which has led me so far as to feel a *contradictio in adjecto* even in the idea of 'direct knowledge' which theorists allow themselves"; [40] and elsewhere he deems this adequate knowledge a "cause of ruin," [41] which is in harmony with that formula to which his entire philosophy converges, *"To recognize untruth as a condition of life."*

What is the philosophical basis of this *partis pris?* This idea which was expounded in the second chapter of this study and which, from a metaphysical point of view, leaving room for the hypothesis of the existence of a *thing in itself,* was expressed in this form: The thing in itself, unique in its essence, not being able to take cognizance of itself except by dividing itself into object and subject, breaking its unity in order to apprehend itself in phenomenal diversity, necessarily conceives itself other than it is. From this metaphysical point of view the illusion of all representation appears to be inherent in the nature of things. To that anti-metaphysicians reply that this illusion is established only with reference to a thing in itself, whose existence they do not recognize. That is sound, but once this thing in itself is suppressed, nothing remains but a succession of phenomena of which one could not say whether they are illusory and differ, as to their object, from the meaning they have for the subject, since they do not exist with any certainty except as phenomena and one would not be able, without falling into the popular illusion, to grant them a purely objective existence. Here, then, it is no longer a question of an equation, one no longer finds face to face two terms between which to estimate a relation of difference or resemblance; one no longer encounters an object and its image, but only a phenomenon which is what it is. Consequently the very notion of truth is suppressed in a still more radical fashion than it was in the preceding metaphysical hypothesis.

Facts of consciousness are the only realities, inasmuch as they are all realities in the same degree and there is no occasion to distinguish among them if some are more or less true than others; such a preoccupation no longer has any sense. The only action it is possible to institute regarding them is to unite the like realities in the same group, that is to say the facts conceived as identical by all consciousnesses and this similarity does not exist in a complete fashion except among those relating to the mechanism of the fact of consciousness itself. In deflecting the word from its metaphysical sense critical philosophy termed *truths* the facts of consciousness of this order: they form the category of logical, mathematical, geometrical truths. But this new conception of *truth,* limited to the mechanism of the fact of consciousness, forfeits all application with reference to the fact of consciousness itself. Besides, it is through the apparatus of these logical, mathematical, geometrical truths, under the action of cause and effect, of time and space that realities acquire their multiple, enigmatic, changing aspect, that they become diversified, show themselves to be irreducible to one another and that, rebellious to any inquiry, they dissimulate their origin. It is by the very virtue of this universal form of the fact of consciousness that the scientist penetrates into the

228

endless labyrinth of causal concatenation or strikes inflexible realities, such as atomic properties which do not permit that one surpass them and which stand like inflexible guards on the threshold of mystery, inexorable, mute, incorruptible, giving no justification of themselves except that that is what they are.

Thus under the action of this double analysis, from the metaphysical, as from the phenomenalist point of view, truth loses its interest, its prestige and its divinity. From the first point of view it implies contradiction, from the second one it only governs a category of realities indifferent to humanity. Everything that impassions, everything that is an object of desire or aversion, everything that is alive is irreducible to the concept of truth in the name of the laws of Knowledge themselves, the only ones upon which men concur in a universal accord. In ethics more than in any other matter the notion of truth must be set aside in order to make room for the conception of reality, for it is in this domain that the fact of consciousness appears in its most undiscernible aspect.

Such is Nietzsche's final conclusion and that is why his last paraphrase of the nihilism of the Critique is found in love songs addressed by Zarathustra to Life, to Life without cause, to Life without aim, to Life completely enveloped in the capricious stuff of its own unique reality.[42]

III.

"Probability, but no truth, appearance of liberty, but no liberty, it is through these two facts that the tree of science avoids the risk of being confounded with the tree of Life." [43] This observation in the WANDERER AND HIS SHADOW reveals in Nietzsche the definitive triumph of the Instinct of Knowledge, whose conclusions have just been stated. It tends to sanction, as a necessity, the intervention of fiction and illusion at the source of every vital manifestation. Now, whoever is conscious of this necessity has already withdrawn from Life. The nature of illusion is not to recognize itself as such, but to consider itself Truth. Besides, it is only possible to be fully conscious of the fatal conditions of the voluntary act when this act sees the energy calling it forth ebbing; it is then accomplished under conditions of weakness and sluggishness, which permit the mind to analyze its mechanism.

What is going to be the attitude of the philosopher deprived of the power to deceive himself, dominated entirely by the Instinct of Knowledge? To what acts, what conduct will he be logically impelled? Since a morality is the ensemble of the acts commanded by a given conception of life, what will be the morality distinctive of a state of pure knowledge?

One can proceed here by elimination and if, after having removed all the modes of activity excluded by a state of pure knowledge, there remains some mode which it tolerates and against which it has no arguments, there will be reason to believe that this special activity, which resists its analysis and which it cannot destroy, is the very one animating the Instinct of Knowledge and without which no knowledge would be possible. Now the mind, which accepts the conclusions of the science of Knowledge in its final consequences, knows that all phenomena, once they have appeared, are linked according to the inflexible mechanism of cause and effect; it knows that these phenomena arise from the unknowable, that it is impossible to call them forth or to modify them, once they have appeared; it is aware that the ego is itself one of these phenomena, so that all interference by which it pretends to intervene is itself involved in the inevitable series of effects and causes; finally it realizes that these phenomena are not susceptible of comparison with one another from the standpoint of a measure of truth, or of goodness. What interest of a kind to give him a consciousness of himself, to determine himself as a phenomenon, what interest can such a mind take in considering this flow of phenomena? Seeing that all other motives have been removed, there remains but one, namely that this mind, which the science of Knowledge forbids ever intervening, is interested in Life as a spectacle. This, then, remains: that Life, inexplicable from the point of view of reason, justifies itself by its representative value. That Life should be a spectacle for a spectator, this may indeed be the word of the enigma, at least for the one in whom the Instinct of Knowledge has become supreme.

Now what quality does one have the right to expect from a spectacle? That it be beautiful and it has been found, too, that in the view of the connoisseur, who has critically sifted all the concepts of finality, supreme good, truth and justice and felt them all to be inconsistent and irreconcilable with life, one concept alone remains intact and that this is indeed that of beauty. Must one not conclude therefrom that the sentiment of the beautiful is the one which remains in the mind, in the presence of phenomena, after the mind has recognized the illusory nature of any effort made to influence them, after it has ceased being a dupe of its own activity and has broken all the ordinary bonds between itself and things, all the relations of material and moral utility? Beauty, then, one will have to say, is the sensation which attaches to the exercise of the pure Instinct of Knowledge. It is the sensation of joy which renders perception possible, the one holding the power to put the knower in relation with the universe and to make the world as representation arise for him.

It has already been noted that the conception of Life as an aesthetic phenomenon is common to Schopenhauer and Nietzsche. When the latter makes it his own, on the threshold of his own philosophical thinking, he looks upon Schopenhauer as an educator and, his admiration for the great man not having weakened as yet, he is still a pessimist. That the world should have no aim, that the aspiration of desire should not be able to trust in a sovereign good, the idea of life being dedicated to struggle, to the crushing of the weak by virtue of a fatal law, this entire ensemble of thoughts is perceived by him in sorrow. But, quite contrary to Schopenhauer, the interpretation of the world as an aesthetic phenomenon, by giving him an explanation, saves him from pessimism and engenders a diametrically different attitude in him: love of life. It is here that the two philosophers separate. For Schopenhauer the sentiment of the beautiful is the joy produced by the discovery of the illusory character of life felt as sorrowful. Life, painful in its essence, that is his point of departure; and for him, as for Hindus, life as illusion, such is the counterpart and the counter-poison of this first proposition. Hence the science of Knowledge, by revealing the illusory character of life, necessarily produces a profound and intense joy in him, who, experiencing life as suffering, believed it at the same time to be real. With Schopenhauer, as with the Hindus, Knowledge always awakens the sleeper at the moment of a nightmare, so that aesthetic joy is the very joy he feels in recognizing, in what he took to be a torturing reality, a fiction and a spectacle.

The inversion of the anguish felt by the active will into the joy it experiences, as soon as it turns into a spectator of its own action, is for Nietzsche also the principle of aesthetic joy. "And thus spake I often to myself for consolation: 'Courage! Cheer up! old heart! An unhappiness hath failed to befall thee: enjoy that as thy—happiness!'" [44]—That is to say: you who suf-

232

fered as an actor, enjoy yourself now as a spectator. But for Schopenhauer the emotion of beauty is no more than a transitory sentiment. The joy of deliverance gives way, in the being whom Life has bruised, to the resolution never to lend himself to a new game: he denies the desire which in the first place induced him to want Life, and absolute renunciation determines in him the end of phenomenal life, the Hindu nirvana or the prostration of the Christian before God. For Nietzsche, on the contrary, the aesthetic sentiment compensates, in the one who feels it, all suffering endured in the course of the drama represented by the instincts. Beauty atones for all suffering.

*

It is this point of view which in Nietzsche gave birth to the conception of the Apollinic spirit and to that of the Dionysiac spirit. In a criticism of himself, written in the last years of his life, he opposes these two conceptions, developed sixteen years earlier in his first work, to the Christian ideal. "Christianity, he says, is in principle essentially and radically satiety and distaste of life for life, which are only dissimulated and disguised under the travesty of faith in another life, a better life." [45] Essential Christianity, like Buddhism, infers annihilation. Now the Greek, according to Nietzsche, feels the pain of living with as keen a sensibility as the Hindu or the Christian. He has heard the reply of Silenus, the companion of Dionysos, to King Midas, who had asked him what was the greatest good for man. "Race of wretched ephemera, sons of hazard and of pain, why do you compel me to say what will not be agreeable for you to hear? The supreme good, forever inaccessible to you, is not to be born, not to be, to be nothing. The good, that comes after it, is for you to die soon." [46] But, in virtue of a

233

superior gift of vitality, the Greek surmounts the pain that goes with life and for that he creates a means for himself: art.

Between grievous reality and his too keen sensibility he interposes the world of plastic representation and here we have Apollinic art. With Apollinic art the suspicion of the fictitious character of phenomenal life insinuates itself as a liberator into the mind of the artist. It is in the dream, according to Nietzsche, that the images of the gods which he will chisel in marble, manifest themselves for the first time to his mind. He forms the habit of observing his dream: in it he sees floating the reflection of his joys, but also of his terrors and all the menaces weighing on him. "These scenes he saw and he sustains them— and yet without being able to remove entirely that fleeting impression that they are but a vision." [47] This suspicion of unreality suffices for him to be interested in his dream, for him to want to continue it, for this dream to become a spectacle for him. When he transposes it and then engraves it in marble, he situates it, thereby and completely, outside of life and beyond any possible reach of pain. Through this quality of unreality, which he imposes upon it, more strongly than in the dream, he enables it to evoke just the idea of beauty, even when it represents the gestures of suffering and anguish. It is thereby that Apollinic art delivers man of pain,—by victory over pain, by converting pain into joy,—instead of freeing him by flight from life in the manner of Christian morality. "To look upon life as a game," this is what Art taught the Greeks. "Earnestness," says Nietzsche, "was too well known to them as pain, . . . and they knew that through art alone misery might be turned into pleasure." [48] Thus art has the place here that morality holds in the Socratic conception and then in the Christian conception. "It is art and not ethics," says

Nietzsche, speaking of his first book, "that is represented as the essentially metaphysical activity of man." [49]

By means of Apollinic art the Greeks learned to capture the most redoubtable realities in the ponderousness, in the immobility of marble, in the bonds of a plastic representation in which they were able to contemplate them without danger. They could enjoy as a spectacle the beauty of the most terrible things. Dionysiac art taught them something more; it lifted for them the veil of the Hindu Maya. Under the sway of a sacred intoxication there awakens in man the feeling of his identity with all the forms of the Universe, and the joy of this initiation finds utterance in the song of the hymns. Whereas in plastic art man reproduces, by line and contour, the multiple disguises under which Life manifests itself to him in external forms, Dionysiac art resorbs in a single mode of expression, human song, the infinite diversity of phenomena: thus it breaks the mirage of their dissimilitude and reduces them to the unity of the subject who perceives them as visions, feels them as sensations and, in virtue of this double right, creates them. What Dionysiac art adds to Apollinic art is the consciousness in the artist of the identity of the spectacle and the spectator. Thereafter man sees himself as the actual creator of all the suffering in which the universe abounds. It is he who endures it, but it is also he who contemplates it and that is for him the justification of Life. Initiated into the mystery of his identity with all things, the beauty of the drama of life compensates him henceforth completely for the suffering he assumes as an actor of the representation.

It is the union of the Apollinic and the Dionysiac spirit which, according to Nietzsche, gave birth to Greek tragedy. The pessimistic conception of life revealed in it, the ineluctable destiny one sees weighing therein on all acts, which stamps the most cruel events with a religious seal, which bends all morality under the burden of necessity and divinizes the horrible, this pessimistic conception "in the Greeks of the strongest, most valiant epoch," [50] is explained by the Dionysiac initiation. It is that which permits the Greek to confront reality. Thanks to it he is able to perceive the fictitious character of the most atrocious evils, and he expresses this consciousness, by which he enthralls pain to make it for him a motive of contemplative joy, in tragic representation.

With the Greek, such as Nietzsche imagined him, in order to designate him as the protagonist of his own thought, intelligence freed from its servitude with respect to the vanity of the aim, the mirages of space and time and the illusion of diversity, manifests, by the production of art, that it has taken possession of the meaning of Life as an aesthetic phenomenon. By the production of the work of art, it announces that it has withdrawn from the scene where it was acting under the spell of illusion, that it has settled as a spectator on the shores of becoming, on the banks of the river on which the barges laden with masks and values invented by the folly of Maya, continue descending the current amid all the noises of Life.—This conception, attributed by Nietzsche to the Greek of the tragic period, is also the identical one which was developed in an earlier study on *Buddhism in the West*.[51] It was shown then how the revelation of the unreality of the phenomenon, a cause of suicide in a depressed race, is a pretext for a new life in the occidental endowed with a superabundance of energy. It was shown, with the particular example of Jean Lahor and his beautiful poems dedicated to Illusion, how a western sensibility, perceiving life as woe, is following this initiation transformed into an aesthetic sensibility eager to perpetuate the spectacle, to describe it, to evoke it and how, once informed and taken into confidence, it now adores

236

and celebrates Life for its beauty with the same ardor with which, in its state of blindness, it used to curse Life for its cruelty.

§

Thus the work of art is the supreme explanation of Life. Where the idea of good, where the idea of truth have failed and have had to confess their inanity, the concept of beauty succeeds in solving the enigma. In the brightest hour, at noontide, aesthetic serenity, dominating the illusion of all pain, awakens in the soul of the knower the sense and the love of life. Hence the morality of the knower will be completely opposed to that of men still a prey to the illusion of Maya. The latter will, in the last resort, want justice, peace, gentleness, fraternity among men, everything that is apt to diminish the intensity of suffering in Life, to make men equal among themselves. Unconsciously, with an earnest desire hidden within themselves, they are seeking attitudes for dying; they extol everything that is likely to put an end to diversity, everything that tends to plunge Life into the repose of the identity of beings and of things. In the belief that they are perfecting Life, rendering it better and more humane, they are laboring to abolish it.

Conversely the knower will love to see Life, and human life too, stimulated by more ardor, more vanity, more self-love, more frenzy in the same way as a reader of a novel is avid for more intrigues, more adventures and wearies of those dull prose compositions in which nothing happens. That there should be instincts subordinate to physical joy and pain, to moral joy and suffering, that the illusion of justice and ideological concepts should come and falsify, foment, confound and inflame primitive instincts, all this delights the Instinct of Knowledge, for it is well that the drama, which it contemplates, be intense and

237

varied. It is also good for the actors to be dupes of their rôles, so that the drama may be well played and that the aim of Life, to be applauded by the spectator, may be realized. This is why the knower loves the vain. "That life may be fair," says Zarathustra, "its game must be well played; for that purpose, however, it needeth good actors. Good actors have I found all the vain ones; they play, and wish people to be fond of beholding them—all their spirit is in this wish. They represent themselves, they invent themselves; in their neighborhood I like to look upon life—it cureth of melancholy. Therefore am I forbearing to the vain, because they are the physicians of my melancholy, and keep me attached to man as to a drama." [52] But the knower loves the wicked especially. "This is, however," Zarathustra says to his disciples, "my third manly prudence: I am not put out of conceit with the *wicked* by your timorousness. I am happy to see the marvels the warm sun hatcheth: tigers and palms and rattlesnakes. Also amongst men there is a beautiful brood of the warm sun, and much that is marvelous in the wicked." [53]

*

Inasmuch as life is a spectacle requiring a spectator, the virtue of the philosopher will consist entirely in being that spectator. All his effort will go to enlarge the qualities of the spectator in himself. He will be obliged to put the needful distance between himself and the scene in which the drama unfolds itself, detach his ego from all that is not contemplative joy, separate himself from any direct joy felt in acts and suppress any appetite designed to satisfy an instinct other than the Instinct of Knowledge. Therefore he must forbid himself any desire for morality likely to gratify the desires of his heart, as well as any passional craving. All these transcended instincts can be treated by him only as means to a more refined pleasure. They are the actors in his theatre and, if he applauds them for the perfection of their performance, he cannot be deceived by their plaints or their sighs, nor can he be a dupe of the presumption of their thoughts and of the thousand little aims that they assign to Life. "But changeable am I only, and wild, and altogether a woman, and no virtuous one: Though I be called by you men 'the profound one,' or the 'faithful one,' 'the eternal one,' 'the mysterious one.' But ye men endow us always with your own virtues—alas, ye virtuous ones!" [54] The Knower, who has heard this avowal of Life, contents himself with contemplating it in its inexhaustible variety. He no longer demands anything else of it than to be beautiful and to realize beauty with an ever growing intensity of energy.

The moment when the knower rises to aesthetic perfection in which his entire morality consists, has for its determining cause the concentration of the total energy, with which he is endowed, in the Instinct of Knowledge alone. The evolution of the universal activity from one to the other of its modes, whose phases have been previously described, receives here, in default of a metaphysical fulfilment, a psychological consecration; it is completed and perfected in the spirit of the spectator. All the energy animating him has now deserted that of its modes in which it was expended in acts. And here we find those activities, which it engendered and which appeared on the world's stage, little by little losing their power to delude. Their game slackens, the last force which animated them, leaves them and the cause, having become anemic, no longer has the power to objectify itself into becoming in new phenomena. All movement is arrested and the ensemble of past and future activities is congealed in the immobile and sovereign pose of the work of art. The spectator enjoying, in the hour of the greatest clarity, the most perfect knowledge, cognizant of the artifices of phenomenal representation, freed from illusion and rid of all fear, contemplates with a complete joy, among the perspectives of space and with the figment of duration, the immense tableau of activities, each grouped in the costume of its rôle, representing with feigned gestures of an admirable precision, in the infinitely varied décor of material forms, the supreme play of the soul, moving in all its rôles, whether it mimes the fury of the instincts, the constraint of moralities or the effort of thought toward philosophies. In the presence of so sublime a spectacle the spectator is far removed from the attitude of renunciation counseled by Schopenhauer. Inflated with all the vigour of the Universe, in the full enjoyment of his instinct of knowledge, far from thinking of having the spectacle cease, he wishes to contemplate it always; he applauds, he exults, he wants the spectacle to recommence unceasingly, to endure forever. He desires life eternally and such as it is. He is an entire house standing up and, roused by enthusiasm, requiring with its bravos and its shouts that the drama begin again.

Thus, from such a point of view, the phenomenal Universe finds its explanation in the phenomenon itself and outside of any metaphysics. The aesthetic phenomenon alone upholds and retains all the others ready, under the action of pain, to be engulfed in nothingness. It even redeems the past, the "It was" "to which run counter the Will's teeth-gnashing and lonesomest tribulation . . ." [55] The will assigns an aesthetic value to the past; it gives it a meaning; in the manifestation of that power through which it intervenes, it recognizes in the past its own endeavor; by that sign it knows itself as the creator of the entire past. This is why Zarathustra teaches: "The Will is a creator." All "It was" is a fragment, a riddle, a fearful chance —until the creating Will saith thereto: "But thus would I have it"—Until the creating Will saith thereto:

"But thus do I will it! Thus shall I will it!" [56] In the last analysis, then, the morality of the science of Knowledge is formulated in a principle of strict aesthetics: Become a good spectator of the Universe, it promulgates, so that the Universe may be for you a spectacle. Know how to transmute every sensation into a perception, withdraw your self from all extraneous sensations, not in order to deny Life, but to perceive it in a unique sensation of beauty, to love it and to desire it for its beauty: *amor fati*. This, in effect, is no longer resignation: it is joy, it is Zarathustra's song of intoxication. It is the laugh and the dance of Zarathustra above all things released from the spirit of heaviness, freed of the bondage to purpose, consequence and necessity. The renunciation of the actor, having become the egoism of the spectator, desires and cherishes the Universe in the heaven of beauty.

IV.

With the first developments of Nietzsche's thought, such as they have just been stated, the Instinct of Knowledge encountered the philosopher, who, rendering it master of power, was to interpret the world according to its will. But it is appropriate to remind the reader at this point that at the beginning of this study, while acknowledging a *parti pris* in favor of the Instinct of Knowledge, we predicted, in the very name of Knowledge, the inevitable triumph of the Vital Instinct, inasmuch as it always creates the modes of a new illusion on the ruins of old fictions. Nietzsche himself took care to justify this prediction. Promulgating the laws of the science of pure Knowledge, loving them first for their cruelty, then for their beauty, that is only a first state of his philosophical thought. He later evolved in the direction of another conception; he took the part of the Vital Instinct, whose existence he seemed to have compromised, and contrived to strengthen it. We shall state further on the reasons and the motives which justify this change. First its physiological cause will be investigated.

Every philosophy, we said with Nietzsche, is the objectivation of a temperament that has taken cognizance of itself. It is a mental landscape which a given physiological state brings forth amid a décor of motives. The temperamental state peculiar to Nietzsche, it was observed further, is the one which is characterized by the supremacy of the Instinct of greatness served by cruelty toward oneself. Hitherto this Instinct was the principle of movement of the philosopher's thought; he transferred it from one place to a higher place and it was in the course of this emigration toward ever more cruel and colder regions that he encountered, loved and described the region where the tree of Knowledge grows in solitude. But this instinct of greatness did not till then become aware of itself; it did not describe itself, nor did it as yet glorify its own tendency in a philosophy. This is what it is now going to accomplish. Accordingly, instead of describing for our benefit the customs and the manners distinctive of the countries it traverses, it is going to divulge its own mechanism, expose the very rhythm of the movement animating it. The means of greatness, that with the aid of which one rises above oneself, this is what Nietzsche is now going to celebrate in the course of that epic philosophy which finds in ZARATHUSTRA its perfect expression.

What means does man employ to raise the waters of rivers above their own level? He constructs dams, which resist their current and contradict it. Presently the waters, which were flowing downward according to the natural declivity of the ground, direct their effort upward; they gather and rise continuously in order to overflow the dike obstructing their course. Like those locks which raise the surface of waters, creating for the boat an artificial depth and lifting it so as to make it rise above the hills, the contradiction of oneself gathers reservoirs and lakes of energy, which elevate the will above itself. It was by this power of damming the exuberance of the instincts, by this engineering science skilled in constructing locks for the will, that Nietzsche rose from an already refined conception of happiness, situated outside of the present time in a power of imagining creative of faith, to a conception of truth which he again surmounted in order to settle on a state of pure Knowledge.

Yet this last stage, commenced, like the preceding ones, in pain and in effort was also, like the preceding ones, consummated in joy. All the grief that the relinquishment of the old moral ideas involved for Nietzsche, being exhausted, the force elevating him is also spent and here he is immobile on the plateau of aesthetic joy which he has just attained, reposing in all serenity in the contemplation of beauty. In such a state the instinct of greatness animating him no longer finds employment and, as it is the true master of that colony of instincts composing the self of the philosopher, since it is the one which has by turns delegated power to the religious instinct, to the instinct for truth, then to the Instinct of Knowledge, it is going to withdraw this power from the last of its representatives and reign itself under its own name. Cruelty toward oneself will now be exercised without dissimulation, no longer under the pretense of realizing the will of some particular instinct, but in order to serve the instinct of grandeur alone, whose unique aspiration is to rise and after it has risen, to rise anew, again and perpetually. As soon, then, as some joyous instinct is manifested in the self, the instinct of greatness will impose the contradiction of itself upon this joy as a step upward, then immediately be on the watch for some new joy in order again to immolate it and to make of its spoil a new degree. The Instinct of

Greatness does not ascend toward a goal; it rises upward, continuously and illimitably, toward the height which can never fail its aspiration. Life is "that which must ever surpass itself." Such is the principle and such the sole meaning of Nietzsche's final philosophy. Zarathustra proves to be the realizer and the hero of this tendency of Life. "For *this* am I from the heart and from the beginning—drawing, hither-drawing, upward-drawing, upbringing; a drawer, a trainer, a training-master. . . ." [57]

Such is also the unique import of the superhuman. The superhuman is not some particular aim: like the kingdom of God, announced by Jesus, the superhuman is a symbol. Every Christian, who realizes in himself a state of perfect renunciation, already possesses the kingdom of God. But every man, who sets as a task for his will the effort to rise ceaselessly above itself, realizes in himself the superhuman. "Life is that which must ever surpass itself"; it is by applying this principle that Zarathustra teaches: "The Superman is the meaning of the earth," and all the value of this definition is in the *sursum* which assigns to man his direction.[58] "What is great in man is that he is a bridge and not a goal." [59] In the superman it is the aspiration toward height which alone is glorified, but the superior species which, by means of this fervent aspiration, man might engender, that superior species would not betoken the fulfillment of destiny; it would itself and anew be subject to the moral law of gravitation toward height. It would have to disappear in its turn and give way to a higher form.

The superhuman, according to M. Lichtenberger, would be the state realized by man when, after having destroyed the table of values which now establishes a standard among things and determines the hierarchy of virtues, he had replaced it with another. This, in effect, is the real aim that Nietzsche proposes to humanity, but it is only a circumstantial aim; once attained this aim will profess its vanity and a more distant goal, perhaps a contrary one, will offer itself to effort in order to stretch anew the spring of the will. It is thereby that the philosophy of the Instinct of Greatness differs from all the preceding conceptions: it does not admit of any presumption of finality. It is the epic glorification of one of the essential modes of Life, of the mode pursuant to which Life evolves ceaselessly toward the future. For Nietzsche Life consists solely in this movement without limit, in the very fact of this evolution. It is in this course, in this bearing and in this dance that he attains a glimpse of the essence and the soul of Life. It is of this grace, this caprice and this ardor that he becomes enamored and his philosophy of the Instinct of Grandeur soars in pursuit of this course, whose aim is nowhere if not in a continual acceleration of its own *élan* and in an ever growing frenzy.

*

There is, we have said, no universal morality, but every will engenders its desire and its repulsion, every living thing thus creating its good and its evil. What, then, is good for the Instinct of Grandeur and what is evil? Good is everything that is apt to tighten the will, to render it stronger, to raise it in the direction of height. "Upward goeth our course from genera on to super-genera." [60] Evil is everything that is of a nature to weaken the will; it is whatever betrays a diminution of energy. "Tell me, my brother, what do we think bad, and worst of all? is it not *degeneration?*" [61]

For the instinct of greatness there is no other good and no other evil than those. There is no other virtue than that which consists in augmenting the power of the will, and the means by which one intensifies volition is, as we have said, the exercise of cruelty toward oneself. "Become hard," Zarathustra says to superior men. Thus cruelty toward oneself is the unique virtue. But that being established, it is evident that such a virtue is going to command of men very different acts according to the external circumstances surrounding them and in conformity with the inward and individual state of their will. The instinct of greatness decrees a common posture, but it cannot specify what definite acts must be accomplished by all. For the same act, virtuous for one, because it implies contradiction of his dominant tendency, will be vicious for another, because it implies, in his particular case, an unconstraint and a softness. Under like circumstances a timid person wins a victory over himself and accomplishes an act of virtue by expressing his thought and his volition forcibly, while an arrogant one achieves the same act of virtue by embracing a contrary conduct. Hence it behooves each one to create his own morality, that is to say, to discern what acts admit for him of the greatest effort, what acts are of a character to elevate him, so that he may afterwards prescribe these acts for himself.

*

Nietzsche, from his particular point of view, formulated a particular morality. He presents it for what it is and does not attribute a universal value to it, but designates it as possibly suiting those, who, governed by the instinct of greatness, have reached the same stage of evolution as himself and are surrounded by a similar landscape of moral circumstances. In order to appreciate the value of this morality one must, therefore, search into the mental and philosophical state upon which it is founded and in view of which it prescribes for itself, in preference, certain acts over others.

246

Now Nietzsche does, at the beginning of his moral life, by virtue of his atavism and his education, realize the Christian ideal: renunciation is for him the easiest act. The Science of Knowledge, to which he has attained, by depriving him of the illusion of liberty, fortified this moral disposition with an added intellectual factor. Finally, a pathological state productive of suffering and reducing his vitality to its minimum, shows him in this philosophy of renunciation the justification and the most favorable interpretation of his inaptitude for living. Everything that ruins and disparages Life, which in him is diminished and which he feels as an affliction, must for him be a cause of joy and appeasement. Once this balance-sheet is established, it is easy to formulate the particular morality, which cruelty practised upon oneself in opposition to such an inner disposition will prescribe. All the postures permitting contradiction of his sensibility are going to become virtues for Nietzsche; for him and for all those, who resemble him, they will be the means of attaining the superhuman.

First of all he wants life, which his sensibility as a sick man denies, more intense. So that it may become so, he expresses the wish that competition among beings grow more formidable, that men be more different from one another, that they institute a more violent struggle for power among themselves. Here, then, there has presently been created a morality in absolute antagonism with the aesthetic morality formulated by the Science of Knowledge, on the one hand, and Christian morality on the other. As a reaction against pessimism, a moral symptom of the physical affliction which has depressed him, and in obedience to the instinct of conservation forbidding him "a philosophy of indigence and discouragement," Nietzsche is going to create in himself and in man the will to love Life.

In his fear as a sick man, who has seen Life close

to being extinguished, he has to condemn that contemplative attitude of the spectator,—artist or scientist—which was the virtuous and triumphant attitude of his preceding philosophy, when the Instinct of Knowledge, master of his thought, was interpreting the universe according to the despotism of its desire. It is because, in effect, the spectator does nothing for the spectacle: he expects everything from the actors. Besides, has not the Science of Knowledge itself taught Nietzsche that, for the purpose of instituting the intrigue of phenomenal life, knowing is nothing, desiring truth is nothing: What, then, does have value for Life? The *non-true* is the answer of the Science of Knowledge, fiction as a creator of the real. Who is the hero claimed by Life? The one, who brings tastes and colors, who puts values into things. He is the one, whom Nietzsche now calls the philosopher.

We must grant him his terminology, while pointing out wherein it differs from the one customarily used. For Nietzsche, having arrived at this last period of his life as a thinker, the one who discloses and describes the science of pure Knowledge, Kant above all others, is a critic. The philosopher, on the contrary, is a man of action; he is the one who imposes a new meaning on the Universe. In interpreting this conception of Nietzsche's M. Lichtenberger has excellently said: "Nothing, . . . in Nature, has value *in itself*, the world of reality is an indifferent matter, which has no other interest than the one we give to it. The true philosopher, then, is the man whose personality is forceful enough to create "the world which interests men." [62] It is, in fact, according to this interpretation that Zarathustra defines the rôle of the philosopher:

"Will to Truth" do ye call it, ye wisest ones, that which impelleth you and maketh you ardent?

Will for the thinkableness of all being: thus do *I* call your will!" [63]

Hence the virtue of the philosopher is to engender strong illusions; for such illusions give birth to appetites, desires, aversions, to this world of reality which interests men. It is from this viewpoint that one must interpret those poems of Zarathustra on *Scholars* and on *Immaculate Perception,* in which the Creator of new values rises scornfully against the *knower* whose entire energy has been centered in the act of looking and who refuses to take part in the game of Life. The knower is that hypertrophied eye or ear, to which is attached a diminutive human form almost deprived of life, and Nietzsche shows us those objective scholars, those contemplators, those conscientious ones of the mind awaiting "open-mouthed the thoughts of others," glorying in the fact that they do not alter reality by the contribution of any illusion. "Real are we wholly, and without faith and superstition." [64] "Perambulating refutations are ye of belief itself" is Zarathustra's reply to them, "and a dislocation of all thought. *Untrustworthy ones:* thus do *I* call you, ye real ones! . . . Unfruitful are ye: *therefore* do ye lack belief." [65]

*

But if such is the condemnation pronounced by Nietzsche, in the period in which he is formulating the philosophy of the instinct of grandeur, against the contemplators, whose crime is the failure to participate in enriching life with tastes and colors, with new passions and desires, one can imagine his reprobation with respect to an enterprise which makes an attempt against the power of Life itself, one which, like Christianity, tends to ruin and diminish Life.

From the point of view Nietzsche has taken he

must, therefore, logically institute a morality which is in all points opposed to the Christian ethic which, may we point out, while heeding the direction of his sympathies and his aversions, was perpetuated in its purest form in Protestantism, and then in the more recent conception of the encyclopaedic and revolutionary spirit.

In truth, and with immediate hostility, the first principle of this Nietzschean morality proclaims inequality among men. "For thus speaketh justice *unto me:* 'Men are not equal.' And neither shall they become so! What would be my love to the Superman, if I spake otherwise. On a thousand bridges and piers shall they throng to the future, and always shall there be more war and inequality among them: thus doth my great love make me speak." [66]

To proclaim inequality among men is simply to make a scientific statement. Accordingly, in his love for what is, by reason of a purely intellectual deduction, Nietzsche has to side with this reality, and the logical result is a condemnation pronounced against pity whose effect tends to combat natural inequality. The instinct of greatness, which compels Nietzsche to cruelty toward himself, therefore determines him to prescribe cruelty toward others equally. "Become hard, all creators are hard." Pity is the most redoubtable reef upon which man can be broken in his ascent toward the superman. Nevertheless, there is, beside this logical constraint, another and more profound explanation of this condemnation of pity which holds so large a place in Nietzsche's work and wounds modern sensibility so keenly. The contradiction of oneself, which is the principle of all the determinations of the philosopher, informs us even here as to the incentive ruling him. Let us suppose that Nietzsche proscribes pity, because he feels pity too keenly, because he realizes the ideal of Christian culture too perfectly.

250

Having reached the point of triumphing over his own suffering, he remains without strength against the suffering of others. His sensibility has been transposed, inasmuch as it now has its roots in the nerves and in the heart of his neighbor. It is there that he will have to be tortured and there that it will have to be surmounted.

Consequently it is a necessity, in some degree a physiological one, that transforms cruelty toward oneself into a cruelty toward others. The principle of this cruelty is an unduly keen sensibility for what concerns the suffering of one's neighbor. It is the pitiful one who dreads pity; but he, who is really hard, does not have to command himself to *become* it. He does not need to beware of pity; he does not know it.

Besides, why would cruelty, useful for oneself as a means of power, not have the same efficacy for others? The weakness, the excessive gentleness, the pessimism and the nihilistic resignation which Nietzsche verified in himself in the period when his vitality descended to its minimum, the symptoms of all these he discovers around him and he assigns to them as a common cause the *Christian phenomenon*. Thenceforth Christianity appears to him as a menace to Life. Life, "that which always wishes to surpass itself," is arrested in its élan toward height by Christian morality. Christianity is, in Nietzsche's view, a disease of Life; it is the gravest of Life's maladies, for it compromises its growth: under the influence of Christianity man's stature ceaselessly diminishes. Therefore Nietzsche will prescribe for humanity the treatment, which he had originally adopted for himself alone. He will formulate for humanity the law of the instinct of greatness and denounce as evil and dangerous all aspirations contrary to this instinct.

*

The aspiration most likely to imperil man's greatness is the aspiration to happiness, since it is incompatible with the means of greatness, cruelty toward oneself: Nietzsche, after Carlyle, but with a very different violence, condemns all eudaemonism. In order to stigmatize the aspiration to happiness, he represents it as the lot of the lowest beings. Thus Zarathustra draws the most contemptuous picture of the last men, who have invented happiness, who "have left the regions where it is hard to live," [67] "Give us the last man" cries the populace immediately: happiness is the wish of the masses. But the virtuous are also a populace, and Zarathustra scourges them: "Ye want to be paid besides, ye virtuous ones! . . . And now ye upbraid me for teaching that there is no reward-giver, nor paymaster? And verily, I do not even teach that virtue is its own reward." [68] And going through the crowd of these men, whom he has vainly tried to elevate above themselves and up to himself, Zarathustra establishes: "They have become *smaller*, and ever become smaller:—*the reason thereof is their doctrine of happiness and virtue.*" [69]

This eudaemonism, which he condemns, Nietzsche finds in Christianity, whether it betrays itself in crude fashion in the mentality of the slave by the hope of superterrestrial felicities or appears in the ascetic in a negative form in the fact of renouncing life, in a flight away from pain. "To blaspheme the earth is now the dreadfulest sin, and to rate the heart of the unknowable higher than the meaning of the earth." [70] Thus speaks Zarathustra.

Therefore here, as elsewhere, it is as a reaction against Christian sentimentality, that the method of hardening extolled by Nietzsche originates, all this therapy able to rouse the energies of Life and to bring them to their paroxysm: necessity of pain which constrains man to augment his strength in order to prevail over evil, necessity of pain as a means of the

252

superhuman and, in order that there may be much pain in the world, necessity of wickedness, of the wickedness of man as a means of pain. "Man must become better and eviler—so do *I* teach," says Zarathustra, "The evilest is necessary for the Superman's best." [71] And Dionysos thinks and expresses himself in like manner, Dionysos the Greek god, who has begun to love man for his boldness and his genius. "I like man, and often think how I can still further advance him, and make him stronger, more evil and more profound—" "Stronger, more evil, and more profound?" queries the confidant of God. "Yes," he said again, "stronger, more evil, and more profound; also more beautiful," replies Dionysos." [72]

*

In this system, then, where cruelty and hardness are virtues, pity remains the most dangerous vice, pity, with all the equalitarian virtues extolled by Christianity and admitted among the drove of slaves, such as that gentleness of the weak, who ". . . anticipate every one's wishes and do well unto every one" in order "that no one hurt them." [73] Here we find condemned all that morality of renunciation, of justice, of fear which from day to day renders men smaller, more miserable, lower and converts the world into an abode of weaklings. It was his pity for man that killed the ancient God. In order that there may be a superman, pity must be surmounted. May those, therefore, die, who ought to die, may those who suffer and who fear Life, disappear from Life; in this way they at least accomplish their destiny.

The same point of view also engenders the double conception of a morality of masters and of a morality of slaves. The morality of masters is, in a word, that of men, who confront the struggle for power instituted by Life. The master knows that there is no other measure than force among activities; he knows that force determines the rank and the degree of goodness. He has, considered as an individual animated by desires and passions, a particular conception of Life; this conception is his own and one which he cannot estimate by the standard of any ideal previously invented, but necessarily, because it is his, he affirms it against any other. War will decide between him and those who possess different conceptions. War is the valid test, the only impartial and fair competition, in fact the only imaginable one. This is why Zarathustra requires of his warriors that they rejoice even when their enemy has triumphed over them, for by this triumph the will of Life is accomplished, power belongs to the stronger, the better is realized. "Your enemy shall ye seek; your war shall ye wage, and for the sake of your thoughts! And if your thoughts succumb, your uprightness shall still shout triumph thereby! [74] For the test to be conclusive, war must be merciless and exempt from pity. The only virtues are bravery and cruelty, audacity, ruse, intelligence, all the manners of being which, according to the circumstances and the age of civilizations, are the most apt to denote strength. The important thing is for the strongest being to impose his thought, his conception of the universe and that there be eliminated all the weak, the sick, all those for whom life would be suffering and opprobrium, *the bad.* "War and courage have done more great things than charity. Not your sympathy, but your bravery hath hitherto saved the victims." [75]

Over against this morality of masters, here is the principle of the morality of slaves. A weakness that wishes to live against the law of Life, revolts against the law of greatness instituted by Life. The slave, then, is bound to falsify and to invert all values. It is no longer force that creates the good; the good exists by itself and necessarily consists in the contrary of force, for otherwise the slave, who is the weaker, would not be able to secure it. Consequently Virtue no longer consists in rushing into combat for the conquest of the best things and in sacrificing one's life to possess them. The weak would be vanquished in this combat; virtue is to renounce the best things, so that, all renouncing them, all may then share *equally* in them, so that each may possess a small part. Virtue is to endure offenses, to pardon them, to be humble, to submit so that, this ideal of the virtuous and the good coming to prevail in humanity, the state of war, in which the weaker is crushed, may end. Thus the morality of slaves tends to retrench from humanity every superior type, to diminish man's stature; its disposition is to act in such a way that Life, which ever wishes to surpass itself, tends continually to sink beneath itself. Interpreting Christian morality in a pejorative sense Nietzsche saw in Christianity the type of the morality of slaves and that is why he turned against it all his hatred of a lover of the grandeur of Life.

*

Thus, starting from this conception of an actual state of enfeeblement of Life manifested or caused by the Christian phenomenon, Nietzsche condemns pity and proposes to the superior man, as a consequence of cruelty toward oneself, hardness toward one's neighbor. It is opportune to recall here that, from the viewpoint of the philosophy of the instinct of grandeur, this morality is only one of circumstance. Cruelty with regard to others is, in a being governed by the instinct of greatness, a consequence of cruelty toward oneself only to the extent that this being has reached the point of deriving his greatest satisfaction from the happiness of others, of undergoing his greatest torment in the suffering of others. The contradiction of oneself then requires the contradiction of others, and the greatest danger for the individual or social being whose sensibility has assumed this outgoing form, is pity which caused the death of God.[76] But the same principle exacts a morality quite the contrary of that characterizing the one whose instincts are completely intent on their gratification: to him, who is not hindered in his *élan* toward power by the consideration of the suffering of others, the contradiction of oneself, a means of greatness, enjoins kindness. ". . . let thy goodness," says Zarathustra, "be thy last self-conquest. All evil do I accredit to thee: therefore do I desire of thee the good." [77]

This remark is of the greatest importance, if we are to disengage from the philosophy of the instinct of grandeur the true morality which it entails and avoid confusing this superior morality with the particular application Nietzsche made of it to the circumstances of his day. The attitude peculiar to the instinct of greatness does, in fact, permit, simultaneously, both that morality of hardness which Nietzsche expounds with insistence, and a morality of renunciation engendering a system of virtues very similar to those commanded by Christianity. If Nietzsche attacked the Christian virtues so violently, it is because, owing to the appraisal he made of the humanity of his time, they seem to him to originate not from too taut an energy, which rises and grows while restraining itself, by constructing sluices for itself, but from a weakness which humbles itself in order to avoid too rugged combats,—not the excess of a force sound enough to coordinate itself, but an anemia and a degeneracy. The precept that has just been cited, on goodness imposed on the one who is capable of all iniquities, this precept which is not unique in Nietzsche's work, shows that even goodness and pity could be explained by a very different genealogy from the one he attributes to them in the present milieu and that, if in our day they develop among the drove of slaves, they could equally, by virtue of a different filiation, arise in the milieu of masters. It is the same with renunciation. What man desires, says Nietzsche, "under the influence of violent emotion" is 'in any case the great, the powerful, the immense and if he happens to notice that the sacrifice of himself satisfies him as well as, or better than, the sacrifice of others, he chooses that." [78]

Thus conceived in its essence this morality of the instinct of grandeur admits of an application everywhere. But this application requires some discernment as a preliminary. Whether the matter at issue concerns an individual, a human group or a race, it is no longer a question of imposing, by way of a panacea, a uniform treatment such as that of the Christian morality; instead one must seek to ascertain what degree of vital energy, that is to say, of egoism animates this being or this collection of beings; then, in measure of this evaluation and in proportion to the excess or the deficiency that has been established, one must institute a method able to retract the energy upon itself or to develop it against the outside. This is what the unconscious of every people or of every race does with the religion it adopts in the period of its puberty: it then measures the force of the curb it gives itself by the impetus which moves it. Afterwards the curb wears out and leaves the social machine some scope in proportion as the energy of the race, having integrated the acts of social utility into custom, has less need of being contained within the limits to which it confines itself spontaneously. Thence the danger of substituting in a race a religious curb devised for another organism for the one which it chose for itself in the divinatory period of the Instinct. Those alone can doubt it who, instead of regarding religious and ethical systems as physiological phenomena, attribute to them, whether they confess it or not, a supernatural origin.

✿

In appraising the philosophy of the Instinct of Grandeur outside of any particular utility, whether it be national or ethnic, it becomes evident that it objectivates into an epopoeia one of the two tendencies which, contradicting each other, constitute phenomenal life and its representation. It is the very principle of movement, of an ascension without limit and without cessation upward. If this tendency existed alone and without counterpoise, life, transported in a vertiginous frenzy toward the future, would not become objectified in any landscape, in any present. The phenomenon would be abolished by speed. But there is another tendency. Zarathustra calls it my born enemy, the *spirit of torpor*. The spirit of torpor is the force of inertia peculiar to everything that is immobile and wants to stand still. By the effect of the spirit of torpor combatting the effort of the Instinct of Grandeur, phenomenal life lags before the mechanism of consciousness in which, by the help of this retardation, are inscribed the landscapes of history.

The spirit of torpor, then, has its useful rôle in the cosmic representation. It also has its protagonist in every mind, whom the present hour satisfies. The philosophy of Nietzsche objectifies the contrary tendency. That is what one must know, in order to profit by it and apply it usefully. Wherever the movement of Life slows down, wherever it manifests a loss of energy, this philosophy is able to reanimate the faltering pulse of activities. It brings with it a principle of acceleration and a power of frenzy; it is the most efficacious and the most admirable means of exaltation. It is the *chanson de gestes* of Life celebrating the beauty, the strength and the agility of its ceaseless élan, demonstrating the mechanism of its ascent upward and how, by the contradiction of itself, it builds the locks where it collects its own flux above the former level.

CHAPTER VIII

SYSTEMS OF METAPHYSICS AND MORALITY FROM THE VIEWPOINT OF KNOWLEDGE

To recognize untruth as a condition of life.

(BEYOND GOOD AND EVIL)

I. Metaphysical and moral systems do not depend on a criterion of truth, but on a criterion of reality.

II. Reality of metaphysical systems. Religions and hypothesis.

III. Reality of the moral phenomenon: Attitude of utility of a physiology. The fictions in which it is expressed: religion, custom and literature.—Scientific conscience, the latest effort of a physiology to promulgate its attitudes of utility. Its protective rôle.—In contrast with scientific mentality, rationalism: a malady of energy and a danger for Knowledge.

With the first part of Nietzsche's philosophy the aim, toward which this study was directed, was already attained. The philosophy of Knowledge, ruining the ancient metaphysical ideas, was realized in its nihilistic perfection, and the mechanism of life, taken to pieces, no longer allowed one to see,—for all the belief in a truth comprehending the substance of things, notwithstanding the faith in a universal finality—anything more than the principle of illusion instituting its movement.

The time has come to pose the questions which had until now been withheld, in order to give scope to those free declarations of the Instinct of Knowledge, emancipated from all servitude and master of its spiritual domain: does, on the one hand, an explanation of the Universe able to calm metaphysical disquiet remain possible? On the other hand, how is one to live? Can a morality be constituted and, if so, upon what data?

*

The answer to these questions is founded on the essential distinction established by the *Critique*, between Knowledge, in so far as it apprehends itself, and Knowledge in so far as it apprehends Being. Knowledge, as far as it apprehends itself, can be defined in a system of laws which inform us at the same time concerning its formal mechanism and the indefinite modes in conformity with which it apprehends Being. These laws are presented in their totality; it is impossible to conceive them other than they are, inasmuch as they show themselves to be everywhere in harmony with themselves, everywhere identical. It is by reason of this universal identity and this character of necessity that one declares them to be *true* and that all science, in the course of which Knowledge describes and apprehends itself, is said to be subject to a criterion of Truth.

It is otherwise with Knowledge in so far as it apprehends Being and it takes care, as has just been noted, to inform the mind thereof in the course of the description which it gives of its mechanism. Thus one is apprised that Being reveals itself to Knowledge only partially, that it remains mysterious in its origins and in its end. What it allows to be grasped of itself, it divulges in sensation. Sensation is for Knowledge the penumbra from which arises the external world with the appetite that it excites. It is, according to Nietzsche's expression, "the weight, the balance and the weigher." Hence Cognition does nothing more than interpret, according to the form of its laws, what Being imparts of itself in sensation, and these laws, situating the object of sensation in time and in space, submitting it to the mechanism of causality, have precisely the effect, since they are respectful of the mystery into which Being withdraws, of screening the object and the desire it carries with it, from any and all definitive determination and construction; their effect is to render the object forever indiscernible in its entirety, in its principle and in its end and desire as well, since both, by the very gesture with which they embrace them, are dispersed in the world of diversity irreducible to identity. Powerless to comprehend Being in its totality through sensation Cognition is, with still more reason, powerless to produce it, to fashion it, to exert an imperative action upon it. For it does not posses any of these powers over sensation in which Being allows itself to be glimpsed according to its will and pleasure: It neither creates nor determines it in quantity or in quality.

Accordingly, whereas the world of Knowledge depends expressly on the concept of Truth, the world of Being never admits of the application of this concept. It was in order to point out this difference forcefully that Nietzsche gave the *non-true* as a condition for Being. Therefore one must understand by the *non-true* the whole content of Knowledge as opposed to its form. The *non-true* is that which does not support any integral explanation, that which avoids any "why" and it is also all the real; it is sensation in its intangible essence, it is the object, taste, vision, desire, everything that involves struggle, conflict, appreciation and fixing of values.

Now, all the errors and all the misapprehensions diffused involuntarily or in a premeditated fashion by philosophy have for their cause the application to one of these two categories—being and knowledge—of the principle which governs the other. It is in this way that the metaphysical and moral systems depending on the category of Being were transferred to the category of Knowledge. By reason of this confusion one wished to reduce them to an identity which they expressly reject, to appreciate and judge them by means of a criterion of truth on which they do not depend at all and which could not attain them. This confusion is the work of rationalism. That term, however, ought not to designate anything but the logical system of the laws of reason, but usage has deflected it from its authentic meaning to the point where one feels constrained no longer to see anything in it except the gross error which was introduced into it, and to recognize that there is no other function than to indicate it.

If one were to persist, with rationalism, in situating metaphysical and moral systems in the world of formal Knowledge, it would be necessary, in view of the impossibility of establishing their truth, to deny their existence. But the philosophy of Knowledge could not sanction a confusion of that sort. Consequently it withdraws them from the formal Category to which one had fruitlessly thought to relegate it and, considering them under the category of existence, it regards them, no longer in the light of truth, but in the light of reality—and discovers them at once.

Everywhere, in fact, where human life appears, it proves to be accompanied by philosophies and moralities. Thus metaphysical and ethical systems reveal themselves as the attributes of a given energy and, by virtue thereof, as realities. One must not ask if they are true—to inquire if a reality is true does not admit of any sense whatever,—but determine their nature and the conditions under which they present themselves. Now one sees them indissolubly linked with a physiological energy outside of which they do not exist at all. Therefrom it must be deduced that to this physiological energy appertain the true reality, the quality, the quantity and the power to produce effects. Metaphysical and moral systems are the shadows in which are represented, in the world of mentality and motivation, this quality, this quantity and this power of causation of the real. Hence they may be defined as mythological realities or even as fictions, in this sense that all representation differs by nature from the object it represents and is never equivalence. But in consequence of an inversion, which is the very essence of the moral world, it is according to this mythological representation, in which reality appears to us, that we appreciate the real; it is to these projected shadows that, for the convenience of language, we attribute the effective power which they figure. What we must, therefore, consider in systems of metaphysics and ethics is, on the one side, their logical harmony, which attests the harmony and equipoise of the psysiological energy they represent; on the other it is their efficacy in determining useful beliefs and acts which bear witness to the strength and the health of this energy. Now, this efficacy is measured by their power to engender illusion. Accordingly it is in this power to deceive that the importance and the true reality of metaphysics and ethics in their variants consist. It is there that any good connoisseur of fictions, shadows and mythologies must consider them in order, by this token, to appreciate the value of the physiological reality which they represent.

II.

From the considerations, which have just been set forth, it follows that the formal laws of Cognition are not qualified to engender systems of metaphysics and morality and that, if such systems exist, it is in the world of historical and psychological reality that they must be sought.

As far as metaphysical systems are concerned history, if consulted, replies that human activities assembled in social groups have never lacked for an explanation of the Universe and the faith that is required to satisfy the discomposure of the mind. As soon as the need for this explanation appears, they find within themselves the power to engender it and to accept it, for they are then in possession of an hallucinatory faculty proportionate to their ardor. It is in this way that religions create paradises and sacred myths with such definiteness.

Holocausts, martyrdoms and holy wars bear ample testimony to the faith which these inventions engender. Later, for less zealous minds or, rather, for those who, under the influence of Knowledge, have compensated in need for enlightenment for what they lost in strength of desire, such strict beliefs are no longer necessary. For them it suffices to know that their conception of the world is not at variance with the laws of Cognition. A system of metaphysics is, for them, no more than an explanation of Being according to the will of a temperament. However well constructed and however harmonious it may be, it could never become truth or an object of absolute faith. It remains an hypothesis. As such, however, it possesses a satisfying virtue for the perspicacious mind, who finds in it an equilibrium and to whom certainty offered in matters that do not justify it, could only bring discomfort and uneasiness.

We have seen Nietzsche give of the world an explanation circumscribed within the interior of the phenomenon and have found him justifying and glorifying Being as an aesthetic phenomenon. Now, this explanation is entirely valid for any being whose energy, unable to objectify itself in the illusion of a supreme good and a finality, feels the emotion of beauty intensely. This emotion, which is established as the *raison d'être* and the subject of the Universe, then provides the mind and its query with the reply and the explanatory principle which it craves.

Besides, does it follow from the fact of Nietzsche having forbidden himself to give an explanation of the Universe beyond the limits of the phenomenon, that such an explanation is improper? Does phenomenal existence have a reverse? Is a thing in itself possible? That, in the main, is the most anxious interrogation which the mind addresses to the philosophy of Knowledge. Now this philosophy would not be able to deny the possibility of a thing in itself any more than it could affirm its reality: the thing in itself, supposing that it exists, is unknowable for itself, such is the only proposition that the philosophy of Knowledge formulates on this point. The interpretations of Hinduism and those of Schopenhauer remain possible hypotheses with the reservation of this restriction, which situates them outside of any state of knowledge and which, moreover, they imply. Now this restriction, despite the consternation it causes at first, is alone able to reassure those, whose metaphysical aspiration is practised by the light and under the control of the Intellect. To the latter the laws of Cognition are known; they are aware that they engender nothing perfect, nothing which, with a finished construction, would admit of an appeasement and a solution. They know that it is by withdrawing the metaphysical solution, as its nature requires, from the domain of Knowledge, by sealing it with the weight of mystery that it escapes all puerility, as well as the law of insatiability governing all desire.

III.

In returning from this exploration of the metaphysical domain we intend to formulate this more immediate question: does the philosophy of Knowledge engender morality? But it is now known that this question can be posed by those alone, who, in the theological manner, see in the faculty of knowing the sources of life, in a category of reason the principle of morality and in truth the cause of the real. The philosophy of Knowledge, as it has just been construed, has precisely for its object to put the mind on guard against these confusions. Hence it cannot have an answer for a question posed in those terms and pregnant with the theological preoccupation which it dissimulates.

But, as it did for metaphysical systems, it considers Life and establishes that moralities exist. The moral phenomenon is revealed as a fact; it is a reality by the same right as a vegetal reality or an animal species. On these grounds it may be the object of a science of observation and it is expedient to concern oneself deeply with its essence, its origin, the conditions of its existence, its different types and the particular forms of its evolution.

In this order of ideas one observes that every human society, once the epoch of pure spontaneity has been passed, imposes upon itself at some moment of its evolution a series of precepts capable of maintaining its health and its strength; that the ensemble of these precepts differs from one society to another, but that none is entirely destitute of it and that it is everywhere the first manifestation of the moral fact. We shall, therefore, define a morality as an attitude of usefulness peculiar to a given physiology. From this one must deduce at once that there is no morality whatever that does not have a determinate physiology, whether individual or ethnic, as its source.

One observes further that every social activity, which formulates its morality, engenders simultaneously the fictions necessary to render it effective. The most customary of these fictions are the belief that the morality peculiar to the race is superior to that of all other races,—presumption being an attitude of everything that is alive,—and then the belief in free will and in responsibility which derives from it. A philosophy regarding the non-true as a condition of life has no reason to marvel when it sees Life engendering fictions. In order to appreciate these fictions and to estimate their value, it concerns itself only, we have said, with searching into the question of whether they have the power to delude and in what degree. Therefore the idea of a sovereign good, the belief in liberty whose illusory character the philosophy of Knowledge established, when a false rationalism was endeavoring to impose them as truths, are considered by the philosophy of Knowledge from the standpoint of a science of observation, treating of the real and not of the true, as elements characteristic of the moral phenomenon at its beginnings in the majority of societies.

In pursuing this inquiry from such a point of view one establishes that these elements of the moral fact appear from the beginning and almost universally in the form of religions. Consequently anyone, who is interested in the science of the moral phenomenon, should study religions with a particular care. Now, by their variety and by their nuances, in harmony with the diversity of human races and groups, they bear witness to their physiological character. Profiting by this evidence one remarks that the social group is able to give birth to a religion only at a definite epoch of its evolution. Like other natural phenomena, such as the fermentation of new wine under the staves, the crisis of teething in the child or the crisis of puberty in the adult, the religious phenomenon presents itself in a human group at a precise date.

As the group moves further away from this date religious law loses its influence over it and the fictions, which it had instituted, lose their illusional power. The philosopher, who observes the moral phenomenon with scientific impartiality and does not pretend, in the manner of professional moralists, to invent it, to fabricate it and to pronounce it, this philosopher does not blame Life for it being that way. A wine that ages becomes lighter; at the same time it gains in bouquet what it loses in quantity. The religion, which a people gave itself, likewise loses the force through which it constrained wills; at the same time the attitudes it commanded, now recorded in atavism, become in individuals natural dispositions. When these virtues have become innate, it would no doubt be dangerous for them to be enjoined with the rigor of yester-year: for not one of these virtues is good in itself and in an absolute fashion. They are of benefit only for being opposed to a contrary tendency the exaggeration of which would harm the social organism and make for a waste of its strength. Thus absolute chastity practised by a human group would imperil this group's survival; but to prescribe chastity for temperaments too impelled toward voluptuousness is only to protect them against a premature exhaustion, besides rendering possible among men associations, whose existence would tend to be compromised by too ardent a struggle for the possession of women. Religion having, as was stated earlier, no value other than that of a curb, it is well that this curb be adjusted relatively to the impulsion of the force the controlling of whose exercise is its aim; it is well for this curb to weaken and to lose of its rigor in proportion as the force of impulsion, whose *élan* it was to regulate, independently adapts itself and restricts itself to its useful task. The same can be said of the spirit of renunciation as of chastity. Renunciation is not inherently good for Life; it is valuable only to the extent that it prevents egoism from incurring the risk of its own ruin, namely, in a social group, in the degree in which it is necessary to allow the individuals of the group to become coordinated. But if it goes beyond this limit, it will bring this group into a state of inferiority over against neighboring societies in which there reigns a lesser spirit of renunciation.

Therefore, as the moral virtues of a society are transposed in custom, it seems useful for the religion, which prescribed these virtues, to see its effective power diminish. Moreover, that is indeed the case and it is also a physical law that a body loses its heat in the measure in which it transmits it to another.

Just as Carlyle was well aware, when a social group has passed the epoch in which it is able to produce the religious phenomenon, the moral principle still contained in it objectifies itself, on the one hand, in custom; it is also expressed and manifested in literature: without the interposition of any fiction whatever, a sensibility, strong and national, interprets in a superior fashion the ideal common to the individuals of one and the same group; in the manner of a suggestion in a propitious environment it acts directly upon other related sensibilities to strengthen, exalt or refine them.

Hence moralities do exist. Far from contesting them the philosophy of Knowledge regards them as essential physiological realities and shows how they are manifested alternately, in the different ages of a social group and concretely, in religion, custom and literature. But, like every living thing, morality is spontaneous; it develops outside of any premeditated intervention of the human mind and the philosophy of knowledge concedes it this character. To voluntarist moralists who reproach it for not being able to found a morality on its own principles, it replies that it does not claim this rôle, if it is not meant for it. In the epoch when they attain to the philosophy of Knowledge, the minds of men may possibly have outreached the time when a morality emanates from them.

That would simply establish that the scientist must not look for the moral phenomenon in this period of human development. Perhaps one would also have to infer from it that minds so placed as to have a viewpoint of pure knowledge, do not need a morality beyond that aesthetic attitude in which we saw them delight at one turn in Nietzsche's philosophy. It would none the less remain established by the philosophy of Knowledge that the moral phenomenon exists and that activities give rise to it under definite conditions and in diverse and successive forms.

✻

Still, are we to gather from this that the philosophy of Knowledge precludes in those, who possess it, all moralizing action on the group to which they belong, on the group which favored and permitted their growth? "All is necessity," says Nietzsche, "thus speaks the new science, and this science is itself necessary." [1] Now, the philosophy of Knowledge, the latest and the most refined product of a physiology, necessarily engenders in turn these free minds who, completely disengaged from the religious prejudice of Truth, regard morality as a science of observation and the moral phenomenon as a phenomenon of utility. In the epochs of advanced civilization, when the religion peculiar to a society sees its illusional power diminish, when custom finds its sway being contested, when alien taste threatens by the invasion of its art and its literature to alter the particular sensibility of the

270

group, the intervention of these free minds is alone able to cull from the ancient fictions ready to founder all they contained of what was useful and essential. These minds alone, seeing that they are as exempt from the new belief in Truth as from any other belief, are not severe on these fictions for having ceased to seem true. Under their ideological disguise of truths, which did not deceive them, they have never failed to recognize their physiological reality. Consequently they will for them be documents to which they will have recourse in order to define and reconstitute the ensemble of the attitudes of usefulness peculiar to the race, attitudes which compose its morality. Thus they restore to the group, threatened with a dissociation, an ideal of itself, an exemplar of its normal type able to strengthen it. It would appear, then, that with the philosophy of Knowledge, the physiological energy of the race, while no longer creating a morality all the elements of which it has already produced, gives itself with the conscience of the scientific mind a new means of objectifying itself. In a society, in which the superior mentality just described had become preponderant, it is likely that this guiding conception of a normal type, representative of the beauty and the health of the group, would prove to have an efficacy equal to that of the ancient fictions for drawing from social energy its greatest effort. For anyone who, with Nietzsche, considers the non-true a condition of life, it could be the object of a new research to determine the fiction or, at the very least, the principle of illusion, in which this scientific point of view would become objectified and by which its efficacy would be recognized.

Can this hypothesis of a human group, in which this impartial mentality would be generally realized, be considered possible? To formulate such a prediction would be hazardous. What one can establish is that this mentality already exists in our day among an élite in every human group of superior civilization. One observes, in effect, that, in the interior of one and the same group, the successive fictions in which morality is represented, do not replace one another abruptly: what happens is that the older ones are in part transformed into the more recent ones and persist alongside the latter. Religion is transmuted into custom and is, among the more intellectual, formulated in scientific conscience; but, after this latter metamorphosis has been achieved, religion and custom continue exerting their influence on a greater or lesser part of the social group, and it is well that all those, who still find in these ancient modes of illusion the aliment suitable to them, not be deprived thereof. It is thus that one and the same ethnic physiology, by modes in rapport with the intellectual evolution of the individuals subject to them, realizes one and the same attitude of utility. It is, therefore, a fact favorable to the health and the vigor of a social group that the modes representative of its morality, however they may differ in degree from the standpoint of intellectual evolution, should coexist and provide the needs of the nation in its entirety; but it is of supreme importance for these modes to emanate from the physiology of the race itself, leaving no room, at least as preponderant influences, for modes rooted in the physiology of another race. Now, in each human society, it is the duty of the most advanced group, the one which has attained to a scientific awareness of the attitudes signifying utility for a race, to be vigilant lest some alien element come in to compromise the vitality of the race and throw anarchy into its organism. That is, in the domain of action, the most immediate task and the one least subject to doubt incumbent upon this purely intellectual group. Alone exempt from all religious prejudice, it is the only one that is capable of appreciating the organic value of religious prejudice. Hence it must take care that the particular religion adopted by the race in the period of its religious fermentation remains a religion of state, the one which is offered to all those with minds so disposed as to continue drawing from the religious fictions the moral sustenance peculiar to the race. It amounts to philosophical sentimentality of a low order to imagine that religions differ among themselves as to the degree of their truthfulness, that they possess a genuine reality, once they are detached from the ethnic organism which produced them. But all scientific minds, to whatever group they may belong, know that religion is a physiological fact, so that a people which allows the religion of another people to be imposed upon itself, is a people vanquished by another in its physiological intimacy.

The most intellectual group of every society will attend with the same care to the conservation of custom, because it is morality in its second aspect. It is true that breadth of Understanding consists in *knowing*, that is to say, in giving to oneself, as a spectacle, a great number of different mental attitudes, attributes of an infinity of organisms; but the force and the health of Understanding and its critical virtue consist in not losing sight of the fact that *knowing* and *living* are two things and that, if it is interesting to know how a bird or a fish breathes, nevertheless one only breathes oneself with one's own lungs and also that one persists in life only by means of one's own moral organism. Scientific minds, then, will be obliged, by reason of the imperious mechanism governing them and, if need be, in opposition to any contrary admiration, to extol for the race to which they belong, the religion, the custom, the literature and the language which developed on the physiological stock in virtue of a natural law superior to all verbal logic.

The attitude which is the most contrary to the scientific spirit, whose supremacy tends to be assured by the philosophy of Knowledge, is that false rationalism instituted by Kant with the CRITIQUE OF PRACTICAL REASON to which became fanatically attached all the mental misfits, all the impotent ones, whose energy, spurious and illegitimate, can objectify itself neither in the rigor of faith, nor in the perfection of custom, nor even in the impartiality of scientific conscience, all those infantile spirits whose retarded religious puberty is manifested and blossoms in an intolerant morality, in a disquieting and equivocal religiosity in a period of evolution which no longer justifies these phenomena. While the diverse positive religions of humanity, daughters of revelation at the time when revelation was fertile, give the appearance of being conceived in conformity with the intention of natural laws and according to the logic of mental anatomy, whereas they still show the secrets of their construction along with the logical beauty of the skeleton, rational religion, with its aspect of a hybrid monster, has its place marked in the secret museum of philosophical anthropology.

Nevertheless, this false rationalism with the universal morality which it engenders, promulgated by Kant, favored by the philosophers of the Encyclopaedia, a spectral revival of the Christian phenomenon with the French Revolution, has been the menace of this century and its great malady. It must be taken for a symptom of anemia and an illness of debility in all the social groups in which it has appeared. For it is for want of strength that a physiology is no longer evidenced in the attitudes of utility which are appropriate to it and that it believes it recognizes itself in an ideological phantom divested of reality. It is at the stage, where it is powerless to engender a representation of itself, that it conceives itself other than it is, that it recognizes itself in alien reflections and, by that false conception, denies and suppresses itself.

The rationalistic phantom is especially dangerous in all countries in which Christianity manifested the

Roman Catholic form, for it borrows its vital appearance and the tinsel of its universal morality from another religious form closer to primitive Christianity, from the Protestant form, the expression of a true physiological reality. Under a semblance of rationalism it is a disguised Protestantism that is offered the mentality of Roman Catholic peoples, and when it imposes itself it indicates, as we have noted, the victory of one physiology over another: its triumph is equivalent, for the race which sustains it, to a defeat on a battlefield. Here, moreover, it destroys all the sources of morality. For, tearing up the roots of religion and of custom, disparaging tradition in which the scientific mind would be able to retrieve the vital elements of the social group in order to reconstitute them in a synthesis, it proposes to races of a high intellectual maturity, in France and in Italy for example, a crude and ill-prepared fiction which could have no hold over them.

Less dangerous for social energy in Protestant countries, it is here more particularly a danger for the mind. For, being confounded with ancient religion and custom by its moral teaching and under the guise of interpreting religion and custom in a more liberal sense, it retains in these modes of the past some minds, whose impatience might have been sharpened by a more stringent rigor, thus gaining the necessary élan with which to bound, beyond the ancient fictions, into the realm of the scientific spirit.

At this point we wish to express our belief that the religious regression with which rationalism, oftentimes under the form of free thought, still threatens to retard the course of intellectual development, will be checked. Beside the admirable line of scientists who, in our country and in neighboring nations, have been the honor of human thought in the course of this century, the genial work of Friedrich Nietzsche is also a symptom which augurs well. This work proves that, if rationalism has a greater hold on Protestant peoples and can be said to constitute a menace to their higher development, these peoples do produce minds of sufficient vigor to oppose to the evil a violence proportionate to its strength. At the end of these pages devoted entirely to analyzing the symptoms of this rationalistic evil which waylays the weak at the egress from religion and custom, we propose the work of Nietzsche as the most efficacious antidote to oppose to a basely sentimental training of reason, as the salt most apt to purify the atmosphere of the mind. By rendering the CRITIQUE OF PURE REASON wholesome after Schopenhauer, by restoring to it its integral sense and entire force of destruction, by opposing pessimism on the other hand, and by showing, beyond the ruins of the ancient metaphysics, Life continuing its evolution with more ardor, above everything, by teaching the value of untruth, Nietzsche reconciled for a time the Instinct of Knowledge with the Vital Instinct. Through this provisional contract, by gaining acceptance of a philosophy of pure Knowledge he renders possible the reign of a scientific modality which, among all the forms of illusion, seems the newest and the richest in promises, the one which, inspiring the élite of humanity with the most confidence, appears to be the one most likely to assure new and curious realizations of the phenomenon we call Life.

NOTES

1. See Havelock Ellis, THE DANCE OF LIFE, Modern Library. Wilmot E. Ellis: THE ART PHILOSOPHY OF JULES DE GAULTIER, University of Washington Chapbook, Number sixteen, 1928. (Seattle, Washington).

2. In his view civilization begins at the point where utility ends. "J'ai toujours estimé qu'il n'est de civilisation qu'au delà de la satisfaction du besoin." This sentence occurs in Jules de Gaultier's autobiography, which he intended for Americans and parts of which Wilmot Ellis incorporated in his book. See also LA GUERRE ET LES DESTINEES DE L'ART, August 1920 and ART ET CIVILISATION, February 1921 in Monde Nouveau.

NOTES TO CHAPTER I

1. Frédéric Nietzsche: PAR DELÀ LE BIEN ET LE MAL (BEYOND GOOD AND EVIL), translated by L. Weiscopf and G. Art, p. 5. Ed. in-8 of the *Mercure de France*.

2. Ibid., p. 6.

3. Henri Lichtenberger: LA PHILOSOPHIE DE NIETZSCHE, P. 104. Alcan.

4. PAR DELA LE BIEN ET LE MAL (BEYOND GOOD AND EVIL), p. 241.

5. The French expression "prendre le Pirée pour un homme" symbolizes confusion. See La Fontaine's fable LE SINGE ET LE DAUPHIN.

6. ". . . Between ourselves he is a man easily led by the nose. He is apt to glory in all our interviews and I have brought him to the point of seeing everything without believing anything."

7. In *Le Misanthrope*.

8. "Monsieur Homais," a character in Gustave Flaubert's novel MADAME BOVARY, a bourgeois pharmacist and type of the stupid freethinker.

9. Victor Cousin: HISTOIRE GÉNÉRALE DE LA PHILOSOPHIE, p. 200. Didier & Cie.

10. BEYOND GOOD AND EVIL (The Free Spirit), par. 25, page 408. Modern Library edition.

NOTES TO CHAPTER II

1. There is no liberty and everything in the world happens according to natural laws;—"Nowhere does there exist any absolutely necessary being, neither in the world, nor outside of the world, as being its cause."

2. "There is a free cause";—"There is in the world something which, whether as a part of it, or as its cause, is an absolutely necessary being."

3. In this connection the reader is referred to some passages discussing intellectualism and different conceptions of vitalism, Page 115 and Footnote 137, in G. M. Spring THE RETURN FROM BABEL, Philosophical Library, Inc., N. Y. 1951.

4. Friedrich Nietzsche: THUS SPAKE ZARA-THUSTRA. Page 247 ("The Convalescent") Modern Library edition. The French translation by Henri Albert (Page 314), Ed. in-8 of the Mercure de France.

NOTES TO CHAPTER IV

1. Friedrich Nietzsche: THE WANDERER AND HIS SHADOW (HUMAN ALL-TOO HUMAN, Part II.) Page 191. Complete Works of Nietzsche, Oscar Levy ed.

2. THUS SPAKE ZARATHUSTRA, page 123. Modern Library ed.

3. ETHICS, Def. VII.

4. Émile Boutroux: *De La Contingence des lois de la nature.* (Alcan).

5. E. Boutroux: DE LA CONTINGENCE DES LOIS DE LA NATURE, p. 160.

6. Friedrich Nietzsche: THE WANDERER AND HIS SHADOW (HUMAN ALL-TOO HUMAN, Part II.) Page 190. Complete works, Oscar Levy ed.

7. Friedrich Nietzsche: BEYOND GOOD AND EVIL."—indeed, our body is but a social structure composed of many souls—"Modern Library, ed. Page 401. Nietzsche, PAGES CHOISES, page 23.

NOTES TO CHAPTER V

1. Max Stirner L'UNIQUE ET SA PROPRIÉTÉ, p. 53. (Ed. de la Revue Blanche). Max Stirner, pseudonym of Kaspar Schmidt, 1806-1856 (THE EGO AND HIS OWN)

2. Francis Bacon (1561-1626) Author of NOVUM ORGANUM.

3. Maurice Barrès, LES DÉRACINÉS. (*The Uprooted*).

4. METAPHYSICAL PRINCIPLES OF MORALITY, Translation by J. Tissot, Preface, p. V.

5. Georges Goyau: L'ÉCOLE D'AUJOURDHUI. Perrin.

6. L'ANÉE PHILOSOPHIQUE (1868) *l'Infini, la substance et la liberté*.

7. L'ANÉE PHILOSOPHIQUE (1868), p. 27.

8. L'ANÉE PHILOSOPHIQUE (1868), p. 7.

9. L'ANÉE PHILOSOPHIQUE (1868).

10. Salente, an ancient eastern Italian city of Magna Graecia supposed by legend to have been founded by Idomeneus, here symbolizes Utopia. The author does not have in mind Sir Thomas More's work of 1516, but refers to "le gouvernement de Salente," as it is found in the famous TÉLÉMAQUE of Fénelon who, as the tutor of Louis XIV's grandson Louis,

the Duke of Bourgogne, composed the work as a picture of an ideal state for the edification of his pupil. The exact location of this Greek city is not known for certain, but it is thought to have been in the heel of the Italian peninsula in or near the modern province of Lecce. Some scholars have identified it with the village of Soleto.

NOTES TO CHAPTER VI

1. Friedrich Nietzsche: THUS SPAKE ZARA-THUSTRA (BEFORE SUNRISE) p. 183. Modern Library edition.
2. DISCOURS SUR L'ESPRIT POSITIF. Ed. de la Société positiviste, page 108.
3. ZARATHUSTRA, p. 127, Modern Library.
4. Edmond Barthèlemy: Thomas Carlyle. Ed. du Mercure de France.
5. Thomas Carlyle HEROES, HERO-WORSHIP (HERO AS DIVINITY) Greystone Press, p. 178.
6. Ibid. (HERO AS PRIEST) p. 246.
7. Edmond Barthèlemy: THOMAS CARLYLE, p. 197.
8. HEROES, HERO-WORSHIP ("The Hero as Divinity") London, Chapman & Hall, 1888, page 28. Masterworks Library, Greystone Press, New York, page 177.
9. SARTOR RESARTUS by Thomas Carlyle, Masterworks Library, Greystone Press, N. Y. p. 121.

NOTES TO CHAPTER VII

* Friedrich Nietzsche: NIETZSCHE AGAINST WAGNER. Epilogue, page 79. Complete Works of Friedrich Nietzsche (tr. by Anthony M. Ludovici.) Edited by Dr. Oscar Levy.

1. Nietzsche: BEYOND GOOD AND EVIL, page 387 (par. 6), Modern Library, New York.

2. BEYOND GOOD AND EVIL, page 386.

3. Nietzsche: THUS SPAKE ZARATHUSTRA, page 123 (par. 34), Modern Library, N. Y.

4. ZARATHUSTRA, page 125, (par. 34), Modern Library, New York.

5. Remy de Gourmont: EPILOGUES, Mercure de France, juillet, 1899.

6. PAGES CHOISES, page 13.

7. Nietzsche, BEYOND GOOD AND EVIL, pages 535-536. (par. 229), Modern Library, New York.

8. LA PHILOSOPHIE DE NIETZSCHE (Alcan)

9. THUS SPAKE ZARATHUSTRA, Modern Library, page 98.

10. BEYOND GOOD AND EVIL, page 536. Modern Library ed.

11. Frédéric Nietzsche: *L'Antéchrist*, p. 241. (LE CREPUSCULE DES IDOLES, ed. du Mercure de France).

12. Remy de Gourmont: D'UN PAYS LOINTAIN.

13. BEYOND GOOD AND EVIL, par. 55, page 440. Modern Library.

14. Quoted by M. Lichtenberger: LA PHILOSOPHIE DE NIETZSCHE, page 95.

15. THUS SPAKE ZARATHUSTRA, Prologue, page 6. Modern Library.

16. BEYOND GOOD AND EVIL, par. 285, page 603. Modern Library.

17. Quoted by M. Lichtenberger: LA PHILOSOPHIE DE NIETZSCHE, p. 95.

18. THUS SPAKE ZARATHUSTRA, page 91. Modern Library.

19. BEYOND GOOD AND EVIL, page 399, par. 19. Modern Library.

20. Ibid, page 397, par. 16.

21. PAGES CHOISIES, page 137 (LE VOYAGEUR ET SON OMBRE)

22. THUS SPAKE ZARATHUSTRA, page 91. Modern Library.

23. THUS SPAKE ZARATHUSTRA, page 183, Modern Library.

24. BEYOND GOOD AND EVIL, par. 231, page 539. Modern Library.

25. THUS SPAKE ZARATHUSTRA, page 25. Modern Library.

26. Ibid, par. 35, page 127.

27. Compare Chapter VI., page 174. The French "goûts et couleurs" is less close to the German original than "a dispute about taste and tasting."

28. BEYOND GOOD AND EVIL, par. 19, page 399.

29. Ibid, page 401.

30. HUMAN, ALL-TOO HUMAN, Part II. (THE

WANDERER AND HIS SHADOW), par. 11, page 192. Complete Works of Friedrich Nietzsche, Edited by Dr. Oscar Levy.

31. PAGES CHOISIES, page 160. (From DAWN OF DAY)

32. Ibid.

33. THUS SPAKE ZARATHUSTRA, page 61. Modern Library.

34. PAGES CHOISIES, page 157. (DAWN OF DAY)

35. THUS SPAKE ZARATHUSTRA, page 215. Modern Library.

36. Ibid., page 217.

32. GENEALOGY OF MORALS, pp. 790-791. Modern Library.

38. Ibid, page 792.

39. BEYOND GOOD AND EVIL, par. 16, page 397. Modern Library.

40. Ibid. Page 601 (par. 281)

41. Ibid. par. 4, page 384.

42. THUS SPAKE ZARATHUSTRA, par. 32, The Dance Song, page 116. Modern Library. Ibid. par. 59, The Second Dance Song, page 252.

43. THE WANDERER AND HIS SHADOW, Part II of HUMAN, ALL-TOO HUMAN, PAGES CHOISIES, p. 122.

44. THUS SPAKE ZARATHUSTRA, page 157. Modern Library.

45. PAGES CHOISIES, page 14.

46. APHORISMES ET FRAGMENTS CHOISIES, page 3.

47. PAGES CHOISIES, page 20.

48. HUMAN, ALL-TOO HUMAN, Part I. (Oscar Levy ed.) page 159.

49. PAGES CHOISIES, page 12.

50. PAGES CHOISIES, page 8.

51. Mercure de France, février, 1898.

52. ZARATHUSTRA, page 157. Modern Library.

53. Ibid, page 158.

54. Ibid, page 117.

55. THUS SPAKE ZARATHUSTRA, page 153. Modern Library, New York, 1954.

56. Ibid. Page 155.

57. ZARATHUSTRA, page 265. Modern Library, N. Y.

58. Ibid, page 6.

59. Ibid, page 8.

60. ZARATHUSTRA, page 79. Modern Library.

61. Ibid.

62. LA PHILOSOPHIE DE NIETZSCHE (Alcan), p. 158.

63. ZARATHUSTRA, par. 34, page 122. Modern Library.

64. Ibid, page 130.

65. ZARATHUSTRA, page 131. Modern Library.

66. Ibid, pages 108-109.

67. ZARATHUSTRA, page 11. Modern Library.

68. Ibid, page 100.

69. Ibid, p. 186.

70. Ibid, p. 7.

71. ZARATHUSTRA, page 322. (*The Higher Man,* par. 5) Modern Library.

72. BEYOND GOOD AND EVIL, page 611. Modern Library.

73. ZARATHUSTRA, pp. 187-188.

74. ZARATHUSTRA, page 47. Modern Library.

75. Ibid, page 48.

76. Compare page 214 and also pages 180 and 181.

77. ZARATHUSTRA, page 128. Modern Library.

78. HUMAN, ALL-TOO HUMAN, Part I, page 141. Complete Works of Friedrich Nietzsche. (tr. by M. Ludovici) Edited by Dr. Oscar Levy.

NOTES FOR CHAPTER VIII

1. HUMAIN, TROP HUMAIN, p. 132.

INDEX